PRAISE FOR *LUCHINO VISCONTI AND THE FABRIC OF CINEMA*

"As Joe McElhaney argues in this persuasive new book, Visconti's insistence on cloth and clothing is more than a lushing-up of the mise-en-scène; it is the privileged expression of latent political-sexual tensions in the filmmaker's worldview. Fabric comes to name the substance and secret of Visconti's style, a veil that McElhaney has the insight neither to lift nor see through but rather to see and make seen in its fully patterned functioning. With an attention perfectly fitted to this style, *Luchino Visconti and the Fabric of Cinema* covers its subject's oeuvre as fully as a cape, while hugging that corpus as close as more intimate apparel."

—D. A. Miller, author of *Hidden Hitchcock*

"McElhaney carefully reframes the historical, political, and sensual dimensions that connect Visconti's work to neorealism and queer cinema. What emerges is a vivid portrait not only of a director's tendencies but of cinema's resources as a 'veiling' and 'unveiling' instrument of desire. This exquisitely observant study primes us to notice 'the cinema of fabric' well beyond Visconti's examples, too."

—Rick Warner, University of North Carolina at Chapel Hill, author of *Godard and the Essay Film: A Form That Thinks*

"In addition to his unsurpassed close readings of all Visconti's major films, Joe McElhaney provides so many kinds of attendant history, with such authority and crystalline economy, that his work rivals the most impressive work on film history that I have encountered. This study demonstrates conclusively that fabric is a central shaping force throughout Visconti's career, and that it affects our reading not only of bodies and the flow and displacements of desire but of every depicted environment."

—George Toles, University of Manitoba

"Joe McElhaney starts from a brilliant insight—the centrality of fabric to our appreciation and enjoyment of film—and explores this through focusing on a director whose presentation of fabric is so defining of what makes his films loved and admired. What makes the study outstanding and important, however, is the way McElhaney draws out the full implications of this focus on fabric, beyond narrative and symbolism, beyond even clothes and fittings or color and pattern, to how fabric works aesthetically in movies, to cut, flow, veiling, draping. Beautifully written and without ever being speciously clever, *Luchino Visconti and the Fabric of Cinema* really does reveal not just that fabric is central to cinema but that cinema is fabric."

—Richard Dyer, King's College London / St Andrews University

"McElhaney's new book performs a task that is as delicate, intricate, and powerful as the body of work he analyzes. In placing the fabric of Visconti's cinema so vividly before the reader, he helps us to understand not only these films' aesthetic sensuality and rigor but also sews Visconti into a broad artistic, political, and historical tapestry. This book marks a milestone in sensitive, beautifully written auteur scholarship and gives us a new Visconti and a new way of seeing—of looking at and through—cinema, all at once."

—John David Rhodes, University of Cambridge, author of
Stupendous, Miserable City: Pasolini's Rome

"In this major study of Luchino Visconti, Joe McElhaney looks at fabric as a lush motif, teasing out the genealogy of Visconti's images across other media as well as the wider film culture from which they emerge. Elegantly interweaving threads of style, history, and sexuality into rich close analysis, McElhaney not only unveils Visconti's cinema but reveals it anew."

—Belén Vidal, senior lecturer in film studies, King's College London

LUCHINO VISCONTI
and the Fabric of Cinema

Joe McElhaney

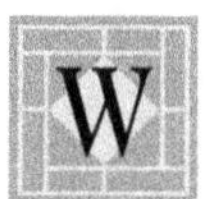

Wayne State University Press
Detroit

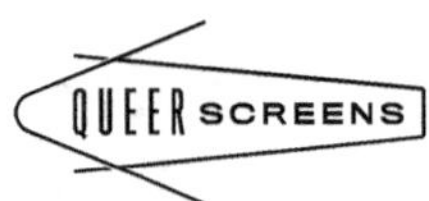

ISBN 978-0-8143-4308-1 (paperback)
ISBN 978-0-8143-4826-0 (hardcover)
ISBN 978-0-8143-4309-8 (e-book)

Library of Congress Control Number: 2020943902

Wayne State University Press
Leonard N. Simons Building
4809 Woodward Avenue
Detroit, Michigan 48201-1309

Visit us online at wsupress.wayne.edu

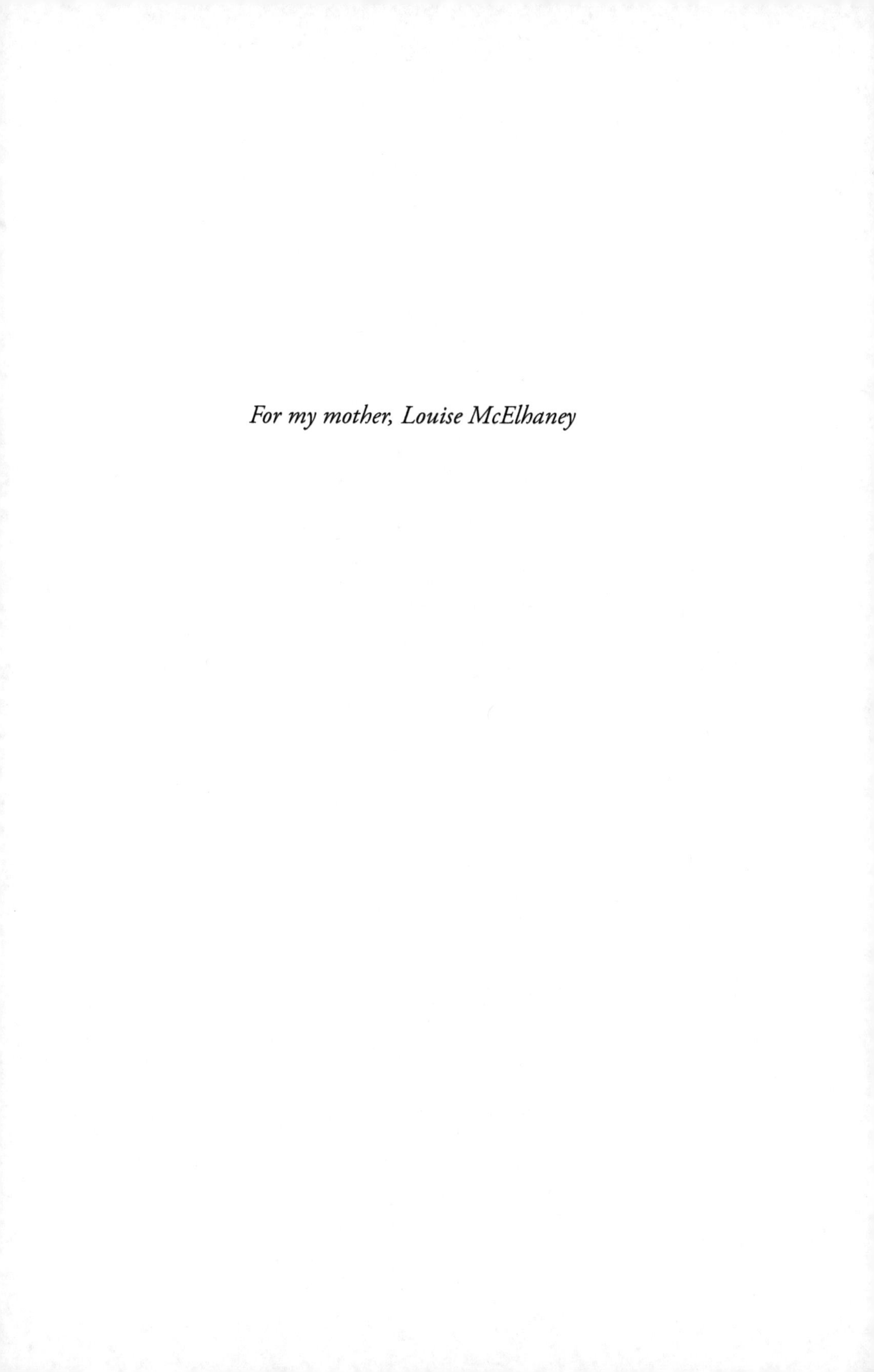

For my mother, Louise McElhaney

CONTENTS

Acknowledgments ix

Introduction: The Cinema of Fabric, the Fabric of Cinema **1**
- Unveiling 1
- Origins and Contexts: Mise-en-Scène 5
- Origins and Contexts: Editing 10

1. Interwoven **17**
- Dirty Laundry 17
- Bursting at the Seams 22
- Knitting and Patching 26
- Bedding Down 33
- Exchanging 40
- Shredding 44
- The Man in the Trench Coat 48

2. The Diva, Draped **55**
- Flowing, Unreeling 55
- A Constant Vision in Black 62
- Projected 71
- Unfurled 74

3. Tight Fits **83**
- Bandages 83
- Fabric and Fog 90
- Tied Together 94
- Dressed for the Weather 97
- Overall 100

4. Classical Forms **105**
- Behind the Curtain 105
- Red 114
- Soiled 121
- Covering Up 126
- Tightening 132

5. Decadent Threads **137**

Prelude: The Witch Burned Alive 137
Historical Tapestries 138
Flutterings 143
Large Patterns 147
Maternal Visions 152
Child Labor 156
Bringing Down the Curtain 164

6. Fading **173**

Beginnings and Endings 173
Lifting the Veil 178
Camouflage 187
The White Angel 193
Deceitful Disguises 198

Notes **207**

Index **221**

ACKNOWLEDGMENTS

I would like to thank David Gerstner for inviting me to contribute to this series he edits. He has been a strong and an enthusiastic supporter of the project throughout its various stages. At Wayne State University Press, my editor Marie Sweetman has been exemplary. Also at the press, my thanks to Kristin Harpster, Kristina Stonehill, and Carrie Downes Teefey. Thanks also to Sandra Judd for her copyediting.

As always, Steve Barnes tolerates my almost continuous states of distraction when working on something like this. Or, really, in relation to almost anything. He deserves a medal for his forbearing.

Most of all, I would like to thank Noa Steimatsky. She has been interested in this book from the moment I first described it to her, and her suggestions, comments, and criticisms of the manuscript forced me to substantially think through the implications of what I was attempting. A great scholar and a great friend.

INTRODUCTION

The Cinema of Fabric, the Fabric of Cinema

Unveiling

In 2008, the DVD/Blu-ray company Masters of Cinema released Luchino Visconti's *Rocco and His Brothers* (1960). In reviewing the disc for *Film Quarterly*, D. A. Miller took note of the apparent limitations of the disc's packaging. In addition to two documentaries and various interviews with the film's creative participants, the package contained a booklet. In it was an interview with Visconti as well as two essays, one by Guido Aristarco and one by Visconti himself, all of these reflecting left-wing discourses contemporaneous with the film's original release. Through such a presentation, with Visconti's Marxism on display, the interest of the film is tied to Antonio Gramsci and the "Southern Question" of working-class migration to Italy's north and framed by debates about the ethical goals of Italian neorealism in the years after its wartime and immediate postwar moment. For all of their value, these approaches are now seen by Miller, when examining the cinema with a different set of expectations, as serving a potentially repressive function. Miller proposes another *Rocco and His Brothers*, one no less political but where criticism has shifted from realism to the film's melancholic beauty. At the center of this beauty are the male bodies on display, those of the Parondi brothers from which the film takes its title. These men and boys are "beautiful for nothing, like garments too fine to wear."[1]

Miller's strategy in this sentence of linking the film's visual beauty with garments is one that will be central to *Luchino Visconti and the Fabric of Cinema*. In this book, I will situate Visconti's films within a trope I am identifying as *the cinema of fabric*. My concern is not with the aesthetics of costume design, nor is the book intended to be part of the literature on the cultural and historical implications of fashion and film, although clothing and (sometimes) fashion are central to my project in other ways. Rather, the cinema I am positing is dominated by multiple *kinds* of fabric, not only clothing and accessories but items of decor, such as curtains, tablecloths, sheets, and drapings. It is a cinema that almost literally *flows*. At times, the films take their cues from fabric, affecting the staging, the movements of the camera, and the editing. But why does this cinema need to flow at all? What does such a need tell us about the cinema in general? And why should Visconti's relationship to it be of interest?

A central argument of this book is that the cinema of fabric arises throughout film history, from the cinema's origins to the present day, and across various genres, national cinemas, and film movements, as well as within the work of various auteurs. Visconti's origins as a director are within Italian neorealism, the most important film movement immediately following the Second World War. Moreover, the movement's influence has been ongoing, as though confirming Visconti's inflated statement that neorealism was "the beginning of the evolution of cinema as art."[2] Within any full-scale attempt to account for neorealism, Visconti looms large. Fabric is central to neorealism, Visconti's use of it having its own implications within that movement. But these implications extend far beyond neorealism. I am thinking not only of cinema preceding and following Visconti but also of ways in which the literary and plastic arts (so thoroughly embedded in Visconti's practice) have given voice to the expressive and rhetorical possibilities of fabric.

As with the work of all neorealist filmmakers, Visconti's cinema in the aftermath of that movement's decline underwent a number of shifts. While never entirely forsaking aspects of the movement, Visconti became an international art cinema director and celebrity figure, adapting major literary texts, collaborating with European and Hollywood movie stars, and working as a director for theater and opera even more extensively than for film. However, Visconti was unlike his early neorealist colleagues in one crucial respect: he was homosexual. He was able to avoid the official censure and oppression of the kind another gay Italian filmmaker with strong Marxist ties, Pier Paolo Pasolini (younger than Visconti by fourteen years and not part of the neorealist emergence) repeatedly faced. Visconti's ability to avoid Pasolini's difficulties is complex, bound up as it is with the protection afforded to Visconti by his celebrity and class status, by his far less confrontational public persona, and by the nature of the work produced. Visconti attached himself to widely recognized Romantic and post-Romantic traditions, a cult of aestheticism Pasolini resisted or, if he used it, he did so in a "scandalous" manner.[3]

In Visconti, far more than we find elsewhere in neorealism, entire environments are dominated by a *need* to express through fabric. We have not simply a world of visual beauty but a highly voluptuous and sometimes agonized filmmaking in which fabrics, repeatedly marked by their mobility, give voice to desires that exceed the films' ostensible subject matter or story situations. In their extended analysis, published in 1972, of Visconti's adaptation of Thomas Mann's *Death in Venice* (1971), Serge Daney and Jean-Pierre Oudart write: "The point of rupture in Visconti's fiction is the point where sexuality appears in the role of the truth of the bourgeois mise-en-scène, of its unveiled secret: the veil is lifted on a forbidden sexual relationship, in the form of a description or a consummation of an act."[4] Like Miller, Daney and Oudart find themselves drawing upon analogies and metaphors of fabric. But it is a fabric tied to eroticism. In a rare example from this period of a direct acknowledgment of Visconti's sexuality, Daney and Oudart refer to the director as an "obsessional homosexual."[5]

Seen strictly in this manner, the fabrics of *Death in Venice* are emblems of a once-repressed desire that are, over the course of the film, subjected to a system of "unveiling." Gustav von Aschenbach (Dirk Bogarde) arrives in Venice, his chilled body covered in gloves, hat, coat, and woolen scarves, all clear markers of emotional and sexual repression. His ongoing attraction for the boy Tadzio (Björn Andrésen) is partly a matter of the boy's physical beauty, here given form through the sustained shots of him in a hotel along the beach. The film's direct articulation of same-sex desire stands in contrast to the world described by Miller in *Rocco*. There, the Parondis are "frequently shown [dressing] or undressing; and as they put on their shoulder-hugging sweaters and tight jeans, or strip down to underwear and boxing trunks, they are attractively drowsy, numb, bewildered—consistently absent-minded, in a word, [they] seem like creatures under enchantment."[6] With *Rocco*, we are confronted with a more "closeted" conception of the image, a "sleepy limbo of latency,"[7] produced under different historical circumstances only eleven years earlier.

Within the context of the cinema of fabric, however, the two films are not necessarily different from one another, the later film merely narrativizing what is already visible in the earlier one, provided one is predisposed to notice such things. The cinema of fabric cannot *simply* be understood as one in which fabric, in its sensuous abundance, becomes a fetishistic extension of the human body and in which, in the case of Visconti, a homosexual director displaces his physical desires for his male camera subjects onto items of clothing associated with these subjects. Such a reading, while still productive

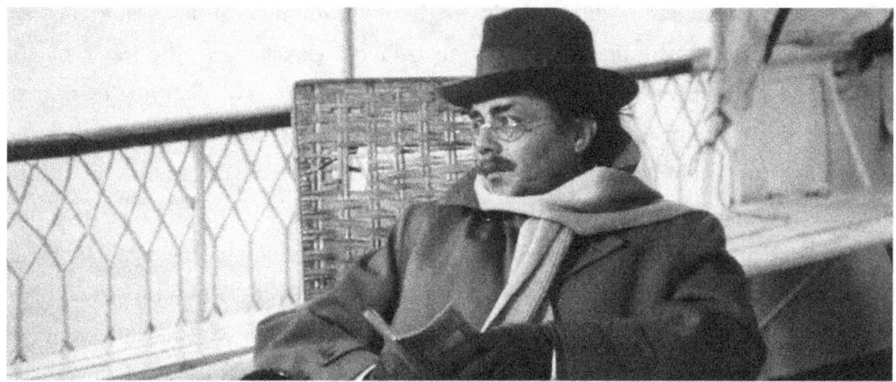

Death in Venice (1971). Layers of clothing as markers of sexual repression.

and one that will be used throughout the book, carries with it the limitations of an interpretive queer hermeneutic. Visconti's cinema is a cinema of desire in its fullest sense, not simply for bodies but also for entire environments, a world of the senses in which fabric becomes a crucial method for shaping these attractions. Miller's focus on the brothers in *Rocco* dressing and undressing would imply that in Visconti such gestures emerge entirely from a preoccupation with male bodies. But the focus on fabric in relation to the female body is still essential, even if such correspondences are less radically charged. What, after all, do Romy Schneider and Silvana Mangano, the female stars of Visconti's episodes from two portmanteau films, respectively *Boccaccio '70/Il lavoro* (1962) and *Le Streghe/The Witch Burned Alive* (1967) undergo but a continuous process of dressing and undressing? Christian Metz has argued that the impulse in certain films to play with edges of the frame and to slowly reveal "has something to do with a kind of permanent undressing, a generalised strip-tease, a less direct but more perfected strip-tease, since it also makes it possible to dress space again, to remove from view what it has previously shown." These "veiling-unveiling procedures" include fundamental punctuation devices such as the fade, the dissolve, and the iris.[8] In discussing Visconti's *Senso* (1954), Jean-Luc Godard writes that each time the male protagonist is about to say something to the female protagonist then "bang!—a fade out."[9] Godard wants something more than he is getting from *Senso*, something the film is not (in a rhetorical strategy typical of Godard) *showing* him. Never mind that *Senso* is not really constructed in the way his comment would imply. For Godard, *Senso*, by not showing certain things, belongs to the tradition of the "great classical film."[10] But what such a critique is, itself, not able to see is something that is not so much absent as veiled and has to be examined with different priorities.

Visconti's cinema, in its constant attraction to fabrics and to veiling, is dominated by a fundamental ambivalence toward not only what it is filming but also the larger forms, movements, and traditions it situates itself within: neorealism, melodrama and historical narrative, the literary adaptation, and the classical and the modern. The origins of such ambivalence are traceable to the contradictions of Visconti's own status as an artist and as a historical and cultural subject, contradictions repeatedly addressed in the literature on him. Central here is Visconti's aristocratic background, on the one hand, and his commitment to Marxism, on the other. For Alberto Moravia, Visconti's class origins give rise to the notion that the society from which he emerges is in a state of decay. Visconti's Marxism allows him to critique the social and economic structures of this society although he remains attached to the values of that world, in particular its aestheticism and strong ties to history and tradition, a conflict "clearly written, for all who know how to read, in each of his films."[11] An issue ignored by Moravia but equally central to this ambivalence would be Visconti's sexuality, which functions as the site of further potential conflict. This sexuality has been, since the beginning of his career, both visible and veiled, disruptive and hidden.

Visconti's cinema presents us with seductive intensities it must pull back from, refusing to fully capitulate, as its ambivalences continue circulating. For all of Visconti's much-remarked-upon fascination with decadence, narrativized in film after film and quite often framed by major historical events confirming a sense of things ending, the experience of the films' images offers other possibilities. In Visconti, the organization, movement, and flow of the images at once confirm the finality being dramatized while also giving birth to other ways of seeing beyond the worlds represented. All of them are what Alexander García Düttmann has referred to as "migrating images" that "do not disclose a meaning in the things to which the things could be subordinated, a meaning which would reclaim them for discourse, but bring them to life as insights into flesh and blood."[12] As we shall see, this flesh and blood is crucially tied to the placement, organization, and movement of fabric.

Origins and Contexts: Mise-en-Scène

In 1917, writing what was a virtual manifesto, Colette called for a new type of cinema artist who would "have to search out the beautiful fold, the weave that catches the light, the obedient drapery, the silken sash, the embroidery with visible design." This new artist would do nothing less than "contribute to the education of cinema."[13] For Colette, such an experience was no less of a reason to celebrate this new art form than films blowing up ships, staging massive crowd scenes, or derailing trains.[14] Colette was establishing a vision of cinema that was feminine, that draped and wove in opposition to a masculine cinema of aggression, destruction, and violence. Within the history of cinema such an impulse was there from the very origins of the form and even before motion pictures were projected. The 1894 Kinetoscopes of Annabelle doing her sun or butterfly dances are not simply images of a body in motion but capture the swirl of the ornate fabrics she is controlling as she dances.

Beyond this early history, a love of draping is apparent in Hollywood films of the traditional studio era in which narrative momentum is briefly suspended in favor of a fashion show. *The Women* (George Cukor, 1939) contains a notable example of this, in which a black-and-white all-female comedy of manners becomes, for six minutes, a Technicolor fashion display. This show is introduced by an unnamed French designer as being devoted to "the rhythmic movement of everyday life" and an opportunity "to study the flow of the new line as it responds to the ever-changing flow of the female form divine." *The Women* establishes itself as a film offering insight into the fundamental nature of female behavior, implied in the definite article of the film's title and often made explicit in the dialogue. This is further confirmed, beyond the diegesis, by the presence of women in the construction of the scenario: The film was based on a play by Clare Booth Luce and adapted for the screen by Anita Loos and Jane Murfin. The fashion sequence in *The Women* is a distillation of what was (and possibly still is) presumed to be a major reason some women went to the movies in the first place: to look at the clothes.

The film criticism of Cecelia Ager for *Variety* in the 1930s is the most important official example of this type of spectatorship in which Ager's focus is on the fashions worn by the films' female subjects. Of the Kay Francis film *Another Dawn* (William Dieterle, 1937), set in North Africa, Ager concedes, "Miss Francis's floating scarves, dervish skirts and feather capes do have a certain merit, ballooning in the sirocco; watching them sort of hypnotizes people, and keeps their minds off the spiritual things she says."[15] This quote is interesting for at least three reasons. First, for how it draws attention, through fabric, to the clichés and conventions of a particular kind of film, these clichés enacted by the female subject. At the same time, Ager's tone is ironic, not only about the film but also about the presumptions of her own status as a spectator who is, by virtue of her gender, supposed to be fixated on such matters. But as her writing also implies, fabric in a film is not simply an adornment but, through its capacity to move, float, and hypnotize, contains a profoundly cinematic idea.

A response to the cinema of fabric, be it swooning, ironic, or both, is not the exclusive province of female audiences. However implicit such audiences might have been for *The Women* on its original release, the film has in the years since then enjoyed a considerable queer spectatorship, responding to the film's camp humor and artifice, to which its costumes are fundamental. That both Cukor and the film's costume designer, Adrian, were homosexual reinforces a sense that another kind of sensibility is on display and that another kind of audience is being addressed. And indeed the history of the reception of the cinema of fabric has sometimes been marked by its anxiety about the feminine and, in particular, about male artists who show a commitment to the specific energies fabric can create, these artists giving themselves over to an effeminate dandyism. Billy Wilder's reference to the homosexual Mitchell Leisen, who directed three screenplays coauthored by Wilder, as a "stupid fairy" for Leisen's detailed attention to the clothes of his actresses at the expense of (for Wilder) more important values within his screenplays is typical.[16]

I would like to draw attention to a Visconti film that will otherwise not be central to the later chapters, *Il lavoro*. Filmed between *Rocco and His Brothers* and *The Leopard* (1963), this episode from *Boccaccio '70* may initially appear to be little more than a divertissement, not only in its running time (53 minutes) but in its scale, the episode entirely confining itself to one large apartment setting. *Boccaccio '70* was a typical producers' film of the period, a portmanteau assembling several major film stars and directors in an attractive package suitable for international distribution. Visconti's episode, while the smallest in relation to its use of a location, was the most expensive of the four episodes (the others were directed by Mario Monicelli, Vittorio De Sica, and Federico Fellini), as Visconti's much-publicized mania for details gave rise to the extreme expenditure. *Il lavoro* was a vehicle for Romy Schneider, already a star in European cinema but who was now undergoing a transformation into a glamorous international figure, largely under Visconti's tutelage. They had worked together the year before, with Alain Delon, on John Ford's *'Tis Pity She's a Whore* (c. 1626) in Paris, a staging controversially lavish in its costumes and décor.

The same opulence dominates *Il lavoro*, which uses Guy de Maupassant's "Au bord du lit" (1883) as a starting point, retaining its basic situation of a wealthy wife responding to her husband's infidelities with prostitutes by demanding payment for her own services. Visconti does not set the film in the nineteenth century, as Jean Renoir had done in his own Maupassant adaptation, *A Day in the Country* (1936). Instead, similar to his process of adapting Giovanni Verga's *I Malavoglia* (1881) into *La terra trema* (1948), Visconti transposed the period to a contemporary one, the setting changed from Paris to Milan, the husband now Italian and named Ottavio (Tomas Milian) and the wife now German and named Pupe (Schneider). Such a transposition engages in a typical Visconti dialectic between a historical past anticipating the present day and a present day persistently attached to the past. The décor in *Il lavoro*, as well as the apartment's architectural framework, suggests a virtual history of the Italian Renaissance (there are Afghan hounds in the film named Da Vinci and Michelangelo) as various modern details (transistor radios, television sets, record players) become points of contrast.

It is Schneider's costumes, though, that are our primary concern. Visconti commissioned Coco Chanel to design this wardrobe. As has been amply documented, Chanel was largely responsible for Visconti's entrée into filmmaking when she introduced him to Renoir, who then invited Visconti to serve as a member of his crew on several films of the mid-1930s, including *A Day in the Country*. Among Visconti's duties on *A Day in the Country* were assembling the period costumes, a process described by the film's female lead, Sylvia Bataille: "Visconti was always there when we tried the costumes on, arranging the drapes. He would put a pin to create a fold, delicately, unobtrusively."[17] In the finished film, though, the delicacy of detail to which Bataille refers is not particularly apparent, due to Renoir so thoroughly integrating the costumes into the film's myriad of visual and rhetorical strategies. Something similar happens to Chanel's own designs for Renoir on *The Rules of the Game* (1939). In that film it is certainly possible to take note of her contribution. But the film does not insist on this. It has other things on its mind. There is no such integrating and diffusing of Chanel in *Il lavoro*. From the moment of Schneider's entrance, approximately twelve minutes into the episode until the final shots, *Il lavoro* is a virtual Chanel fashion show.

The tone of Maupassant's story is dry. Dialogue predominates, and there is little descriptive detail. In the Visconti, everything is detail, abundance. Contrasts are established between the immobility of items of décor and the flowing lines of fabric. This contrast is conceived in terms of the masculine world of business linked with Ottavio and his various male associates (these associates totally absent from Maupassant) and the feminine world of Pupe, one of Persian kittens in contrast to her husband's Afghan hounds. The early section of the film, centered on Ottavio, is frantically paced. But from the moment Ottavio steps into Pupe's bedroom, things become languorous. As Ottavio enters, the camera follows him in a tracking shot from right to left, both husband and camera discovering Pupe lying on the floor, writing and smoking, as she listens to records. She is dressed in an archetypal Chanel outfit, a tweed suit with a matching hat, pink blouse, and two-toned high-heeled shoes. But it is Visconti's presentation of this moment which deserves attention.

As she writes and talks to her husband, she adjusts the movements of her body. Face down, she then rises to a seated position while turning in profile as she quietly reads aloud, stretches her body over toward the record player, and lifts the player's arm up. As she walks about the room talking to Ottavio, more details of the outfit are revealed as the "new" Romy Schneider is likewise revealed. She takes off the hat and jacket, has dinner, talks on the telephone, undresses and bathes, then puts on another outfit: gold brocade with fur hat and stole. All of this dressing and undressing calls attention to the movement and texture of these fabrics. It is not just a display of the finished outfit on the star but a filmed record of the levels of construction, clothing at once ornate and lighter than air, emphasizing the "flow of the female form divine."

"I belong to the period of Mann, Proust and Mahler," Visconti once famously stated.[18] This historical positioning of his aesthetic has multiple implications that will be addressed throughout the book. For now, though, there is *The Captive* (1923), the fifth volume of Marcel Proust's *In Search of Lost Time* (1913–1927). Proust writes of the great interest the Baron de Charlus takes in women's clothing, treating it with the same attention to detail as he does paintings. Such an interest, though, arouses the anxiety of "scandalmongers" and "over-dogmatic theorists," who regard such an interest as a way for the "invert" to compensate for a sexual attraction to his own gender. Charlus will, for reasons tied to his social downfall, later acquire the derogatory nickname of "the dressmaker." Marcel the narrator is skeptical of such a facile assumption about inverts even while partly endorsing it, since "this is indeed sometimes the case." The invert demonstrates a love for women by showering on them his taste and discrimination. Marcel refers to such a love as "platonic" even as he acknowledges that this is a "highly inappropriate adjective" for what is transpiring here.[19] Is Visconti doing this to Schneider? One could argue "this is indeed sometimes the case." But at other times the presentation turns her body into an erotic spectacle offered to the camera and the desiring viewer, one in which fabric is always linked with her flesh. After she has taken a bath, she dries herself with an enormous green towel, and there is a rapid zoom into her where we can see drops of water and perspiration on her back, shoulders, and neck, her hair hanging in damp strands, calling attention to the texture of her skin. The zoom is partly motivated by Ottavio's point of view. But it also exceeds this, as though the shot is as much for the benefit of the spectator as it is for the husband.

Chanel's designs create an image of a specific type of twentieth-century woman, wearing clothes that had a chic simplicity, moved expressively, and could be worn in a number of different social situations. "The Chanel woman," Roland Barthes writes, "is not the idle young girl but the young woman confronting the world of work which is itself kept discreet, evasive."[20] In our first view of Pupe, an "idle young girl," her tweed suit indicates a woman who is now ready to confront this world of work. While Chanel was enjoying great commercial success after her return to fashion in 1954, criticisms of her designs for harkening back to prewar ideas persisted. In Michelangelo Antonioni's *Cronaca di un amore* (1950), the young, wealthy Paola Fontana (Lucia Bosé), whose husband is the owner of Fontana Fabrics, goes to a salon and is told by the owner that, while Chanel had once been a magnificent designer, Fontana would have been too young to remember her. Much of the immediate postwar hostility toward Chanel, though, has its basis not simply in her now seemingly "old-fashioned" modernity but in her complicity with the Nazis during the Occupation of Paris, a complicity that points to the frequently close ties between fascism and modernism. Visconti himself later admitted to not being immune during the 1930s to fascist aesthetics.[21]

For Barthes, though, Chanel's clothing resists the very notion of fashion. In its relentless search for the new, fashion depends upon "a violent sensation of time," whereas Chanel is driven toward the "eternal beauty" of women, one more closely linked with images derived from art history. Chanel rejects "perishable materials" and instead "the very thing that negates fashion, long life, Chanel makes into a precious quality."[22] These images of Schneider parading about are likewise predicated on violent sensations of time. A young German film star whose recognition up to this point had largely been roles that cited or evoked German history and culture prior to Nazism, a Nazism to which not only Chanel but Schneider's own mother, Magda Schneider, had been linked. A star who had, in effect, been stuck in a past not of her own making now at last broke free and became a modern, international figure.[23] But she did so by appearing in an adaptation of a story by a nineteenth-century French writer and was situated within décor spanning historical eras and cultural citations. In the midst of this were the Chanel outfits representing a "timeless" female modernity, their fabric moving within and about all of this décor. Fabric is implicated within a system that traverses history, culture, and sexual desire.

Origins and Contexts: Editing

Let us imagine another cinema of fabric, through another manifesto. This one was written in 1923 by Dziga Vertov, and in it he places his work in opposition to the industrialized, capitalist mode of production of "cinematographers." For Vertov, the latter turn out products that, in their persistent ties to earlier art forms, do not address the fundamental nature of what a motion picture camera can produce. Vertov refers to himself and the other "kinoks" as "a herd of junkmen doing rather well peddling their rags."[24] The reference to rags is not incidental when placed within the context of Vertov's work and of the cinema of fabric. "In undressing a flirtatious bourgeoisie and a bloated bourgeois," he writes, "and in returning food and objects to the workers and peasants who've made them, we are giving millions of laborers the opportunity to see the truth and to question the need to dress and feed a caste of parasites."[25]

In writing on Vertov's *The Man with the Movie Camera* (1929), Annette Michelson draws a link between this film and Karl Marx's analysis in *The German Ideology* (1846/1932) of the rise of weaving in a nineteenth-century urbanized Europe. She notes Vertov's linkage of images of weaving in factories with the "cranks and spindles of the filmmaking apparatus"[26] and how the editing structure of the first two-thirds of the film has a "rhythmic pulsing of energy" that "culminates in the identification of filmmaking . . . as now directly and explicitly related to the paradigmatic form of industry: textile manufacture, itself seen as central in the economy's production."[27] For Michelson, such linkages are part of the film's "seamless organic continuum" and one linked as well to Vertov's Marxist dialectics.[28]

Vertov's Marxism is far removed from the romantic and often-androgynous cinema of fabric described thus far and is resistant to queer, camp readings. Nevertheless, women are fundamental to this new type of image making. *The Man with the Movie Camera* does not simply, as Michelson argues, link textile manufacturing with film editing. It shows it is *women* who are engaged in these rhymed activities, especially the woman working at the editing table assembling *The Man with the Movie Camera*, Yelizaveta Svilova. Throughout the film, the women engaged in labor and leisure are part of the film's relentless allegorizing of its own methods. At almost literally the halfway point in the film, a woman gives birth, the baby still attached to a crucial "fabric" of life-giving, the umbilical cord, and Vertov and Svilova are presenting us with a new Soviet society as new images of women are also being brought to life, liberated not simply within the social world being captured but also through the (female) labor of assembling the film's footage.

It is in the work of Sergei Eisenstein, though, where we find the early history of montage being not only tied to the cinema of fabric but elevated to the level of queer erotics. *Battleship Potemkin* (1925) is as useful an example as any. Much has been written on this indestructibly canonical film and its montage structure based on visual conflict within and across shots and where fabric becomes one of the motifs structuring the montage. As with Visconti, the reception of Eisenstein's films has adjusted itself in relation to increased acknowledgement of the director's sexuality. Eisenstein's, after being under-researched or even denied for many years, has now become myth, available to be appropriated for diverse purposes. In his later years Eisenstein's interest in bisexuality as an aesthetic image and philosophical position stood at the center of his interest in an art that could, as Yuri Tsivian writes, "embrace contradictions, to nutshell a conflict, to cause a collision; in other words, to shape what he calls the montage-image."[29]

In *Battleship Potemkin*, fabrics assume a heightened presence. The film contrasts the literal and symbolic heaviness of some phenomena with the comparative softness, even sensuality, of others and these have connotations in terms of the struggle for political power. An example is the sequence of the off-duty sailors asleep in hammocks on the battleship. A variety of shots illustrates the idea of sleeping sailors. The shot with which the sequence begins could loosely qualify as a master, but due to the cluttered framing and low-key lighting it is difficult to get a fully particularized view of the sailors; instead we have a generalized image of collective male bodies enveloped in the fabric of the hammocks. On one level, this is consistent with the film's political agenda, in which, in the words of an early intertitle, "the individual personality, having hardly had time to become conscious of itself, dissolved in the mass and the mass itself became dissolved in the revolutionary élan." But the cutting into gradually closer views of the men establishes another kind of contrast in that not only are faces and bodies individualized but the framings vary and the men even lie in the hammocks in different ways, creating a strong graphic of criss-crossing lines from shot to shot. Moreover, several of the men are either shirtless or have their shirt buttons opened. When an officer emerges from above deck and walks through the hammocks, he stumbles and, in anger, illogically blames a sleeping officer. The sailor is sleeping facedown and, in retaliation for the imagined offense, the officer whips the sailor's back, the gesture covered in three, slightly overlapping shots. What is most vivid about this imagery is the muscled back of the whipped sailor who, after turning over to look at the officer walking away, returns to his facedown position and weeps, the muscles of his back indicating this along with an intertitle, "Hurtful."

The sailor's back acquires its erotic force (as erotic as the back of Romy Schneider as she dries herself with a towel in *Il lavoro*) through several elements: the relationship between the back and the ways his skin captures the light; the relationship between the back as a type of mobile surface coexisting in the same frame with the hammock and rumpled sheet of the pillow into which he is crying; and the strikingly feminine image of maleness here, the sailor responding to the beating by crying like a child. Or a woman. As the film cuts into the closer views of the various men, sunk into their hammocks, the shots often evoke a body encased in a womb, the womb slit open for a cesarean. The symbolic potential of such images in a film that is also about an event anticipating the Bolshevik Revolution is not anecdotal: the Soviet Union is being "born" here. Vertov films a literal childbirth in order to produce a symbolic image of a new socialist utopia. But he remains tied to a certain biological imperative. For Eisenstein, images of birth are capable of being produced under multiple, shifting conceptions of gender even if, in the case of *Battleship Potemkin*, this involves a marginalizing of women from the process.

A foundational principle of Eisenstein's writings is cinematic pathos, loosely defined as "whatever 'sends' the spectator into ecstasy."[30] Such a response is twofold, partly tied to the images on-screen and the other occurring in the mind and body of the spectator. The spectator, aligned with the filmmaker's attitude toward the subject, "ecstatically" follows "a personage gripped by pathos" and, in the process, "goes out of himself." This occurs because in the imagistic structure there is a "radiating out into the surroundings and environment of a personage, that is, when his very surroundings also are presented in, say, his condition of 'frenzy.'"[31] However, we do not "go into *nothing*" here. "To go out of oneself inevitably implies a transition to something else, to something different in quality, to something opposite to what one was. . . ."[32] This "leap" is explicitly situated by Eisenstein in relation to materialist dialectics, "a transition from quantity to quality. A transition to opposition."[33] Strictly in terms of fabric, in *Battleship Potemkin*, hundreds of townspeople rise up in anger over the death of Vakulinchuk at the hands of the ship's officers. In the midst of various shots of individuals and groups expressing this need to rise up, Eisenstein cuts to a young

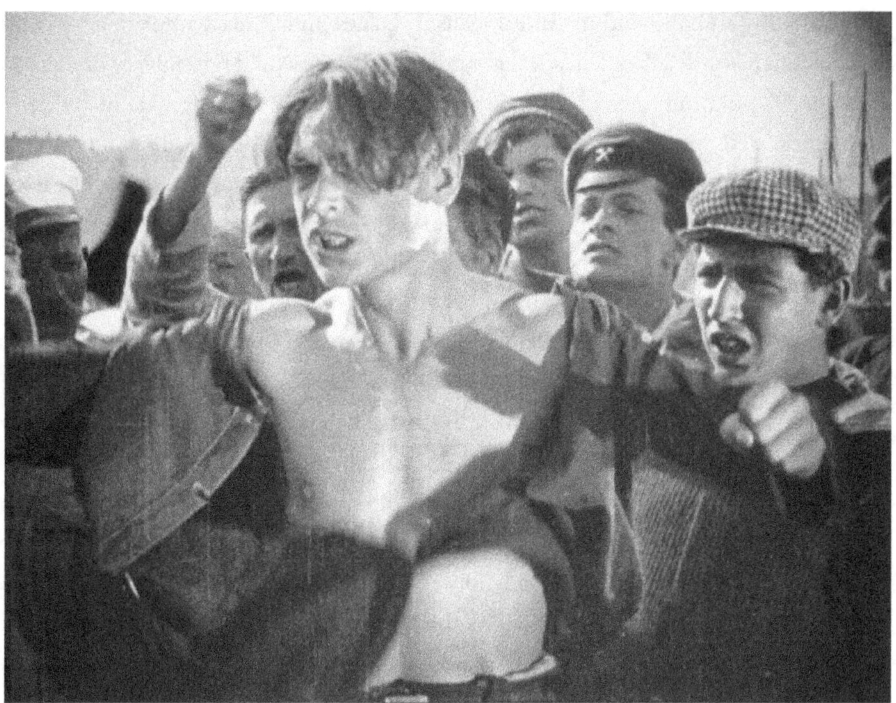

Battleship Potemkin (Sergei Eisenstein, 1925). Ecstasy through the tearing of the shirt.

man who, in his excitement, rips his shirt open, exposing his chest. The shot is very brief, as though to hold it any longer would mark a passage into an overtly *sexual* gesture of rising up. This image of a male body, his ecstasy communicated above all through the tearing of the shirt, has the potential to override the more pressing need to create an image of political resistance.

Let us imagine, then, another way of making use of Eisenstein's arguments as they may also be understood in relation to Visconti. This need to go out of oneself, to transition into something new, opposite to what one was, is also deeply romantic. This romanticism has potential in terms of queer aesthetics in which neither the events being perceived *by* the viewer nor the position *of* the viewer are static but are in an almost constant state of negotiation. There is in Eisenstein an intensity with which he approaches the work of art in which the creator/spectator is also refusing to normalize the work through conventional critical strategies. I shall return to Eisenstein in several passages in the book as a useful point of contact and contrast with Visconti: in their commitment to both Marxism and aestheticism; in their tying of these commitments to a cinema also documenting problems of history and cultural identity; and in the articulation of an erotics of cinema in which fabric becomes crucial.

In situating Visconti within critical realism, Daney and Oudart argue that Visconti is "completely unversed in dialectical materialism since it would put his very practice in question."[34] Built into such an argument is an assumption that dialectical materialism is the most desirable of methodologies for explicating social, political, and economic relations as well as for applying these to an analysis of aesthetic practices. But the issue here is not whether Visconti is "unversed" in dialectical materialism. Such a claim has built into it a presumption about what an aesthetic object must do before that object has even been produced. Eisenstein's films directly emerge out of a Communist revolution, and the goals of his early filmmaking practice are strongly tied to that moment. Visconti's first film was made during the declining years of a fascist dictatorship; and as he continues to make films in the aftermath of the war, he does so in a country where the left-wing desire for political dominance is the site of continuous struggle. In terms of the histories of cinematic form up through the time when Visconti began to emerge, dialectical montage would have been of limited to no use. Aside from the fact that this style of editing was indelibly tied to an earlier film movement now two decades old, the initial impulse behind this montage was produced under different political conditions from Visconti's. His roots in neorealism situate his work within a movement in which montage is downplayed in favor of a mise-en-scène attempting to interrogate the very nature of what an image must now represent.

In *Bellissima* (1951) there is a revealing sequence in regard to editing in neorealism. Stage mother Maddalena (Anna Magnani), anxious for her young, untrained daughter to make her acting debut in a film by director Alessandro Blasetti, manages to invade the workroom of a film editor, Iris (Liliana Mancini), at Cinecittá studios. Iris is editing the various screen tests of little girls for Blasetti and has already finished the one for Maddalena's daughter. In the midst of a conversation with Iris, Maddelena suddenly recognizes her as the star of *Under the Sun of Rome* (Renato Castellani, 1948), one of a number of now rarely discussed films of the neorealist era that partook of neorealist tendencies, including the use of nonprofessional actors such as Mancini. In *Bellissima*, though, Mancini explains that her lack of professional acting skills limited her chances at a career. She is now "reduced" to being an editor. In contrast to *The Man with the Movie Camera*, in which Svilova's intervention is fundamental to the project, in *Bellissima* editing is a gesture of survival in the cinema after one's dreams have been dashed.

Nevertheless, such pessimism about editing is complicated by the larger example of Visconti's filmmaking, in which the cut (even within the framework of analytical editing) frequently has enormous weight. We sometimes see this with a particular forcefulness when the cut is making itself felt in relation to fabric. One example will suffice for now and it is from his first film, *Ossessione* (1943). The cut in question occurs at the very end of a sequence in which the lovers are kissing in the bedroom of the adulterous wife, the kiss reflected in the mirror of a clothes cabinet belonging to the woman's grotesque husband, from whom she is desperate to escape. As the lovers kiss, the cabinet door slowly opens of its own accord, "like a curtain opening," as Ivo Blom phrases it,[35] revealing the husband's jackets and ties hanging there. As the camera tracks into these items, the image dissolves to a long shot of the husband bicycling down a road, unaware of the situation involving his wife. Most obviously what we have here is a conventional foreshadowing of the husband's murder, one that will be committed by his wife and her new lover. But the clothes divorced from the body of the husband, when combined with the uncanniness of the closet door opening and the dissolve to the oblivious husband, reduce the husband to little more than a spot on the landscape. Such strategies are not simply dramatic but tied to the social implications of a film produced during the declining months of Italian Fascism, in which death and decay are everywhere and where the "bloated bourgeois" aspects of the husband have their own implicit ties to an oppressive regime.

Two methods of understanding the cinema of fabric are now apparent and will be central to much of what follows here, one method built upon mise-en-scène (movement and volume within the shot) and the other upon montage (with editing itself becoming a type of weaving, now potentially tied to social, political, and historical ambitions). Both of these methods are central to Visconti.

INTERWOVEN

Dirty Laundry

In the history of Italian cinema, 1960 is the year of three monumental films: Federico Fellini's *La dolce vita*, Michelangelo Antonioni's *L'avventura*, and Luchino Visconti's *Rocco and His Brothers*. Their international success led to a significant Italian cinema revival, marking the first time the Italians were able to command this scale of attention since the emergence of neorealism roughly fifteen years earlier. And while *Rocco* has clear links with Visconti's earlier work, the film is also, in important respects, unlike his preceding films. When *La dolce vita*, *L'avventura*, and *Rocco* opened, they were taken to indicate new directions for Italian cinema that extended and critiqued the film movement that galvanized audiences immediately after the Second World War. "Do you think neorealism is dead or alive?" a reporter asks Sylvia (Anita Ekberg), the Hollywood star visiting Rome in *La dolce vita*. The question, like so many posed in *La dolce vita*, is never answered. From the time of its release up through the present day, *Rocco and His Brothers* has always been understood as the least formally innovative of the three films. Its ostensible classicism, though, is of a very particular nature.

Arguments for *Rocco*'s classicism are largely traceable to the film's novelistic dimension. Of particular relevance is how the film draws upon the forms of the nineteenth-century naturalist novel, where the realism is constructed through the accumulation of details and symbolic meanings, making use of extended descriptions of environments and the human figures within them, as in the work of Maupassant, Gustave Flaubert, Émile Zola, Giovanni Verga, Fyodor Dostoevsky. In 1946, Visconti staged a production of Dostoevsky's *Crime and Punishment* (1866), and the character of Rocco would, in its impossible "saintly" nature, have some of its basis in Prince Myshkin from *The Idiot* (1869). When Sam Rohdie writes that in *Rocco* "even the most banal detail seems overcharged," it is a response to this type of nineteenth-century realism.[1] Whether this literary heft disqualifies Visconti from fully belonging to neorealism is another matter. Guido Aristarco has argued that Visconti was "the first director in Italy to formulate a critical neorealism and the first to narrate films with the sweeping narrative scope of the novel."[2] What such an inclination on Visconti's part entails is indicative of an ambivalence of wishing to belong to a significant film movement while choosing to remain somewhat outside of it, as though commenting on the nature of this movement as much as participating in it.

It is not uncommon in the critical literature on realism and naturalism to refer to how its forms and motifs are "woven" together. This, in itself, is tied to the most basic element of the storyteller "spinning" a tale for an enraptured listener, even as it is also tied to the formal constructions of art in general, in particular arts that are temporal in nature and in which the aesthetic expressivity is often a question of this dense interweaving. In *The Brothers Karamazov* (1880), Dostoevsky has the Devil (in reality, a hallucination of Ivan Karamazov's) refer to "such artistic dreams, such complex and real actuality, such events, or even a world of events, woven into such a plot, with such unexpected details, beginning from your highest manifestations down to the last shirt button, as I swear even Leo Tolstoy couldn't invent."[3] It is Zola, though, who will, in *Au Bonheur des Dames*, elevate fabric to the most heightened of naturalist visions. In this novel on the emergence of the Paris department store, Zola writes of how

> lace shivered, fell back and hid the depths of the shop behind a disturbing veil of mystery; even the lengths of cloth, thick, square-cut, exhaled tempting breaths, while the coats on the dummies threw out their chests, endowing them with souls, and the great velvet overcoat swelled, warm and suppliant, as though across living shoulders with a beating breast and swaying hips.[4]

For the cinema, such anthropomorphic language has enormous possibilities, even though many Zola film adaptations fail to take full advantage. Eisenstein argues the "plastic side" to Zola's writing is, in its linking of human beings with the details of their environment, and in its desire to plunge us into the totality of a setting, "very close in [its] nature to cinema."[5] In Visconti, such an impulse is clearest in *Ossessione*, an unauthorized adaptation of James M. Cain's *The Postman Always Rings Twice* (1934). The debates as to whether *Ossessione* should be understood as an early neorealist film or a late example of thirties naturalism found in French cinema of that decade, such as Renoir's modern-dress adaptation of Zola's *La Bête Humaine* (1938), persist. For now, though, I would stress the importance of an early neorealist erotics, one with ties to nineteenth-century naturalism but articulated at a very different historical juncture. In its visual and dramatic density, *Ossessione* is as close to the world of Zola as it is to the world of American crime fiction to which Cain belongs. As in Zola, we find in Cain an attempt to document violent and sexual impulses with ties to the natural world. But Cain's language is, in contrast to Zola's, cryptic.

When we stopped it was in front of an undertaker shop in Hollywood, and they carried me in. Cora was there, pretty battered up. She had on a blouse that the police matron had lent her, and it puffed out around her belly like it was stuffed with hay. Her suit and her shoes were dusty, and her eye was all swelled up where I had hit it.[6]

Visconti retains the basic idea of a world covered in dust and grime, the filth extended to the clothing worn by his protagonists. But the film supplements and inflates Cain's universe.

Cain's novel is only 116 pages long. Visconti's film lasts for 140 minutes. On the fourth page of the novel, Frank Chambers (Gino in *Ossessione*) has his first look at Cora Papadakis (Giovanna in *Ossessione*). She is tersely described as someone who "wasn't any raving beauty, but she had a sulky look to her, and her lips stuck out in a way that made me want to mash them in for her."[7] What she is wearing as he spots her, the details of her home and work environment of Twin Oaks Tavern, none of this interests Cain as part of Frank's initial impressions. It is enough to describe the tavern as "nothing but a roadside sandwich joint, like a million others in California."[8] In Visconti's film, the trattoria where Gino (Massimo Girotti) meets Giovanna (Clara Calamai) is implicitly "like a million others" (consistent with the sociopolitical tradition of realism) even as the film plunges us into the details of this particular totality.

The attention to detail in the décor of the trattoria is of a kind in which Visconti's cinema will never cease to revel, in this case a world of forlorn and decaying abundance even amidst economic and material scarcity. But it is the initial encounter between Gino and Giovanna that has attracted the greatest detail of attention, in particular for its strategy of playing within and against various expectations. The encounter was designed as a shock for Italian viewers contemporaneous with the film's release, since both actors are "dirtied up" in a film intended to be a provocation to the Fascist cinema within which both actors had made significant appearances. Calamai's hair, bleached blonde in her most notable roles prior to this, is darkened, her appearance closer to Corinne Luchair's Cora in the French version of the Cain novel *Le Dernier tournant* (Pierre Chenal, 1939), although Luchair is otherwise filmed in a more conventionally glamorous way. Prior to *Ossessione*, Girotti and Calamai had major roles in films by Alessandro Blasetti, Girotti in the allegorical adventure *The Iron Crown* (1941) and Calamai in the tongue-in-cheek historical work *The Jester's Supper* (1942). But the contrast between these two films and *Ossessione* is not simply a matter of the presentation of the actors. Blasetti literally envelops these films in curtains, in sheer or ornate fabrics and creates androgynous environments of sexual sadism and masochism. In *The*

Iron Crown, Girotti is introduced wearing only a leopard-skin loincloth. His body is shaved, in contrast to the extremely hirsute body he presents in *Ossessione*. Early in *The Jester's Supper*, a man rips Calamai's chiffon gown as a threatened prelude to a sexual assault. The assault never transpires but the ripping briefly exposes Calamai's breasts.[9] The provocation of the eroticism in *Ossessione*, then, is one of context and form, attributable to the film's ties to naturalism. What Visconti does with his two stars, but especially Giroitti, is a dual process of at once "degrading" them, making them literally dirty, and, at the same time, reinvigorating them, making them desirable in another way, with a desire no less tied to the properties of cinema than the idealization in their earlier films.

In the opening sequence, Gino is at first only filmed from the back and side as he moves through the front of the trattoria, his face hidden as the camera takes in what he is wearing: a suit covered in dust with large tears in the elbows of both arms of the jacket, and his feet in moccasins, as though only the lightest of fabrics separates Gino's feet from the earth. There is nothing Chaplinesque about this image of a wandering, homeless male, but rather a sense of ruination. Nevertheless, it is also a typical star entrance, a slow buildup to the reveal of his face. Neither Gino nor the viewer sees Giovanna as she sings "Fiorin Fiorella" in what will turn out to be the kitchen. "Like Dante's Circle with the wanderer Ulysses," Geoffrey Nowell-Smith writes of Giovanna in this opening, "she entices Gino (significantly) by her singing."[10] But when the faces of both stars are finally revealed, there is an imbalance in their respective presentations. When Gino steps into the kitchen and discovers the source of the singing, Calamai's Giovanna receives the first close-up, shot in high key, the light evenly spread across her face, flattering to her but otherwise unremarkable. Giovanna is first looking down, polishing her fingernails. She quickly looks up at Gino, then looks back down, and then (a delayed reaction) quickly looks back up, slightly tilting her head as she now scrutinizes him. The cut to Gino is a quick tracking shot toward him, the lighting on this face more detailed than that given to Calamai: a key light hits the left of his face, his nose casting a discreet shadow on the face's right side; a small amount of fill light reaches this side as a flower-printed curtain hangs behind the left side of his face. We are seeing Gino through Giovanna's eyes even as the camera is supplementing her look with its own. Once Gino steps into the kitchen, the slight suspension introduced through this presentation is broken as he brazenly walks around, helping himself to food, and insultingly refers to the grotesque obesity of Giovanna's husband, Bragana (Juan De Landa), who is outside the trattoria. These exchanges are captured in wider mobile shots showing details of the large kitchen. Gino removes his jacket, revealing only a soiled, sleeveless T-shirt underneath. The sight of his exposed back causes

Giovanna, as she suddenly turns around to look at him, to literally stop in her tracks. For a cinema of fabric, though, it is the rags and towels that droop on the walls that create an indelible sense of the environment surrounding Giovanna.

Such attention to forlorn detail is a naturalist transposition. For Eisenstein, Zola is typical of the naturalists "going out of themselves" in the pressure they put on details, thereby elevating pathos to "an event that is by no means obliged to be pathetic" even as Zola remains mindful of the structure of the condition he is describing.[11] In *Thérèse Raquin* (1867) Zola describes the décor of the shop belonging to Madame Raquin: "On one side, there were a few articles of clothing: fluted tulle bonnets at two or three francs apiece; muslin sleeves and collars; and woolens, stockings, socks and braces. Each item, yellow with age, hung pitifully from a wire hook, so that the window, from top to bottom, was full of whitish rags that took on a mournful appearance in the transparent gloom."[12] In his 1953 modern-dress version of the novel, Marcel Carné reproduces none of this detail and the shop is simply a background, the fabrics looking clean, new, and immaculately ordered. *Ossessione* comes closer to Zola, with the rags and towels in Giovanna's kitchen taking on a "mournful appearance in the transparent gloom."

During Frank's second encounter with Cora in *The Postman Always Rings Twice*, her outfit is described as "one of those white nurse uniforms, like they all wear, whether they work in a dentist's office or a bakeshop. It had been clean in the morning, but it was a little bit rumpled now, and messy. I could smell her."[13] Tay Garnett's Hollywood version of *The Postman Always Rings Twice* (1946) retains a whiteness linked with Cora (Lana Turner, whose hair is bleached) and sustains it for much of the film. But it is a white that never becomes soiled. *Ossessione* does not participate in this type of visual irony but appears to build upon a description of Cora from a passage late in Cain's novel in which Frank observes her getting off a train wearing a black dress "that made her look tall, and a black hat, and black shoes and stockings . . ."[14] Giovanna is largely associated with black, so that the sense of white declining into visible filth is eliminated. It is as though the grime is thoroughly embedded in her, a blackness that will also be linked with her own death. The image of a woman in black will recur in Visconti although its implications will shift from film to film. In *Rocco and His Brothers*, Rosaria (Katina Paxinou), the Parondi matriarch, is enshrouded in black, partly as an indication of her status as a widow but partly because in black she can extravagantly perform the *role* of grieving. When she is reunited with her oldest son, Vincenzo (Spiros Focás), at Vincenzo's engagement party to Ginetta (Claudia Cardinale), she disapprovingly comments that he has stopped wearing mourning clothes. Moreover, Rosaria's black clothing removes her from any bodily display. It is as though these shrouds *become* her body, desexualizing her. In much of the early part of *Ossessione*, Gino's T-shirt is not only soiled but somewhat too small, unwittingly displaying chest muscle and with a nipple periodically exposed.[15] Such an eroticizing of the male figure has naturalist precedents, particularly if applied to working-class figures equated with primal desires. In *Thérèse Raquin*, Zola describes the male protagonist, Laurent, as someone about whom "you could sense the swelling, well-developed muscles beneath his clothes, and the whole body, with its thick, firm flesh. Thérèse examined him curiously from his hands to his face, feeling a little shudder pass through her when she reached his bull's neck."[16]

The struggle in *Ossessione* is one that recurs in Visconti, in which the human subjects, in their intense need to look at an object of desire, are at once creators and spectators of images. The camera is ambiguously aligned with these human subjects while also giving itself the power to move through and articulate its own desires in relation to what it sees and creates. If Gino is much more strongly marked as an object of desire than Giovanna, it is less clear who has the greater force in controlling such states. Early in the film, after Bragana leaves Giovanna alone at the trattoria, Gino is working on the water pump outside when he hears Giovanna sing the same "siren song" that first lured him into the kitchen. Gino throws down the pump and walks toward the trattoria and stops. As he decides to move forward, there is a cut from a close-up of him framed from the waist up to a reverse angle, forward tracking shot, moving toward the trattoria's entrance. When the mobile shot begins, it implies his point of view, but the implication is almost immediately challenged when Gino walks into the shot from the left, the movement now suggesting the camera's autonomy. Whatever "natural" attractions are occurring between the protagonists, they are also drawn together by forces larger than themselves. But as Gino hears Giovanna's voice and moves forward, he wipes his hands on his T-shirt, a gesture of further rubbing the sweat and dirt into the fabric. The gesture itself equally implies something autoerotic, the dirty, decaying shirt placed against Gino's chest intensifying him as a naturalist image of desire, offered to the camera and to the (potentially desiring) spectator.

Bursting at the Seams

The title of *Rocco* most obviously evokes Mann's tetralogy *Joseph and His Brothers* (1926–43) as well as *The Brothers Karamazov*. Aristarco argues the film may be seen partly as a reference to Rocco Scotellaro, who wrote poetry devoted to the peasants of his region.[17] And Henry Bacon has drawn attention to how Visconti and his screenwriters made use of more contemporaneous Italian literature, including the work of Carlo Levi and Giovanni Testori.[18] One may speak, then, of a self-conscious fusion in *Rocco* of not so much classical and modernist forms of realism as multiple versions of these forms, subject as they have been to changing historical and cultural conceptions. These fusions, I would argue, lead to a certain experience of the image with ties to cinematic pathos.

As in Eisenstein, a Marxist awareness of economic and social oppression becomes a driving force. But in Visconti this is caught up short by a passage not so much from quantity to quality as from one quality to another, this other quality being an erotics that cannot be contained by explicit social or political agendas. The older Parondi brothers, Rocco (Alain Delon) and Simone (Renato Salvatori) "burst the bounds of the ordinary," as Rohdie puts it, in a film that regards "the ordinary as repressive." Visconti creates a world in which one must move toward "a depth beyond the normal."[19] Crucial for creating this is the relationship between the texture of bodies and faces and the texture and forms of fabric, even as these remain tied to the film's sociopolitical ambitions.

Early in the film, Rocco gets a job in a laundry owned by a beautiful, older woman, Luisa (Suzy Delair), and staffed by young women. Rocco is established here and in much of the first section of the film as fundamentally an innocent. In one shot in the laundry sequence in which he announces the arrival of Simone, a wooden doll is visible on the far left, Pinocchio, another Italian innocent who finds himself descending into a nightmarish underworld. The women who work at the laundry dote on Rocco but in an almost platonic manner. To the women, Rocco is their "sleeping beauty" in need of a kiss to awaken him. (Luisa, in contrast, has had trouble sleeping the night before.) It is as though they are speaking to a prepubescent child, more feminine than masculine, even as their sleeping beauty reference implies a form of gender reversal.

Simone's arrival at the laundry brings a very different sexual energy to the proceedings. Rocco mainly stands off to the side in the laundry, the bulk of the activity occurring center and left as the women move about. It is as though he is observing the action more than participating in it. When Simone enters, however, he immediately begins exploring the space, such an exploration clearly bound up for Simone in terms of the women there. One laundress (Adriana Asti) tells Simone that customers come, undress, and then go out brand new. That such a miraculous process of taking off one's dirty clothes and then quickly having them cleaned is also expensive does not intimidate Simone, who insists, albeit ironically, that he has money. This laundry becomes the site of bourgeois privilege in which others literally do your dirty work. In virtually every shot of the sequence, dirty and clean jackets, pants, shirts, and dresses hang or are piled up and displayed. But the conveniences of this world are inaccessible to those who work there, with Rocco even lower in the class pecking order than Luisa's female employees, hence his tangential physical placement in the space.

Luisa's entrance, brought about by her hearing the commotion Simone has caused, does not break the sexual and class tensions Simone has created but intensifies them. The screenplay describes Luisa's entrance as being marked by "another curtain, of the same material as that forming the dressing room" then "suddenly pulled aside."[20] In the final film, she does not pull the curtains aside and instead she is framed by them at the entrance to the rear of the laundry. Initially unaware Simone is Rocco's brother, she is attracted to him, eyes quickly scanning his body, and she offers him one of the dressing rooms. But Luisa refuses to clean Simone's shirt because it is too frayed, a clear indication of his class status. Even so, this does not inspire Luisa's revulsion but, like a protégée of the Baron de Charlus, Simone is desirable because of his "rough trade" appeal, and she folds over and examines the frayed shirt in a way exceeding a simple evaluation of its wear and tear. In a wide three-shot, as an undressed Simone holds the dressing room curtain over the lower part of his body, she looks first at his chest (covered in a sleeveless white T-shirt), then at his shirt while she insists, smiling, there is nothing she can do, as her eyes quickly look him up and down. Simone's covering of his body is only partially successful, and he is soon almost entirely visible in his underwear to Luisa as he mechanically holds the curtain in his hand.

Their encounter comes to an end when she closes the dressing room curtain, the curtain briefly dominating almost half of the frame. But this is immediately followed by a cut to Luisa walking toward the main space of the laundry, curtains draping this entrance that also serve to frame this shot. Rocco enters middle right, carrying a basket of clean laundry, and walks over to Simone. Luisa is at the far left, in the foreground, and as Simone and Rocco talk she examines Simone's trousers. Her smile and the examination connote both her sexual attraction to the owner of those pants and the gestures of a businesswoman with a pragmatic task before her of cleaning for someone whose class status is decidedly lower than that of her usual customers. In fact, the conversation between the brothers and Luisa is over money, with Rocco's wages being the final sacrifice he makes for his brother in helping him to pay for his laundry adventure. Simone continues to hold the dressing room curtain over the bottom half of his body. But the gesture indicates more of a slight embarrassment over the financial arrangement being discussed for his benefit than it does a display of sexual modesty.

Near the end of the shot of Simone covering himself with the curtain, and after Luisa and Rocco have exited the frame, Simone surreptitiously looks down at a table of dress shirts. Still holding the curtain in front of him, Simone takes a shirt off of the table. A match-on-action shows the theft continuing in a closer view, the camera tilting up from Simone's chest to his face, as he quickly closes the curtain. The next cut, however, takes us to other side of the curtain, a slightly low-angled shot. The curtain now hides Simone's activities from the women in the main space of the laundry. For the spectator, Simone is visible, admiring himself in the mirror as he holds the folded shirt in front of him and then stuffs it into his bag. On the level of narrative construction, the spectator's privileged view of Simone's action functions as a piece of dramatic irony. But it also provides a privileged view of his body in an otherwise private space, the various fabrics heightening our experience of the environment and the unfolding dramatic situations. But the fabrics here are not only sexual. When Simone reaches for that clean, white shirt on the table, it is a gesture of resistance, a refusal to accept his lot in life that stands in contrast to the passivity of Rocco, whose saintly nature causes him to accept what is handed to him.

Such a moment bears comparison with a sequence in *La terra trema* involving Lucia Valastro (Agnese Giammona), the younger sister of the Valastro fishing family. As Lucia and her older sister Mara (Nelluccia Giammona) are doing needlepoint, Don Salvatore (Rosario Galvagno), the local policeman, arrives and tempts Lucia with a silk scarf, dangling it through the window. He tells her she was born to wear fine things, speaking to her as though he were the Mephistopheles of the island. He compliments her on her beauty and tells her that she does not belong in a village but in a large city where she will find the material rewards to which she is entitled. Earlier in the film, as Lucia puts sheets on a bed she tells a fairy story to the youngest sister about a king's son who falls in love with a girl when he sees her thimble. Throughout Visconti, the bed becomes a space to which the protagonists and the

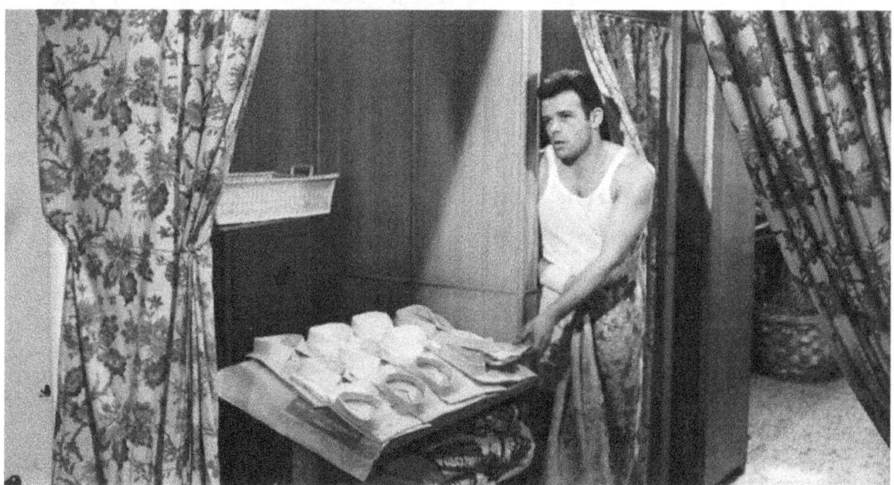

Rocco and His Brothers (1960). Reaching for the shirt as a gesture of resistance.

films are drawn, not only for sleep and sexual encounters but also as sites of new potentials, in which desires are articulated in ways outside of the various dominant cultures being represented. Sheets, blankets, and pillows are used in an expressive manner exceeding, even in restricted economic situations, mere functionality. Such potentials, though, are invariably short-lived, as the material reality of the surrounding world intervenes. For Eisenstein, "the bed is the real sphere of man's activities: it is here that he is born, he loves, he dies."[21] As Lucia tells this story, she sits on the bed and dreamily looks off, as though the combination of clean white sheets and a fairy tale in which a thimble becomes the locus of attraction between a man and a woman is her entrée into the world of fantasy. While Lucia initially attempts to keep a physical distance from Don Salvatore, the sight of the dangling scarf is too much for her. As Mara continues to focus on her needlepoint, her sister walks over to the window, where she touches the scarf and rubs it against her cheek before finally pulling herself back against the wall and claiming such an item is too luxurious for her, then collapsing onto the bed. And as she talks of her love for silk scarves, earrings, and a necklace, there is a cut to Mara holding her knitting in her lap and putting her chin on her hand. The scarf, like the shirt Simone steals, is tied to the desire for class ascension, one even more impossible in *La terra trema*, where the problems facing the characters are much more socioeconomic than in *Rocco*, where the socioeconomic problems coexist with problems of both a mythic and an existential nature. By the time this scarf is being dangled before Lucia, her family's already limited financial means have been decimated and the destinies of both sisters now are clearly linked with the humbleness of their needlepoint. But the scarf is also, like the shirt and all of Simone's own clothing, a type of sexual object. Even though Don Salvatore repeatedly stresses he is a friend to Lucia, he implicitly expects sexual favors for this gift, ones that could conceivably ruin Lucia's reputation in the village. And, in fact, her mildly flirtatious exchanges with him will do just that, even without her acting on the temptations of the scarf. The manner in which the issues in *La terra trema* receive articulations through fabric, then, are different from those in *Rocco and His Brothers* and for reasons very much tied to the urgency of the neorealist moment in which *La terra trema* was made.

Knitting and Patching

In writing on Roberto Rossellini's *Paisà* (1947), André Bazin locates much of neorealism's interest in the documentary-like nature of its images, in its visual and dramatic sketchiness closer to the elliptical, journalistic impulse of contemporary American literature, and in its deliberate absence of overt aestheticizing.[22] With regard to Vittorio

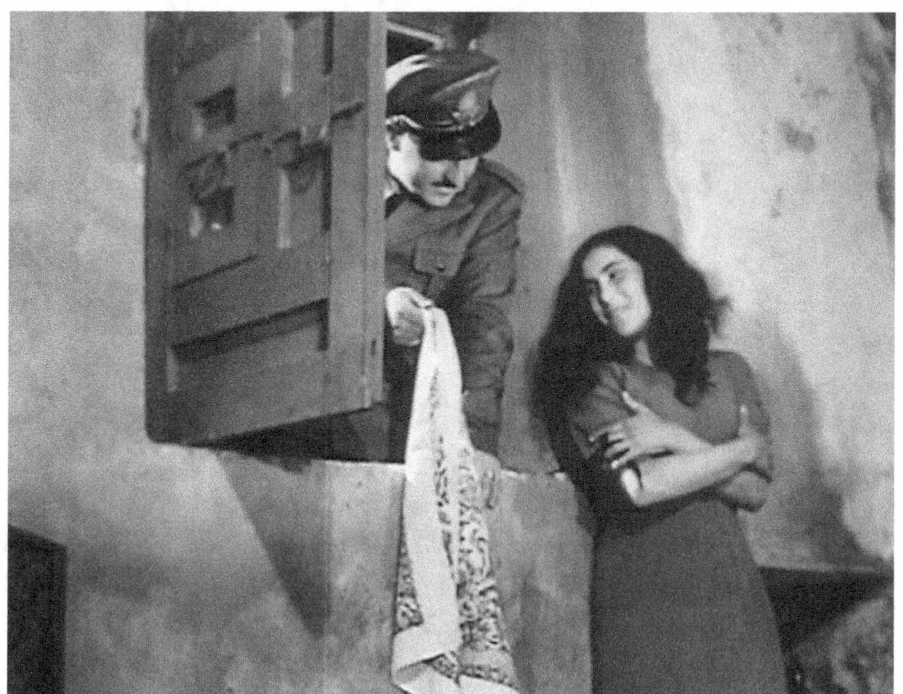

La terra trema (1948). Temptations of the scarf, an entrée into another world.

De Sica's *Bicycle Thieves* (1948), Bazin draws attention to how neorealism has given itself over to the "disappearance" of the story, the actor, the mise-en-scène. The more uneven rhythms and tone of Rossellini are replaced in De Sica by a comparatively seamless editing style and meticulous screenplay construction that nevertheless create an effect of "respect" for the reality of its subject matter and in a way consistent with the larger goals of neorealism.[23] Bazin's counterexample is Vertov, in which "everyday events" are situated within a "dialectical spectrum of montage."[24] Bazin posits a neorealism that "knows only immanence. It is from appearances only, the simple appearance of beings and of the world, that it knows how to deduce the ideas that it unearths. It is a phenomenology."[25]

For the cinema of fabric, *Bicycle Thieves* is of particular interest in relation to the early canon of neorealism. The decision by Maria Ricci (Lianella Carell) to give her husband, Antonio (Lamberto Maggiorani), their bed sheets so he can buy back his bicycle from the pawnbroker allows for the basic situations and conflicts of the film to occur. She strips the bed and carries the sheets into the kitchen, where she tosses them into a corner, as a laundry bucket filled with another set of sheets is waiting to be washed. She pours water into this bucket as the film dissolves to bundled sheets being passed through the pawnbroker's window. When the husband goes to another window with his receipt for the bicycle, he sees through this window a man carrying what is presumably the bag he and his wife have brought. The camera pans with this man as he walks across the room and, in long shot, wall-to-wall racks reaching the ceiling are now visible, piled high with bag after bag of laundry. The man begins to climb these racks as the camera continues to pan, as well as to tilt, following his movements. But there is a cut before he has completed the journey, as though the movement, like the bags themselves, is infinite. Those bags are, on the most immediate level, a realistic notation arising out of the economic despair of postwar Italy. But the sheer volume of them gives rise to other interpretations. When Maria earlier states that the family can temporarily do without sheets, she is acknowledging that fabric is a luxury when it comes to economic survival. The laundry bags at the pawnbroker's are not quite junk (since they have the potential to be resold). But within the immediate context these sheets become material surplus. In addition, the sheets are tied to human use, to the bodies lying on them. The Riccis receive less money for them than anticipated because most of the sheets, while washed, are used. The laundry bundles piled on top of one another become extensions of a human body, as expendable as the objects surrounding it. After this, however, *Bicycle Thieves* moves on and does not employ fabric as a structuring idea. Instead, it is the bicycle that will become the film's central image of muchness, even as these sheets are the precondition for the bicycle. It is up to Visconti, of the major neorealist directors, to systematically pursue a more sustained approach to fabric.

With *La terra trema*, though, Bazin is disturbed by the evidence of formalism and of an "aesthetic participation in history."[26] In contrast to *Battleship Potemkin*, in *La terra trema* there is "no moving eloquence to bolster its documentary vigor."[27] These words were written in 1948. Four years later, in *Cahiers du cinéma*, Amédée Ayfre would write on neorealism and *La terra trema* in ways of more immediate relevance to this book. Ayfre and Bazin share many of the same concerns in relation to neorealism, including its phenomenological possibilities. But Ayfre implicitly responds to Bazin's misgivings by arguing that the film's visual beauty and self-conscious formalism are no less authentic than the "deliberate neutralism" found in *Bicycle Thieves*:

> Like those figures which can be seen in depth or relief at will, a Vermeer painting can be a diligent lace-maker at her window or a skillful chromatic effect in blue, silver-grey and very pale orange, radiating out from a pulpy, velvety, almost flesh surface. The same experience can come from Visconti's genuine Sicilian fishermen. The glory (in almost the theological sense of the

word) he shrouds them in does not veil them but is what enables them to be seen.[28]

Ayfre joins company with Miller, Daney, and Oudart in relying upon the language and metaphors of fabric in order to evoke the experience of a Visconti film, although in this instance for very different reasons. For Ayfre, to shroud a human figure has less to do with fetishism and displacement than with revealing the mystery of God's universe and of grace itself, even as such a transcendent interpretation does not necessarily foreclose a secular one.

Foreshadowing *Rocco*, itself conceived of as a loose continuation of *La terra trema*, the film has several crucial sequences involving the brothers dressing and undressing. But the clothing of the men is comparatively tattered in contrast with what is worn by the professional actors in *Rocco*, the latter film offering a more stylized conception of the working-class "real." Of the Parondi brothers undressing in *Rocco*, Miller writes of how such actions evoke a "sleepy limbo of latency" in which "all things seem possible, because none [of the brothers] has submitted to the mangling limitations of social realization and rule."[29] Such a limbo is not foreign to *La terra trema*, in which the choreography of dressing and undressing is so strongly tied to the men rather than the women. In the film's opening, the women go through a typical early morning ritual of cleaning the home and getting things ready for the returning men. But they are already dressed, with Mara helping Lucia to put on a scarf as the final touch, these actions becoming quasi-hieratic. Noa Steimatsky has drawn attention to a theatrical realism at work in the film, the use of locations suggesting "a conception of nature as a contained, determinant, humanized stage—and a conception of reality as itself such a set."[30]

A major example of this is the sequence in which the Valastro sisters and their mother (the mother holding a baby) stand on the harbor rocks as they anxiously wait for the men to return from the sea. Described by Nowell-Smith as a sequence having "a straight emotional charge that is reminiscent of Eisenstein,"[31] it opens in long shot, the women in silhouette standing on the rocks and looking out to sea. The camera, which is at a three-quarter side view of the women, begins to slowly pan left, away from them to the crashing waves as a setting sun begins to break through the overcast sky. *Battleship Potemkin* opens with a brief montage of a violent sea, waves crashing against a rocky shore. But there are no human figures in the shots and the film immediately claims these images for political metaphor, for a latent revolution about to rise up. While *La terra trema* is the most explicitly Marxist of all of Visconti's films (particularly evident in the voice-over narration and in the dialogue of the oldest Valastro son, the politicized 'Ntoni), Visconti's sea is not called upon to signify in the manner of Eisenstein's, nor is its violence particularly naturalist. The sea's power is larger than the human fantasies and struggles projected onto it.

After the pan out to the sea, there is a cut to a closer group view of the women, all of them standing in full profile, carefully positioned in the low-angle frame. Lucia is in the front, on the highest rock, looking out and holding her youngest sister, Lia; Mara is several feet behind but also several feet closer to the camera, on a lower rock; and the mother is at the far right, slightly higher than Mara in the frame but slightly lower than Lucia and her sister. The bodies of the women are very still. The primary images of movement are the black shawls on the women, as they flutter about due to the high winds. Lucia not only stands higher and is closer to the sea than Mara and her mother, she is the only one here whose head moves as she scans the horizon. Lucia is the one female member of the Valastros with a strong desire to experience a world beyond Acitrezza, a world represented by that silk handkerchief dangled through the window of the home she and her family will be forced to move into after they have lost the mortgage on their prior home. Mara is the older sister and is in the foreground. But her essential passivity leads to her being lower in the frame, whereas her long-suffering mother is relegated to the far right and rear of the shot. The various cuts into closer views of the women are all done at a low angle: first Lucia and Lia, then Mara and her mother (Mara right foreground, mother left background), then a single of the mother before returning to Lucia and Lia, this time with a tighter two-shot, and finally a single on Mara, who looks down, as though resigned. The sequence ends with a long shot of all the women, filmed from behind as they look out, the sea dominating the frame, as they then slowly turn and walk away.

The low-angled, tableau-like shots here impart a mythic quality to their struggles, taking place on a "humanized stage" in which reality becomes a set. But it is arguably the movement of the black shawls that has the greatest expressive power. Their blackness already implies a Trojan Women–like mourning. And while the images of the women here indicate a family unit, their differences are also indicated not only in the blocking but in how the shawls are draped around them. Lucia does not cover her head but, "freer" than her mother and Mara, she simply drapes the shawl around her shoulders as her long hair blows in the wind. Her little sister beside her, though, has her head covered, as do Mara and Mrs. Valastro. The youngest sister's face is exposed, whereas Mara and the mother use part of the shawl to cover their mouths from the wind. In the two-shot of Mara and Mrs. Valastro, the covering of mouths with the shawl draws a link between these women of two different generations. Mrs. Valastro firmly keeps her shawl over her mouth, whereas Mara keeps covering and uncovering her mouth, Mara implicitly destined to inherit the same social position as her mother. Beyond this, the movements of their shawls become an expression of not only anxious waiting but also the collective melancholy and helplessness of all the Valastros in the face of natural and economic disasters.

Visconti's general approach to fabric in the midst of poverty differs sharply with the films of his neorealist colleagues. For example, contrast the decaying coats and sweaters worn by Pasquale (Franco Interlenghi) and Giuseppe (Rinaldo Smordoni) in De Sica's *Shoeshine* (1946) with the sweater worn by Vanni (Antonio Micale), one of the younger brothers in *La terra trema*. For De Sica, the clothes on the boys are realistic details integrated into the film's larger socioeconomic portrait of postwar Italy, the clothes suggesting found objects that, in their original conditions, would have been beyond the economic reach of the world of the boys. While decay in the clothing is evident, there are no framings drawing particular attention to this. For Visconti, Vanni's sweater is also a realistic notation but something more, an object over which the camera lingers. In one sequence late in the film, Vanni returns home, soaked from the rain, with money he has earned, and he stands with his back to the camera, facing an open window looking out toward the sea. As he does so, we are given time

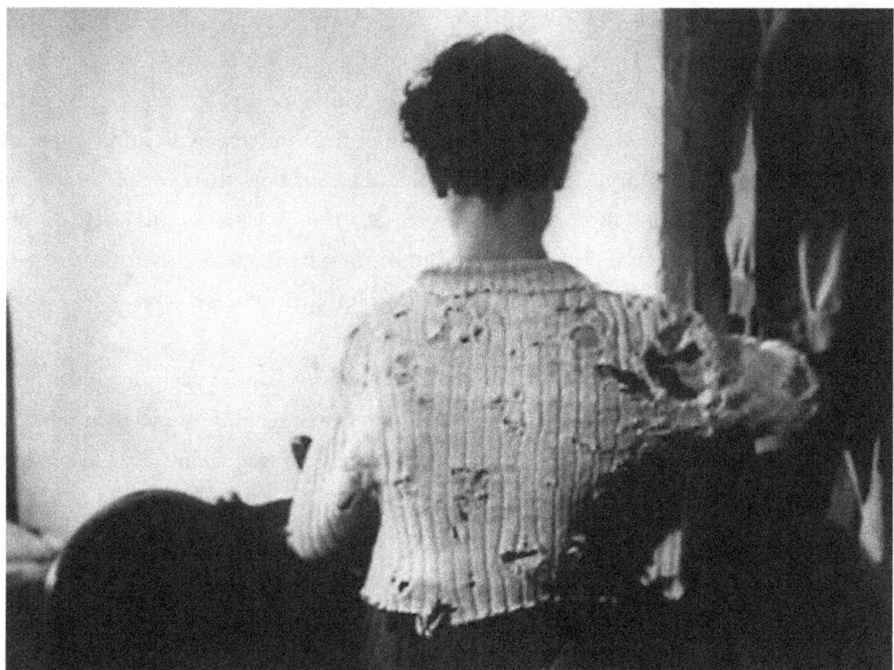

La terra trema. The paradoxical beauty of the decayed sweater.

to scan the sweater, to absorb its paradoxical beauty, before Vanni turns around and speaks to his brothers.

This moment is situated within yet another sequence of the men undressing, with the oldest brother 'Ntoni (Antonio Arcidiacono) taking off his sweater, revealing a muscled back and chest, before he slowly walks across the room and puts on a T-shirt. As he walks back to the bed, Vanni is standing on it, back to the camera and visible from the neck down, now wearing only boxer shorts, and the two brothers get into bed together. Within the realm of the fiction, we understand these to be brothers and that this environment is not incestuously homosexual. At the same time, we may experience such moments in ways not strictly tied to the potentially repressive alibi of story and fictional characters. That is to say, we are also looking at "real life" individuals (unrelated by blood) moving in front of a camera. And these images of putting on and taking off clothes and doing so in front of other men carry with them a particular sexual charge.

La terra trema is not utterly singular among neorealist films in creating an image of homosocial male bonding with homosexual possibilities. Parker Tyler sees the "true friendship pacts" between Pasquale and Giuseppe in *Shoeshine* as "potentially homosexual." While noting that "sex as such never enters the action," Tyler adds that "it doesn't have to. It is perfectly, palpably implicit. Despite the sordid harshness of this Damon-and-Pythias story, a pure and tender homosexuality threads it and survives when it is over."[32] De Sica gives us a tracking shot of various boys in the reform school showering, nude. Although Pasquale and Giuseppe are not among the boys in the shower, the somewhat superfluous nature of the shot creates an atmosphere of possibilities. And the film includes enough prepubescent boys there for the eroticism to be denied at the same moment it is offered. *Shoeshine* creates an intensity, almost romantic in nature, between the two boys. But the film has none of the erotic aestheticism of *La terra trema* (which otherwise has no implied same-sex love story), thus muting its more extreme potential.

In the "aesthetic participation in history" of *La terra trema*, the rhythms of the film are notably slow, the actors moving in an attenuated manner. The slowness no doubt has much of its basis in nonprofessional actors having to execute complicated staging ideas within a film relying on extended takes, depth-of-field shooting, and sometimes intricate camera movements. As a political film showing idealized male bodies in relation to political struggles, it is the inverse of *Battleship Potemkin*. For Eisenstein, the sleeping, half-dressed men of his film finally rise up and take action, doing so within a highly elliptical, montage-based work, its seventy-five-minute running time but one indication of its economy of form. For Visconti, in a film over two and a half hours long, sleep becomes a state toward which the men succumb, as though defeated, unable to enact the ecstatic images of resisting that dominate the male figures in Eisenstein.

In *La terra trema,* there are shifting energies between male and female, masculine and feminine and in which the men are often more beautiful than the women. Some of this has its basis in Verga's *I Malavoglia* and its occasional references to men whose beauty or feminine qualities are, in turn, tied to fabric. Alfio, a character not used in the film, is a bachelor described as someone who "knows how to sew and do his wash and darn his own shirts." Once married, "his wife will go around with the donkey cart and he'll stay home to raise the children."[33] A detail from the novel reproduced by the film is the description of the photograph of a uniformed 'Ntoni in the navy, in which he "looked like the Archangel Michael in the flesh, with those feet planted on the carpet and that drapery above his head, just like the drapery above the Madonna of Ognina, so handsome, so licked and polished that even his own mother wouldn't have recognized him."[34] 'Ntoni's beauty in the photograph is reinforced not only through the clothing he is wearing but through the fabric of the mise-en-scène surrounding him.

Women are often at the edges or backgrounds of the frame, weaving or knitting in a world in which the clothing of the men otherwise is worn, patched. The one exception is when the Valastros go into Catalonia in order to take out a mortgage and the women help the men dress. Upon his happy return, 'Ntoni has a reunion with his girlfriend, Nedda (Rosa Costanzo), and 'Ntoni is still wearing a nice shirt, a sweater vest, and a tie. But Nedda playfully pulls the tie off of him, a prelude to lovemaking but also a gesture that indicates such garments are not part of 'Ntoni's natural order. If the decayed male clothing achieves such a force it is also because the very notion of the fabric tear is part of a larger visual patterning. The opening sequence is built around things being torn, not clothing but fishing nets, in which tears are everywhere and the *men* must do the stitching, as though the nets are an extension of the fragile nature of the entire community. But the men soon find themselves metaphorically caught in netting of a more severe nature, tied to economic oppression. When 'Ntoni later discovers Nedda has gone away, he walks along the shore where men are repairing sails and nets, a world from which he is now excluded. The film's resolution requires 'Ntoni to put back on the shirt with holes and his patched pants. As he steps outside of his home, returning to his job as fisherman, he sees his two younger brothers, also in rags, all of this serving as an image of defeat, the possibility of political resistance indefinitely delayed.

Bedding Down

In a 1954 review of *Senso,* Bazin offers a different interpretation of *La terra trema* from the one he offered six years earlier. He now sees that the Valastros "were not dressed in rags, they were draped in them like tragic princes. Not because Visconti was trying to distort or simply interpret their existence but because he was revealing its imminent dignity."[35,36] Such a shifting view is in itself indicative of the ambivalences generated by Visconti's aestheticizing through fabric, in particular when such aestheticizing is tied to the spectacle of male beauty. For Daney and Oudart, much of Visconti's fascination with the proletariat is symptomatic of a bourgeois fascination with "the dirtiness of the object of desire." Visconti finds the proletarian men of his films desirable *because* they are dirty and thereby make *him* dirty as well, confirming his own belief that the class system from which he emerges is decadent. At the same time, Visconti sees them as not dirty at all but as aristocrats (like him), "tragic princes" displaying their "imminent dignity."[37] On this last point, Daney and Oudart refer to Proust and the propensity of the Baron de Charlus to pursue young men clearly beneath his station in life who are then elevated by the Baron to the status of equals in his social world. Daney and Oudart's rather florid Marxist and Freudian reading of Visconti gives sharp articulation to the sexual and social undercurrents of the films. But broader context in relation to Italian cinema during this period is needed. In Rossellini's early neorealist films *Rome, Open City* (1945) and *Germany, Year Zero* (1947), fabric is a largely negative force in a world in which Nazism is conflated with homosexuality. Such an approach contrasts with what is found in *Ossessione*, where the war is never overtly represented and where homosexuality (and fabric) assumes a very different function.

Hence the importance of Spagnolo (Elio Marcuzzo). There is no equivalent in Cain's novel or the other film versions. Spagnolo embodies one of two alternatives for Gino beyond the world represented by Giovanna—the other option tied to Anita (Dhia Cristiani), a character who does, in fact, have an equivalent in Cain, Madge Allen. But it is Spagnolo who transforms the implications of the film. As has often been noted, his assumed name of Spagnolo (real name: Giuseppe) would, given the historical context, have implied a tie to the Republican forces of the Spanish Civil War. This, according to one of the screenwriters on the film, Mario Alicata, was Spagnolo's purpose in an earlier draft of the screenplay. Gino was intended to have been, for Alicata, a "positive character" who had returned from Spain and "gone on the road to promote Socialism and anti-Fascism."[38] (How this would be achieved in a film made during the Fascist period is unclear.) Visconti, though, has claimed credit for the character's "entire creation," someone who was "the arch symbol of revolution and free thought," and also addressed "social and poetic problems."[39] Given Alicata's unhappiness with the final result, it is safe to assume that, whatever Visconti's Marxist sympathies, revolution and free thought assume different implications for him than for the likes of Alicata.

The "social and poetic problems" Spagnolo introduces are threefold. The first is that he articulates a certain philosophy of the nonmaterial. This is not lived through asceticism but through a cavalier approach to capital. Spagnolo refuses property and fixed ownership, bringing the character close to philosophical Cynicism. Instead of owning things, he is a traveler. The second is that he is deeply Italian in a pre-Fascist sense. He identifies himself as an artist but the art he practices is a type of hucksterism, telling fortunes in market squares. This is less a sign of Spagnolo's "unsavory" nature than it is a way of tying him to the Italian folk culture and its vernacular customs and gestures that Fascism was intent on eliminating, bringing him close to the early world of commedia dell'arte. If Gino's entrance as a "tramp" in the opening sequence resists the evocation of Chaplin, Spagnolo comes much closer to Chaplin's Tramp, in not only his clothing and bowler hat but also his poetic ties to the dispossessed. (He otherwise, though, lacks the Tramp's comparative innocence.) The third is that he is implicitly homosexual, thus becoming another alternative for Gino attempting to break free of Giovanna's hold over him, which is not simply sexual but tied to the very things Spagnolo opposes. And these problems receive sharp articulations through fabric.

After their initial meeting on a train, Gino and Spagnolo check into a rundown hotel, where Gino drops his suitcase and clothes spill out. The clothes are Giovanna's, as is the suitcase, the result of his angrily storming away and leaving her along the road after she changed her mind about running away with him. Among these items are silk stockings, which Spagnolo picks up as he jokingly asks Gino if he sells women's apparel. Gino's angry response to Spagnolo—to stay out of his business—allows for the stockings and all of Giovanna's clothing to be not only a metonym for the feminine (and possibly for Gino's own repressed feminine, i.e., homosexual, side) but also the indexical signs of a very specific woman whom Gino continues to carry around with him. The contents of this suitcase form a point of rupture between the two men, circumventing the possibilities of Gino and Spagnolo firmly becoming a couple, sexual or otherwise.

They share a double bed, and the hotel's landlady, oblivious to Gino's appeal, is only concerned his decrepit shoes will spoil the clean "honeymoon sheets," as Spagnolo ironically refers to them. Such irony, though, also hints at the sexual possibilities in the relationship between the two men. In an excellent analysis of the use of landscape in *Ossessione*, Giuliana Minghelli refers to how the film draws upon the "intimacy of the bedroom" as a "site where questions of identity, history, and belonging . . . are mournfully confessed."[40] As Minghelli notes, the film's major characters "are exiles with the shady pasts of *vagabondaggi* and destitution; for all of them, belonging, at best a confused utopian yearning, is tied to shame and resignation."[41]

But in the hotel bedroom sequence we also see a tendency in Visconti to stage sequences of seduction in which the seducer is pursuing something larger than sex. As in the scarf sequence from *La terra trema*, what we have in *Ossessione* is the desire for one person to convince another to engage in a rethinking of his or her entire way of life. Minghelli describes a later shot of Gino and Spagnolo looking out at the sea, their legs draped against the outdoor wall, as one in which the sea becomes a "site of freedom that literally lifts the characters outside the claustrophobic plot to a higher plane."[42] Far behind and above the men, in a low-angle shot, is a church in which various individuals (mainly, if not entirely, men) can be distantly seen walking on the roof. Eventually one man is alone here, his white linen suit causing him to stand out, mirage-like, even though he is filmed from a considerable distance. For Minghelli, such an "oneiric appearance is the promise of freedom and utopia in this new friendship of Gino's."[43] But back to the hotel.

As the men get into bed together, Spagnolo tells Gino he needs to get away on a ship and that the sea breeze will clear his mind of Giovanna. When Spagnolo utters the line of dialogue that Gino will be free again if he follows his advice there is a cut to a medium shot of Gino lying on his back, his soiled T-shirt once again exposing much of his chest, the far right of the frame cutting him off just below the waist. He looks up and over at Spagnolo and twice questions the word free. Spagnolo is on the far left of the frame, in profile, the left third of his body cut off. He is entirely in shadow, in contrast to the light bathing Gino. Spagnolo's physical presence is briefly abstracted as the emphasis is now placed on the words he is uttering to Gino, his voice becoming a mild form of incantation that has the potential to pull Gino away from Giovanna and toward the "social and poetic" life Spagnolo has created for himself. This freedom he is espousing, though, is paradoxical, since Gino is also (with no visible effort on his part) exercising a type of spell over Spagnolo, erotic in nature.

These two melancholy male figures sharing a bed has, certainly within the context of the film's production, an even bolder element of provocation than the more blatant staging of the first encounter between Gino and Giovanna, since that earlier moment is still framed within the context of heterosexual relations. Mauro Giori has drawn upon a number of published responses contemporaneous with the film's release in which writers were taken aback by the image of two men sharing the same bed, by the ambiguity of Spagnolo's motivations, and by the eroticism with which Girotti is treated.[44] The composition of the shot of the two men in bed presents two distinct possibilities for living a certain kind of life. Gino alternates between staring at Spagnolo and staring off into space, held by what Spagnolo offers. But the possibility of a fusion of these two worlds of light and shadow is suspended.

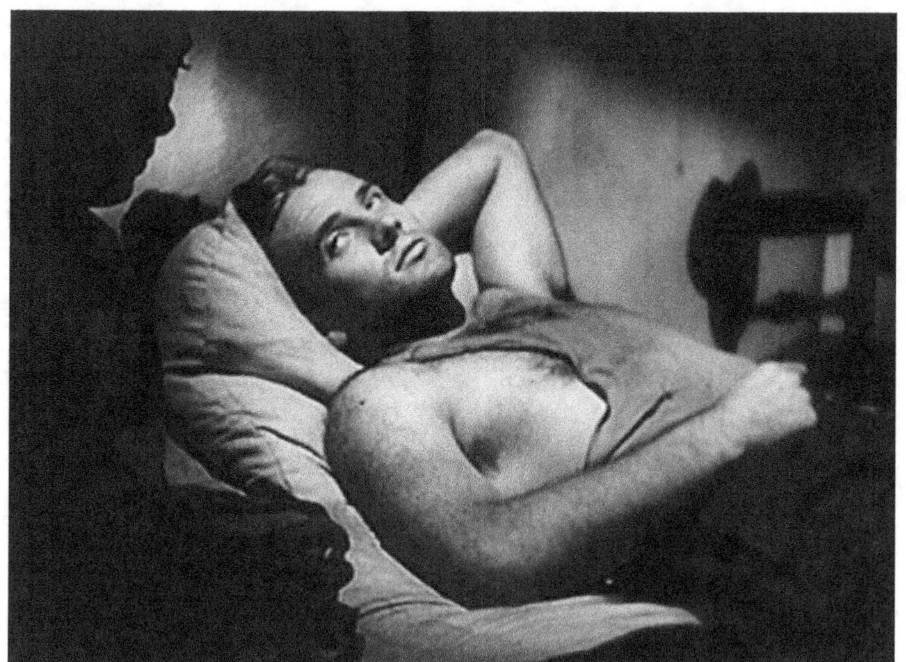

Ossessione (1943). The lure of all-male adventure and the fetish of the soiled T-shirt.

After their murder of Bragana, Gino and Giovanna are successfully managing the trattoria. Gino's clothes are new, he looks freshly bathed, and his hair is combed and brilliantined. But the domestic world he once desired now stifles. He opens a window framed by lace curtains and unbuttons the top of his shirt, as though the repressive nature of what he is now experiencing is contained within this gesture. And it is at this precise moment where Spagnolo rematerializes, walking in the market square and looking about, as though searching for Gino. With his shirt suddenly unbuttoned like this it is as though Gino is making himself available again to Spagnolo. Their reunion evokes the sequence in which Spagnolo temporarily convinces Gino to accept his way of life as they sit on a wall and look out to sea. Here they are along a riverbank. But the choice of location and the framing have none of the implications of the earlier sequence. Along the riverbank, Spagnolo takes off his jacket and sits on it (setting up a contrast between what Gino has become and what Spagnolo remains) and again attempts to convince Gino to accompany him. But the tensions between the two men have their basis in two unresolvable issues: Spagnolo's sense that Gino has betrayed him, not simply by returning to Giovanna but also by rejecting his entire philosophy, and Gino's inability to overcome his deep-seated ambivalence about both options available to him. All of this culminates in Gino physically attacking Spagnolo.

There is a shot at the end of the section of the film dealing with Spagnolo's return that encapsulates Gino's situation. After Spagnolo has gone and all of the customers of the trattoria have cleared out, Gino walks away from the inn and toward the highway. In the foreground of this shot is a table with dirty dishes and glasses on it. On the far left, taking up a quarter of the frame, is a dark cloth moving in the breeze. This image is at the core of the film's concern with being on the move, being mobile, and enjoying freedom, on the one hand, and being tied to home, property, and ownership, on the other, while the slight of movements of the fabric signify a melancholic impossibility in relation to both of these options.

It is Anita who introduces yet another possibility, a variation on both Spagnolo and Giovanna, and fabric becomes key to these additional possibilities. Her entrance is markedly unlike her entrance in the Cain novel or in Chenal's film. In Cain, Madge meets Frank when her car stalls in a parking lot and he helps her to start up the engine. In the Chenal film, the car is stalled in a garage but the nature of the meeting is otherwise the same. Madge's ownership of this car announces her financial security as well as links her with the mobility Frank now desires. In *Ossessione*, Gino and Anita meet in a park when her ball of yarn is taken away by a boy playing a prank and Gino steps in to rescue her. Anita's knitting is, writes Minghelli, a "last ironic remnant of the lost home, its security and affections."[45]

In the Chenal film, Franck (Fernand Gravey) and Madge (Florence Marly) are in a luxurious hotel room, its large windows covered with what look like expensive chiffon curtains. It is here that Madge briefly convinces a skeptical Franck to run away with her as she offers a utopian vision of living in the mountains. (In this manner her function is close to Spagnolo's.) Anita, though, is far more passive and does not take these initiatives. She is a dancer but one who is also frequently on the road. Like Spagnolo, she is a traveler but one with, as we will soon see, firmer ties to family and bourgeois gentility. Also as with Spagnolo, there is an implication she may be tied to a "forbidden" sexual status, in her case prostitution. Much of the literature on the film presumptively describes her as a prostitute, but the evidence for it is ambiguous and, if she is one, this is not something Gino fully recognizes. He does not, in fact, so much attempt to comprehend the woman he just met as project his own desires onto her.

For Gino, the décor of Anita's rented room becomes a potentially transcendent realm away from the nightmare of poverty. When he steps into her room for the first time (she isn't there), the right side of the frame is dominated by white chiffon draping for her bed, the sight of which causes Gino to momentarily pause. The whiteness of the fabric suggests not only purity, a cleansing of his past, but also a movement away from the literal dirt, dust, and mud linked, in different ways, with Spagnolo and Giovanna.

As he walks across the room, he spots a chiffon gown she has left hanging outside of the dress cabinet and he lovingly strokes it, at one point placing his hand under the fabric. Suitcases are stacked against the wall but the atmosphere is also domestic, as Gino observes the framed photographs of her family on the wall and dresser. In *La terra trema*, the photographs the Valastros have of themselves in their home are guarantees of their status as a family unit, and Anita is likewise linked with family, unlike Giovanna, who not only does not refer to family but is also given no precise location from which she originated. (Gino, it is made clear, is originally from Senigallia.) A bottle of cologne is also on the dresser, the cologne something Gino not only samples but then wipes on his jacket. The gesture is an echo of the one he performs earlier in the film, as he hears Giovanna's siren song, but there it was sweat and grime he wiped onto the fabric. The wiping of the cologne onto his jacket, on the other hand, is far less sexual even as it also announces his gradual immersion into the realm of a very ironically framed refinement. All of this décor indicates Anita having personalized the space in a feminine manner. This contrasts with the hotel room Gino shares with Spagnolo, defined by its transitory nature, the absence of any personal details because in Spagnolo's world one is always on the move, unattached to anyone. When Anita eventually enters, she sits on the bed and raises a piece of the chiffon draping as Gino sits with

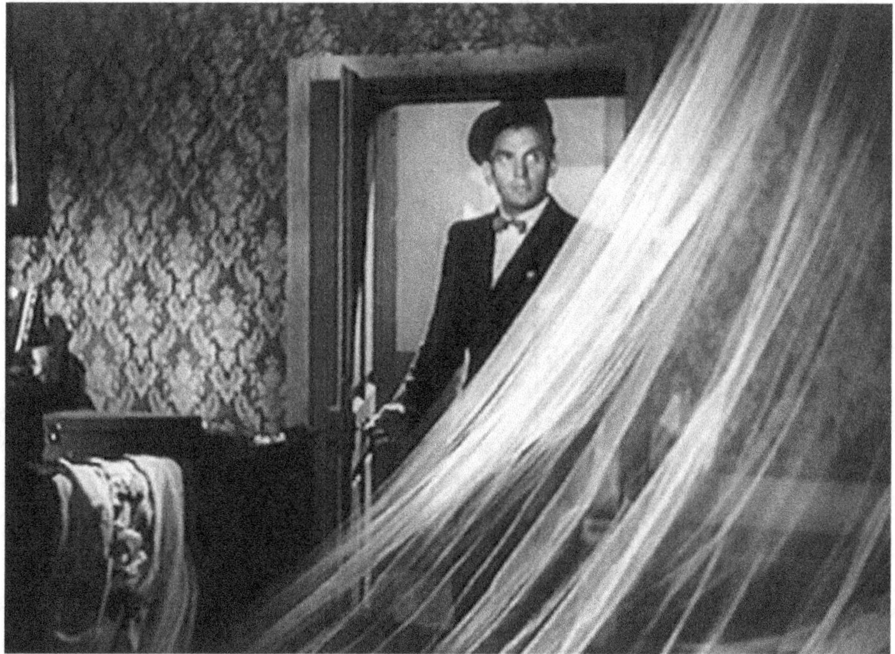

Ossessione. Draping as marker of the feminine.

her. He puts his arms around her and a tentative atmosphere of gentility is created, in contrast to the naturalist eroticism of his world with Giovanna. (Gino rejects a more direct sexual advance from Anita here.)

In this space of becoming clean, Gino confesses to the murder of Bragana, and here the white chiffon draping assumes yet another function. Gino lies on Anita's bed, wearing a shirt, but with the transparent chiffon draping dominating the right side of the frame now partly veiling his face and upper torso. The camera slowly tracks backward, Gino's face first turned away from the camera and then turned toward it, but his eyes looking upward and just missing a direct gaze into the camera. Historically, such a composition is more strongly linked with the filming of women and, in particular, female stars. But here it is Gino who is veiled and who becomes the passive and beautiful object of desire, less for Anita (whose subjectivity has little weight) than for the camera. As the camera reaches the end of its reverse track, Anita is shown sitting on the bed, listening. Gino is finishing his description of the murder as one in which he was unable to resist the power of Giovanna looking at him, as though she had cast a spell, the murder transforming him into a state from which he can never return. Gino has "gone out of himself" but in a negative way, the fabric draped across the bed becoming the central marker of this loss.

Exchanging

It is often very cold in *Rocco and His Brothers.* The Parondis, arriving from the south to the north, experience a sudden drop in temperature, thrusting them into a new world in which they must not only adapt but also dress differently. And coats will become central to the film. Great importance is given to the brothers wearing layers of clothing, sweaters, coats, and scarves before they go out even as their clothing also indicates their individual personalities. In the opening sequence, the ways in which Simone flings back his coat are a foreshadowing of his various acts of hubris central to his downfall. But the cold temperatures, no less than the heat in *Ossessione* or the damp in *La terra trema*, are a precondition for the men to ritualistically dress and undress. Soon after the Parondis arrive in Milan, there is an early-morning snow, prompting Rosaria to send her boys out offering their services for shoveling. Before leaving, Rocco wipes his hands with a dishrag. But this item does not have the forlornness of the rags in *Ossessione*. Instead, it is productively used. As the boys shovel, they have an energy, roughhousing and smacking one another on the rear end, quite different from the languorous rhythms of the Valastros. Rosaria tells Rocco to wear her sweater when he goes out with his brothers in order to shovel. He protests that it is a woman's sweater but Rosaria wins the argument. This becomes one of a number of moments in the film in which clothing is exchanged (sometimes across genders), stolen, and regarded as items of not only erotic but also (as we have seen in the laundry sequence) socioeconomic significance.

When the prostitute Nadia (Annie Girardot) makes her entrance into the film and into the Parondi apartment, officially on the run from her violent father, she is scantily clothed, wearing a thin dress, and the brothers search for a coat with which to cover her (they suggest that she use an old coat of their father's), although the search is completed by Rosaria, as this coat begins to feed into the film's circuit of exchanges. The apartment's décor is dominated by clothes hanging out to dry. But the damp fabric also implies clothing that has clung to the body of the individual who has just worn it. When Nadia eventually escapes from the apartment, she takes the coat with her but slips off her dress, a kind of naturalist animal-like leaving behind of something. (Ciro can be briefly seen sniffing Nadia's discarded dress.) Her affair with Simone will soon follow.

Later in the film, Nadia meets up with Rocco and she returns a stolen necklace (wrapped in a handkerchief) given to her by Simone. We have already seen this theft when Simone, in the midst of a seduction of Luisa, moves his hand (shown in close-up) over this piece of jewelry, the image dissolving to Rocco in the family apartment stitching up his boxing trunks. This aggressive action of Simone's is contrasted through the dissolve with Rocco's gentle, feminine action of sewing, but sewing an item of clothing tied to violent male-on-male spectacle. Comparisons have often been made between *Rocco and His Brothers* and Arthur Miller's play *A View from the Bridge* (1956), staged by Visconti in Rome in 1958. At the center of the play's dramatic conflict is the barely repressed erotic attraction the Italian American protagonist Eddie feels for his young niece Catherine, related by blood to his wife, Beatrice. Intensifying and complicating this is the arrival of two cousins of Beatrice's who move in with them, with one of the cousins, Rodolpho, developing a romance with Catherine. Eddie begins to suspect Rodolpho of being homosexual, with such tenuous indicators as Rodolpho's blonde hair and tenor singing voice. At one point in the play, though, he also draws attention to Rodolpho's sewing ability and his skill in adjusting the size of one of Catherine's dresses: "He takes the dress, lays it on the table, he cuts it up; one-two-three, he makes a new dress. I mean he looked so sweet there, like an angel—you could kiss him he was so sweet."[46] The hysteria Eddie feels for Rodolpho has its origins in two contradictory, scandalous desires, one for Catherine and the other for Rodolpho. For a man to sew is not only the marker of the feminine; it also has the potential to turn such a male into an object of desire for another male. In *Rocco and His Brothers*, though, it is less Rocco, however adept he might be with a needle and thread, than Simone who will more centrally become a male body desired by another male, whereas Rocco remains confined to the desiring gaze of women. As Nadia and Rocco sit in her car, she reaches into his coat and tells him he is nice and warm, while asking him what he has on under the coat. Nadia and Rocco have not yet begun their affair but her tentative seduction of him here is, typical of the film, enacted through a relation between fabric and a sexualized body. We might then see Nadia as someone who is, like the clothing items of the film, exchanged, even as she participates in and often generates these actions.

Contrast such an emphasis on the exchange of clothing with what is found in *L'avventura*. In Antonioni's film, the dressing and undressing of Claudia (Monica Vitti) and Anna (Lea Massari) in the lower level of the yacht, while giving off a somewhat sexual charge as they smile, look at each other, and laugh, with Anna handing Claudia her blouse, become part of a larger pattern in the film in which the shedding and exchanging of clothes are tied to disappearance around the vacillating figures of various women who are at once points of attraction and negation. Much later in the film, the actress Gloria Perkins (Dorothy de Poliolo) sets off a frenzy of desire among reporters and the other men who are following her, and this is primarily tied to the form-fitting dress she wears. She tells the reporters she wants all women of the world to dress like her. "Oh, not like this, though," she suddenly says, as there is a cut to a close shot of her dress, filmed at the hip but displaying a rip in the fabric generated by a faulty zipper. This slightly open tear has a clear vaginal connotation, fabric forming a continuity with the female body. In *Rocco*, the women are not embodied in this manner. Near the end of *L'avventura*, after Sandro (Gabriele Ferzetti), Anna's boyfriend and now also Claudia's, disappears in the early morning hours, Claudia goes into his room, takes a shirt out of his open suitcase, and embraces and sniffs it. But she quickly tosses it back into the suitcase, its inadequacy as much a question of the film's inability to eroticize the male body as it is a question of Claudia's desire for Sandro himself rather than his shirt. No such blockages are at work in *Rocco*.

Simone is brute physicality, impulsive, violent, overtly sexual. Rocco is, as the dialogue will explicitly state, saintly. His saintliness, though, is predicated on a certain ideal of male beauty closer to the physically ravishing Joseph described in *Joseph and His Brothers*. But Rocco has none of Joseph's belief in his own specialness and in which Joseph, as George Lukács writes, "imagines others love him more than they love themselves."[47] Delon will soon specialize in playing narcissistic characters, including for Visconti in *The Leopard*, but his Rocco is without conventional ego. Rather than Nadia "contaminating" Rocco, he "elevates" her to his level, a movement nevertheless precipitating much of the tragedy in the second half of the film. If Rocco is a feminized sleeping beauty, the beauty of Mann's Joseph reaches a point of physical intensity in the description of the coat of many colors, which is "long and ample, both a dress and a robe." This "virginal garb" of Joseph's is "as finely spun as if made only of a breeze, a vapor, of nothing," even as it is also "heavy from the embroidered images scattered everywhere across it."[48] Rocco is associated with simpler clothing, befitting his character, who, like Spagnolo, embodies ideals, in Rocco's case those of a pure Christian and Roman Catholic origin, tied to his never completely severed relationship to the South. Catholic iconography dominates much of the décor. But unlike Rossellini, Visconti shows no interest, either in *Rocco* or elsewhere, in exploring the sacred. If the film reproduces, and the characters enact, Catholic gestures and iconography, it is above all because such matters are part of this social world and not because the film itself has any commitment to them external to the project at hand. The contrasts between Rocco and Simone are strongly in place in order to frequently suggest that the forces and desires animating this world are, like the clothing being worn, caught in circuits of exchange, in which nothing is stable.

After Nadia gives the jeweled pin back to Rocco, he returns home and lies on a bed as the camera slowly moves toward him. He is wearing a clean, sleeveless T-shirt, one arm raised back, exposing a tuft of underarm hair on a body otherwise conspicuously smooth. Rocco looks directly into the camera, this look ambiguously motivated in terms of the story situation. He is talking to Simone about Nadia and tells Simone he has just seen her, prompting Simone's angry rejection of her. It is clear, however, that Rocco has begun to be drawn to Nadia. But Rocco is also about to leave home in order to join the navy, and the look off is also tied to a sense of uncertainty about the future, not only in relation to Nadia but also about himself and his family and the new situations facing them in Milan. The shot is a visual and rhetorical echo of shots from two earlier films. The first is from *Ossessione*, described earlier in this chapter, Gino's confession to Anita of killing Giovanna's husband and of the spell Giovanna cast over him. Nadia has likewise cast a type of spell over Rocco, and his gaze into the camera is one indication of this, as though their fates are now intertwined. However, neither Giovanna nor Nadia are simple agents of destruction as they likewise find themselves implicated in situations over which they have little control and in which they will both die.

The second is from *La terra trema* when, late in the film after the Valastros have lost their fleet, 'Ntoni is out drinking at night with various men who represent the lowest rung of his socioeconomic world. They are drunkenly wandering through the streets and trying to keep out of the eye of Don Salvatore. The sequence ends with an extraordinarily long take that begins with 'Ntoni standing in between two of the men as they watch Don Salvatore safely leave the vicinity. 'Ntoni will move out of the shot as other activities of the cavorting men are shown by the mobile, panning camera, the clothing little more than remnants of what it might have once been, holes and patches abounding. One of these activities involves two men dancing, their bodies very close together. Even if we allow for the possibility that such same-sex dancing is by no means uncommon in social environments in which opposite-sex partners are in short supply, this image remains bold. The two men continue to dance while moving down the street, eventually becoming shadows. 'Ntoni eventually steps back into the shot, looks toward the camera, and for a few seconds it appears as though he is about to look directly into it. This never firmly occurs, though, as 'Ntoni does not turn away from the camera but steps closer to it, moving to the far right of the frame as he now looks off. But what is he seeing? We get no reverse angle. The look itself is directed at something beyond the confines of this small island. It is the kind of look, articulated in different ways and under different conditions, that recurs in Visconti: the look beyond the immediate reality, the longing for the ineffable. In this image, though, what particularly captures the light is 'Ntoni's white woolen scarf standing out amidst all of the shadows. A slight breeze causes the scarf to move and as it begins this movement, the film dissolves from 'Ntoni to the next sequence. Behind 'Ntoni is one world, entirely of men and political uselessness, men who have no interest in "improving" their lives. The irreparably decayed clothing is one indication of a world turning in on itself. But is this homosocial world one with the potential to be homosexual? The intimacy of the two men dancing with one another is startling in this regard. Is it, in the midst of what we are witnessing here, an image of sexual desire being expressed not possible in the more "civilized" world of the island? Or is it to be taken as part of 'Ntoni's downfall, as the dancing men disappear into the darkness? That woolen scarf in the breeze adds the finishing touch of ambivalence and melancholia to this moment, as though 'Ntoni's desire for any kind of economic autonomy has become impossible.

Shredding

For Sigmund Freud the origin of ambivalence has much of its basis in "man's relation to his father."[49] *Rocco and His Brothers* was originally to have opened in Basilicata, with the funeral of the Parondi patriarch. For financial and logistical reasons, the sequence was never shot. But the published screenplay describes this planned opening, set in the pouring rain as the father's coffin is lowered into the "wild and stormy" sea.[50] The Parondi brothers are dressed in black as they stand on a rocky cliff, most likely meant to evoke the Valastro women waiting for the men to return from the sea. Such a sequence would have stressed the importance of the newly absent father to the narrative that followed. For Rohdie, an absence of a father in *Rocco* suggests the removal "of the very basis of what is legal and social," including sexual relations.[51]

Unlike Vincenzo or Ciro, Rocco and Simone never fully adapt to the modern values of the North although their responses take different forms, contributing to the intensity of their relationship with one another. The potential Rohdie sees in this failure to adapt is a "pure" expression of homosexual desire within which Nadia serves as the doomed mediator.[52] However, the images suggest something more complicated and for reasons that cannot be simply ascribed to the story and characters. Moreover, Rosaria herself, while tied to the melodramatic extravagance so central to the film, never questions the dominant social order, becoming no less a source of ambivalence than the father, who functions more as a fading signifier of a diminished patriarchal order than as a symbol of its ongoing power. But the question of Nadia as mediator is vital, and the rape sequence is one of two crucial enactments of her function in this regard.

Simone is effectively *metteur en scène* of the rape, seizing control of both Nadia and his brother. Rocco is forced to witness the degradation of a woman he has attempted to morally elevate into a "real Saint Agnes," as she is elsewhere ironically referred to by Ivo (Corrado Pani), one of Simone's friends who assists in the rape. (Saint Agnes is the patron saint of rape victims.) Simone takes off Nadia's panties and throws them at Rocco. She is wearing a trench coat, its pale color perhaps an indication of her desire for a cleansing of her past now that she is with Saint Rocco. But a trench coat is also a form of protection against rain and damp, and the coat will prove inadequate in relation to what she is about to face. When Simone throws her panties off they do not land precisely on Rocco's head but lightly graze his face before they fall to the ground. The potential for a transcendent form of sexual desire is suddenly reduced to the functioning of genitalia, represented by the panties. When Nadia gets up after being raped, the back of her coat is covered in mud and she is holding her high heels. Her dream of being "made clean" by Rocco has now been literally reduced to the level of dirt by Simone, forcing her to be like him again. But Rocco undergoes a displaced form of rape here in being forced to witness his brother raping Nadia: both Rocco and Nadia must be humiliated or there is no satisfaction for Simone. In this primal image of brother against brother there is something of the brothers turning against Joseph in Mann's novel, ripping Joseph's coat of many colors as a form of collective rape but one that is also a rape of the mother since the coat is not only tied to the mother (like Rosaria's sweater Rocco is forced to wear) but also is as feminine as it is masculine, as female as it is male. Mann describes how, in seizing the coat and rendering Joseph naked, the brothers ripped and shredded it, the mother's garment, and the son's as well, so that both wore it by turns, becoming one by means of the veil, god and goddess. His furious brothers had unveiled him without mercy—as love unveils the bride in the bedchamber, so their rage had unveiled him and known him as he stood there naked, shudders of deadly shame pass through him. In his mind the ideas of "unveiling" and "death" dwelt close together—how could he not have held the tatters of the garment to him and begged, "Don't rip it!"[53]

Simone does not simply want Rocco to come down to his level but to "unveil" him in front of witnesses, to "make a woman of him," and Nadia is the means through which Simone is able to achieve this.

Nadia returns to Simone but entirely due to Rocco's insistence. Earlier in the film, Nadia has a monologue in her bedroom that she delivers to Simone in which she describes her impoverished, postwar childhood. Her silk stockings are hanging out to dry, signaling this bedroom as a feminine environment. As she talks to Simone, she walks over to her closet and puts on a thin negligee as we can also see that the windows to this room are covered by two layers of curtains, as though blocking out the world. In the aftermath of the rape and the resumption of her relationship with Simone, her undergarments and stockings hang in a bedroom once again. But it is a space that is not her own; it is Simone's, in the Parondi apartment. The undergarments now connote an almost negative feminine force, her resentment as palpable through these items as it is through her dialogue. When Ciro enters their bedroom to discuss the scandalous nature of the relationship, he has trouble navigating his way through the undergarment clutter, which lacks the sensual force of the wet clothes of the Parondi brothers during their first encounter with Nadia.

Nadia's murder at the hands of Simone, near the end of the film, is a culminating moment in the structure of exchange and mediation and is a case where parallel editing, in itself another type of exchange—of filmed images—is central. Nadia's murder occurs as Rocco is in the boxing ring, and the two events, while occurring at more or less the same time, are also symbolically linked. Such a rhetorical approach has been consistent throughout the film but reserved for moments in which the final shot of one sequence will then ironically announce the first shot of the succeeding sequence. Beyond this, sequences, gestures, large and small events in *Rocco* do not stand alone as a simple succession of dramatic moments but are linked, as though the events have been "stitched" together, the needlework made partly visible.

For the murder sequence, Simone wears a black coat, Nadia a white one. The whiteness of her coat less connotes a purity than serves as an ironic sign of her degradation:

she has by now left Simone and is prostituting herself in this remote location, the terrain flat and the water shallow. It is shallow waters and flat terrain that will surround Gino and Giovanna near the end of *Ossessione* as they lie sleeping outdoors in the sand, Giovanna wearing the jacket from Gino's pinstripe suit. In the sequence that immediately follows, the film's final one, their car swerves to avoid crashing into an oncoming vehicle and plunges into a river. This kills Giovanna and is a car accident death "correcting" the false one the couple had staged in relation to their murder of Bragana. In the last shot of the film, the camera tracks in to Gino, wearing his pinstripe suit suddenly reduced to rags, as he weeps. Gino has not only returned to where he began but has been taken one step further toward arrest, negation, and despair. At the same time, Girotti as Gino is no less beautiful than he is elsewhere in the film, the torn shirt partially exposing his chest, the shredded garment creating a fetishistic image of forbidden desire that is too much for the mechanics of the final developments of the story line. Gino is alive but again outside of a world to which he is ambivalently attached. Simone, while no less caught up in a similar system, is far less passive than Gino and more likely to take aggressive action although this will have no less dire consequences, as the final encounter with Nadia demonstrates.

Throughout the sequence, Simone and Nadia continually pull toward and away from one another, a physical enactment of their entire relationship. But this also creates a sense that the roles of pursuer and pursued are exchangeable, with no simple opposition between victim and victimizer. When she first runs away from him he pulls off her coat, revealing her black dress underneath. But she is unable to run very far because of the shallow water blocking her movements. As Simone continues to chase Nadia, the coat he holds (particularly in wider shots) becomes a spot of white, almost losing its representational status. Their initial physical struggle as he is holding her, him constantly telling her he loves her, her saying she hates him, prompts a cut to Rocco in the boxing ring, accepting his fate, as though wanting to be hit. As Cecci (Paolo Stoppa) shouts to Rocco to cover himself, Simone repeats the exact line as we cut back to the couple, Nadia against a tree, where the line now refers to the coat Simone tries to use in order to protect her from the cold. Rocco and Nadia have seemingly submitted to their fates. If earlier in the film Nadia seductively reached into Rocco's coat pocket, here it is Simone who reaches into his own coat pocket and takes out a knife, prompted by Nadia's reference to Simone destroying the only good thing in her life (i.e., Rocco). Nadia slowly walks along the lake, as though beckoning Simone, coat first on her shoulders, before she leans against a lamp and drops the coat to the ground. Spotting the knife, she opens her arms to Simone in a grandiose gesture, at once an act of seduction and an assumption of a crucifixion pose.

The intent behind the cross-cutting between Simone's repeated stabbing of Nadia and Rocco alternately hitting and being hit in the boxing ring is, by virtually any standard of rhetoric, quite clear. But as Simone begins to plunge his knife into Nadia's body, she decides she wishes to live. Her cry of anguish, though, arrives too late, and the ambivalences driving the film are now irrevocable. Where the sequence gains much of its force (aside from the horrifying spectacle of Nadia being stabbed) is in how Rocco now begins to gain strength, as though resisting Nadia's fate: he wins the match. Her murder transmits a perverse energy, revitalizing Rocco at the same moment it is destroying Nadia and, in a different way, Simone. As part of the Dostoevskian dimension to the film, Simone now acquires the desperation of Raskolnikov in *Crime and Punishment* after his murder of Alyona and Lizaveta, where Raskolnikov's clothing centrally figures. Dostoevsky writes of how a "strange thought" came into Raskolnikov's head in which "perhaps all his clothes were covered with blood, perhaps there were stains all over them, and he simply did not see, did not notice them, because his reason was failing, going to pieces . . . his mind darkening. . . ."[54] After murdering Nadia, Simone wipes the blood on his coat and attempts to wash his hands by placing them in the shallow water, both of these actions pathetic in relation to the act he has just committed. His movements as he runs away are furtive, animal-like, his body hunched, as though confirming his earlier reference to himself as a beast, his blood literally and symbolically everywhere.

The Man in the Trench Coat

He makes his entrance about thirty minutes into the film. Simone is practicing in the ring with another man and, in frustration at the man's instructions to punch faster, he quickly walks away. The camera tracks away from Simone, moving left to right and at a slight diagonal across the gym as other boxers practice on the floor. At the end of its journey, the tracking camera finds Rocco practicing, but alone, watching himself in a full-length mirror. The movement is interrupted by a fast zoom toward Rocco as he stops and looks into the mirror. A cut now takes us closer to Rocco but the framing adjusts itself a bit farther to his right so that we see what he sees, in the reflection: the boxing promoter Diulio Morini (Roger Hanin) entering the gym, accompanied by two women.

The zoom announces a discordant element in the midst of an otherwise elegant dolly. This discord, as will soon become clear, is tied to Morini as a sexually desiring subject. When Morini walks farther into the gym he does not move toward the beautiful and saintly Rocco but toward Simone. He is drawn toward not platonic ideals but physical realities. Morini is wearing a fedora and a pale-colored trench coat, which not only contrasts with what the other men in the gym are wearing but creates an image of a man bundled up, as though repressed. He appraises Simone by opening Simone's mouth and examining his teeth, treating him like a racehorse or a slave. (He specifically compares Simone's teeth to those of a wolf, the film never letting go of its naturalist implications.) Immediately after this exchange, Simone, buoyed by the attention he has just received, jumps in the shower and begins vigorously washing himself. He is soon joined by Rocco, who stands next to Simone, and by an unnamed third man (the latter stands slightly behind the other two), creating something close to an ecstatic homosocial and homoerotic image. But an interruption in this short-lived paradise occurs and again it is Morini who is the source, as he walks into the shower room, still fully bundled up, his two escorts (one in a fur coat, the other in a darker colored trench) loitering in the extreme rear of the shot. As he moves forward, he steps into and out of shadows. The unnamed man in the shower walks past Morini, who does not even give the man a glance. Morini's look is very focused on one individual: Simone. Rocco and Simone, unlike the third man in the shower, never cross over from the space of showering to the space where Morini is standing. These become two distinct realms, as a shivering Rocco senses the "danger" involved in Morini's fixed attention toward his brother in a way Simone himself, dazzled by the material possibilities of Morini's appraisal of him, does not. As Morini stands against a wall, looking intently at Simone and constantly making a gesture of stroking his thumb against his cheek, the low-key lighting and the evocation of the autoerotic of the thumb gesture indicate the forbidden desires Morini embodies.

Through boxing, Simone and Rocco quickly gain access to capital and some measure of social success as they also become spectacle. In the introduction I referred to *Under the Sun of Rome* in terms of its relationship to the editing room sequence of *Bellissima.* And the boxing sequence of Castellani's film is of some interest in relation to *Rocco.* Castellani will often shoot the male protagonist, Ciro (Oscar Blando), in a blatantly erotic manner, the camera positioned at the boy's hips as he moves, or from behind or on his shoulders as he walks. At one point in the film, as he goes to answer the doorbell in his underwear, he can be clearly seen adjusting his penis and testicles. *Under the Sun of Rome* takes from the De Sica/Cesare Zavattini films of this period the idea of the lost or stolen item marking a point of crisis in the narrative, the item in this film being a pair of white tennis shoes given to Ciro by his father. One of Ciro's attempts to get money in order to replace the shoes is to fight in an amateur bout of boxing. However, the shorts he is given are too big for him and they keep slipping off, so we are repeatedly shown very brief views of his naked rear end. This sort of farcical male eroticism is foreign to Visconti. But the literal slippage of the boxing shorts is another articulation of what it is Morini is looking for in the dressing rooms. Castellani's film is set during the Occupation of Rome, thereby creating an atmosphere of secretiveness, characters speaking in code, a world of casual pickups, prostitution male and female, and infidelities, brought about not in spite but because of the Occupation. Even so, the resolution depends on a reconciliation with the values of the father. Both parents die on behalf of their children and Ciro must grow up and become an adult, part of the symbolic order. The film finally insists on an upholding of conventional social relations, even as many of its images imply other options.

Rocco and His Brothers is neither as coy nor as conservatively "innocent." For Morini, it is less the spectacle of men in the ring attracting than it is the areas "offstage," where his look at men like Simone can be more intensely focused, if only in subterfuge. In the sequence immediately following the one in the shower, Simone is, through Morini's machinations, promoted to the comparatively prestigious Cerri's Gym, and Morini comes to his dressing room after the fight to congratulate the victorious Simone. Morini is even more thoroughly bundled than in our first view of him, wearing a heavy coat, thick scarf, hat, and padded leather gloves. The gloves give Morini the freedom to touch Simone's face, ostensibly to ask about the cut on his cheek but also for him to achieve, however briefly, a form of physical intimacy not possible with the naked hand. That this gesture, used twice, is intuitively perceived by Simone as quasi-sexual is indicated by the way Simone, after being touched, feels his cheek again, as though attempting to reclaim it. Morini holds up Simone's discarded boxing trunks and announces to the entire room that their purple color is favored by both champions and showgirls. His masculinity via boxing is celebrated by Morini even as Morini simultaneously "reduces" him to the level of the feminine. This is also a form of humiliating him in terms of his proletarian status, purple signifying vulgarity, the reference to showgirls assuming double duty. Such an insult in terms of his class origins is not lost on Simone, as his facial expression clearly indicates. In fact, Simone ignores the dinner date Morini has set up for the two of them and spontaneously goes off with Nadia, as a disappointed Morini sits in his car. It is by now perfectly obvious that Morini's two ever-present female escorts (or attendants), whose coats often visually play off of what Morini himself is wearing, are baits, lures Morini uses to attract men, as Morini huddles in his trench coat.

Near the end of *La terra trema*, a mysterious man tempts Cola with Lucky Strike cigarettes. As women do laundry in the background, Cola and the man walk off together, smoking, and discuss something we cannot hear. The man is dressed in a manner similar to what Morini will later wear: a fedora and a trench coat, in this case the trench coat made of what appears to be black vinyl. Older men in trench coats luring younger, more gullible men away, tempting them to forsake the values of one world in favor of another, evokes sexual predation. In the case of *La terra trema* this possibility is elided when it transpires that the man is a smuggler and it is this illegal world Cola will soon accept as his own. However, the same-sex atmosphere of the moment is further teased out. As the smuggler and a barefoot Cola, the seat of his pants covered in large, decrepit patches, walk away, they become smaller as they recede into the middle rear of the frame. Two young men, also in rags and patches and barefoot, walk over to the far right of frame, as one puts his arm on the shoulder of the other and they look at and discuss the situation of Cola and the stranger. The gesture of one young man's arm resting on the shoulder of the other would, in a different context, signify very little. In this context, though, it creates a seductive male-on-male image. One male couple, their clothes falling apart, assesses another male couple (one of them immaculately dressed, the other in tatters, an image of the vulnerably available) as the latter walks away, confirming suspicions one might have about the intent of the mysterious man linked with illegal activity. A man in a trench coat, in both *La terra trema* and *Rocco and His Brothers*, comes to embody the very force of closeted desire, of seduction through material means rather than sexual ones.

In the incessant parallels, rhymes, and exchanges of *Rocco*, Morini will come to be linked with Luisa in their shared desire for Simone. (Simone will steal from both of them.) While potentially scandalous due to age and class differences, Luisa's attraction to Simone is within the bounds of heterosexuality, enacted through and around the freshly laundered shirts of other men. Morini's seduction of Simone occurs in Morini's apartment. In this apartment, for the first time we see Morini with no coat, no hat, no protective armor and his desire for Simone more directly articulated than it has ever been, whereas Simone is bundled up, in a dark coat and scarf. Before the apartment's décor is fully visible (Morini is keeping the lights low as a prelude to seduction), he takes off his sport jacket. A desperate Simone, drinking heavily, tells Morini he needs a lot of money. The cut to Morini after this line is uttered shows Morini standing at the far right of the frame, the low-key lighting obscuring much of the detail of the setting and most of his face. What stands out in this shot is his white dress shirt capturing the small amount of light and, just below the shirt, his hands on his hips as he listens to Simone. This gesture is striking because, although Morini elsewhere attempts (like the Baron de Charlus) to give a performance of masculinity, this is an effeminate pose, as though in his own surroundings and with the object of his desire finally willing to submit to him (for a fee), he can let down his guard.

What takes place between the two men here is a symbolic boxing match. Before physical blows are struck a hostile verbal exchange occurs. The sexual excitement for

Morini is not in spite of but because of Simone's degraded state, "the dirtiness of the object of desire," but one who has also become something of a fallen god, a one-time Apollo as Morini refers to him here. When a fist fight ensues between the two men, it is Morini who wins, and the cut to a close-up on the face of the disgraced Simone after this shows him wiping his face, an echo of the gesture he performed earlier in the film and also in relation to Morini touching him, in the dressing room, with a gloved hand. (He touches him on the cheek twice with his naked hand here, the second touch abruptly repudiated.) The gloves are now off.

During these later exchanges, a television set becomes the major light source, and it is showing some sort of documentary on Renaissance painting. This part of the sequence has been the subject of several different analyses, inevitable given its strangeness. Just before the very moment Morini turns off the TV and the lights go out, implying the sexual act about to occur, we can see a detail from Titian's *The Bacchanal* (1519–20). In this detail, two women sit close together, one leaning into the other. To use the language of cinema for a moment, the two women are framed in an overhead shot so we see the draping of their dresses along with the cleavage of one woman and the exposed shoulder of the other. In the context of this sequence, the image suggests lesbianism but one serving as a backdrop to male homosexuality. No sooner is this image offered, though, than Morini turns the set off and the image cuts to black. Should we take all of this as a major instance of Simone's downfall, as some have argued? Titian's *The Fall of Man* (1565–70), visible at one point on the television, and with the set abruptly switched off, plunging the room into darkness, might very well signify that "the two men then do something that cannot bear the light of day."[55] Given Visconti's long-standing fascination with the downfall of civilizations and of the individuals within them, this is not a far-fetched reading. One may even situate this moment within a certain neorealist tendency of representing the homosexual. In *Bicycle Thieves*, for example, there is the pedophile who tries to pick up Bruno, the pedophile representing another kind of economic option in the midst of postwar poverty, the loss of innocence for the sake of capital. But Simone is neither a child nor innocent, and the conditions surrounding this encounter with Morini are markedly different.

The cut immediately following the switch off of the TV takes us to the kitchen of the Parondi apartment, where the fully socialized Ciro, wearing an immaculately clean white T-shirt, is washing his face in the sink before he then walks across the kitchen to the windows where women are seen in the apartment complex hanging out laundry on railings—all of this making clean after the "filth" of gay sex. Far more than any other character in the film, Morini embodies the look of the camera itself at these men. But it is also a look that is "bundled up," looking with intensity while retreating into shadows, even as these shadows are no guarantee of safety. In *Time Regained* (1927), Proust writes of how the look of desire Charlus directs at a Senegalese soldier "who passed into darkness" is one Charlus imagines not being noticed by others. But "the Baron was mistaken, the intensity of contact and of gaze was greater than propriety permitted."[56] In *Rocco and His Brothers*, the shadows from which Morini imagines he is safely looking, in his heavy clothing, are what the camera is drawn toward and makes visible.

In the sequence soon after this, Vincenzo, Rocco, and Ciro arrive at Morini's in response to Morini's report to the police of Simone's theft. The brothers here are either in dress coats or in tweed, with suits underneath these coats, the wardrobe indicating economic or social stability. But daylight also makes fully apparent what had only been intermittent in the apartment the previous evening: the striking contrast between the man whose profession ties him to the world of boxing and the décor of his apartment, which suggests an aesthete, with paintings, mirrors in rococo frames, statuary, and decorative lampshades. Such décor in cinema already has a certain history, particularly in American film noir, of implying that the inhabitant of the space is gay or sexually ambiguous, as with the apartment of Waldo Lydecker in *Laura* (Otto Preminger, 1944). The photos of boxers here, along with the hanging boxing gloves, while officially announcing Morini's profession, also become male pinups and fetishes. The silk robe Morini now wears is fully of a piece with the decor, as though he is now willing to at least temporarily assume a role as a homosexual aesthete. In its closeted bourgeois respectability and display of material wealth, this apartment is the antithesis of what Spagnolo offers Gino in *Ossessione*.

What I would particularly call attention to in this sequence, though, is one of the paintings on the wall, Van Gogh's *Portrait of Armand Roulin* (1888).[57] In the first shot of the sequence Morini is standing in front and to the right center of the frame, the Van Gogh behind him as Roulin looks out at the spectator. In much of the sequence, the staging will move Morini or the brothers over to the painting and then away from it as they speak and walk about, without them ever noticing the painting itself. Within the context of the film, the seventeen-year-old Roulin becomes absorbed into the parade of male beauties. In the portrait, Roulin's face is supplemented and enhanced by the attention Van Gogh pays to the folds of the jacket and to his hat, these details only fleetingly visible in this sequence from a black-and-white film, which also robs the painting of its play with the yellow of Roulin's jacket and the blue of his hat. Meyer Schapiro has written of how the execution of the portrait is "soft and tender," offering a "frank, loving vision" in which Van Gogh shows "his delight in the presence of a young individual."[58] In this sequence, though, Roulin becomes a dandified figure,

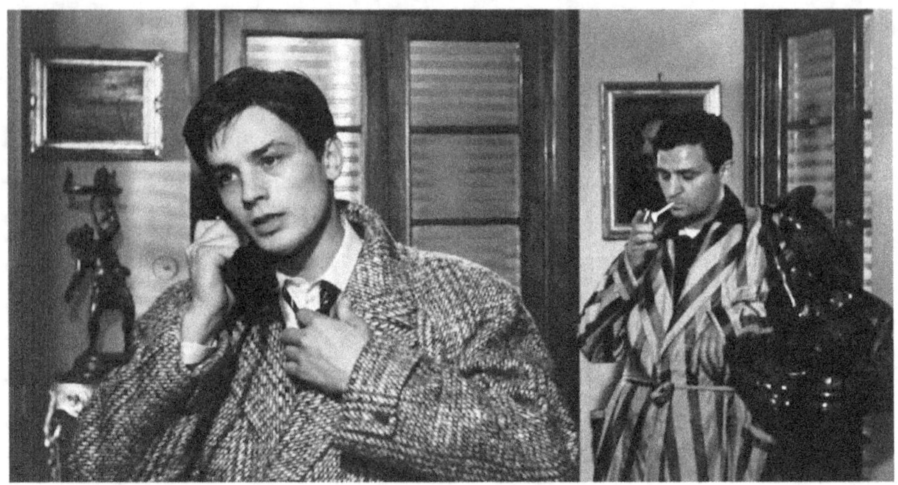

Rocco and His Brothers. Clothing that suffocates.

almost decadent, and one around which the sequence gravitates. This Roulin is not the object of a "frank, loving vision" but a sexualized object, perhaps a young version of Gino, his jacket and hat not yet subjected to the ravages of poverty.

At the end of the sequence, Rocco (observed by Morini) is on the phone with Cerri and accepts a deal to return to boxing as a way of paying off Simone's debt to Morini, as the cycle of exchange central to the film continues. But as Rocco resigns himself to this, he opens his coat and pulls at his shirt and tie. In *Joseph and His Brothers*, when Jacob mistakenly believes Joseph is dead he tears off his clothes in grief, in which action "he did not stop at his outer robe but, evidently pursuing some savage plan, in fact tore to shreds everything he had on, casting the tatters aside one after the other, and stripped himself naked."[59] Rocco does not completely undress and he is not plunged into grief. But the clothes that once signified an integration into the modern world of Milan are now suffocating him. In *Ossessione*, as we have already seen, when Gino feels suffocated in running the successful trattoria he throws open a window and unbuttons the top of his shirt. But the crisis there is more of an existential one. Saint Rocco must make a conscious decision to literally take the blows, the punishment his brother by rights should be receiving. His clothes suddenly do not fit. He will never belong to this world, as the gesture of pulling at his clothes prepares him for the cycle of dressing and undressing for the boxing arena that will be his destiny.

THE DIVA, DRAPED

Flowing, Unreeling

In between *La terra trema* and *Rocco and His Brothers*, Visconti directed three features, *Bellissima*, *Senso*, and *White Nights*. (*White Nights* will be addressed in the next chapter.) *Bellissima* and *Senso* are, as *Rocco and His Brothers* would also be, films that involve a rethinking of the implications of Italian cinema's neorealist ideals during a period of increased uncertainty about the movement's future. Of the two films, *Senso* has been widely understood as the boldest intervention, with Guido Aristarco going so far as to declare it a "revolutionary film that brought our cinematic history to a new peak."[1] An expensive studio endeavor, with Visconti working in color for the first time, *Senso* is also the first of his films to address history, in this instance the final period of the Risorgimento during the Third Italian War of Independence. *Bellissima* is set in a vividly realized present day markedly unlike the one in *Ossessione*. The atmosphere of economic despair from the earlier film now gives way to a Roman working class living in the midst of Italy's postwar "economic miracle." In contrast to the first two Visconti features, *Bellissima* shows us a world of, if not abundance, at the very least order. But *Senso* is Visconti's first film in which a literal aristocracy (as opposed to the "symbolic princes" of *La terra trema*) plays a central role, although it is an aristocracy in the midst of (if not actively participating in) its own decline.

Senso is based on a novella of the same title by Camillo Boito published in 1882 from which Visconti's film retains some elements, but it is in other respects a work of very different concerns. Beyond this source, and in a manner typical of Visconti as we have seen in the previous chapter, the film evokes multiple literary traditions and forms. *Bellissima*, on the other hand, is based on an original screenplay, cowritten by Francesco Rosi and Suso Cecchi d'Amico, from a story by Cesare Zavattini. For this particular chapter, however, it is less literature that is my concern in relation to fabric than how fabric is tied to very self-consciously articulated and closely related ideas of the theatrical and the cinematic. And while the filming of men was central to the previous chapter, with women assuming a crucial but nonetheless intermediary function, I now want to reverse this. The major female characters in *Bellissima* and *Senso*,

Maddalena Ciccone and Livia Serpieri, and the two actresses portraying them, respectively Anna Magnani and Alida Valli are, in their extravagant emotionalism, women with ties to the Italian tradition of the diva. In Italian cinema, the diva achieved a peak of importance during the silent era, immediately prior to World War I, when the diva film constituted a virtual genre. The theatrical gestures and artificial dramatic constructions of the diva film, and the cult surrounding such figures as Lyda Borelli and Francesca Bertini, would appear to be the antithesis of neorealism. Typical of Visconti's historical dialectics, though, he revived the diva in *Bellissima* and *Senso* but in such a way as to both critique and expand upon (if not celebrate) the diva cult and the presumptions of early neorealism. And in each of the films this revisiting of the female-star-as-diva is one in which fabric is central.

In the case of *Senso*, the revival is related to the function of both melodrama and opera, a strategy of which Visconti could not have been clearer in stating in interviews, even as this overt use of melodrama was also tied to realism: "I tried to make [*Senso*] with maximum realism, at the same time giving it this element of Italian melodrama."[2] Whereas André Bazin would refer to melodrama as a "demon" Italian filmmakers "are not entirely capable of resisting,"[3] Visconti would invert such an argument and transform melodrama into a privileged form through which realism could be articulated. "In real life," Visconti stated, "there are melodramatic people, just as there are illiterate fishermen in Sicily."[4] His frequently quoted declaration that his love for melodrama arose because melodrama straddles the borders of life and theatre is fundamental to the operation of *Senso*, a world without the "illiterate fishermen" of *La terra trema*. Within and beyond these borders, the diva becomes "this rare creature, whose role in the spectacle should be reassessed. In the mythologies of our time the diva is the incarnation of the rare, the extravagant and the exceptional."[5]

The diva is also central to opera, and it was soon after finishing *Senso* that Visconti began to direct opera for the stage, most notably his productions with Maria Callas in the 1950s. Visconti described seeing the overweight Callas in a production of Richard Wagner's *Parsifal* (1882) in 1949. "'She was still enormous," he said; "she was half-naked in the second act, covered with yard on yard of transparent chiffon: a marvelous temptress, an odalisque.'"[6] Callas would become, for Visconti, an embodiment of the theatrical sublime. Crucial to this first experience of her for Visconti, though, was not simply the voice and theatrical presence but a sense of the mythical and infinite created through the "yard on yard" of chiffon only partially covering her. By the time she began to appear in Visconti's operas, she had famously slimmed down. Callas's costuming in her work with Visconti was fundamental to their theatrical presentation, and the literature on the Visconti/Callas productions is filled with tantalizing descriptions of gowns made of white silk, of red silk encrusted with jewels, of bustles with long trains, and of pleated robes in silk brocades. However, Visconti would later refer to Callas as a "monstrous phenomenon. Almost a disease. A kind of actress that has passed for all time."[7] The diva, then, is a crucial site of ambivalence in Visconti, a sickness from which one must attempt to recover, not only because of the intensity of emotions she generates but also because she is something out of the past. At the same time, this sickness is the very point of attraction, tied to the need to succumb to a force larger than oneself, a diva swathed in fabric. But what sort of past, what sort of history is embodied in and through her? And how are the fabrics that surround her part of this? Of the two films being addressed in this chapter, *Senso*, by virtue of being a historical melodrama set among the richly appointed upper classes, is by far the most wide-ranging in its use of fabric. *Bellissima*, though, is not a minor exercise even if its images of fabric are not as extensive as those of *Senso*.

Both films open with excerpts from operas, in *Bellissima*, "Saria possibile?" from Donizitti's *L'elisir d'amore* (1832) and, in *Senso*, from Verdi's *Il trovatore* (1853), "L'onda de' suoni mistici pura discenda al cor!" sung by Manrico and his lady love Leonora, as well as a somewhat abbreviated version of "Di quella pira l'orrendo foco" sung by Manrico. The Donizetti is a comic opera, the Verdi a grand opera, announcing the tone of the films to follow. The Verdi is an opera of flames, delirious visions, and mistaken identities but also of enchantments and spells. When torn between political commitments and romantic ones, it is the former that must win out, and this is precisely what occurs in "L'onda de' suoni mistici pura discenda al cor!" The Donizetti is also an opera of spells and, in this instance, of potions (the elixir of the title). But these elixirs are not real. They are sold by a huckster, in an opera of not only unrequited passions but sudden reversals in which romantic love ultimately wins out, as it invariably must in such a comic enterprise. "Saria possibile," though, is not about love or magic potions. It is an ensemble piece, of village women gossiping, and female chatter will be crucial to *Bellissima*, forming another kind of fabric for the film. Millicent Marcus notes that the "seamless flow of words" dominating the film's soundtrack is "matched by the uncut flow of images on the celluloid strip."[8] Language and fabric flow in this film, constantly unreeling. The lead singer in this ensemble piece from the Donizetti who is spreading gossip informs the other women it was a *tailor* who gave her this information. And in the film to follow, it is the construction and purchase of a dress that will be central to the narrative.

Early in the film, there is a sequence set in the shop of a seamstress. It opens with a mobile master shot leading from a corner of the shop (two women are in the left and right foreground of the deep focus image, ironing) as a shop assistant (Nora Ricci) emerges from the rear center carrying a yard of tulle. As the camera follows her into the main area, a wide shot shows an environment filled with fabrics of various shapes and textures. The assistant holds up the tulle for stage mother Maddalena, who is hoping to find the right material for a dress for her young daughter, Maria (Tina Apicella), one the girl will wear for her screen test at Cinecittà as part of a massive talent search for an unknown to play the lead in a new film. The women in this space never stop talking, this talk accompanied by comic gestures. Maddalena and the seamstress discuss possibilities for the girl's dress, much of the discussion revolving around the relative softness or hardness of the fabrics with which Maddalena is being presented and which she will sometimes touch. The seamstress offers to make a satin leotard based on one worn in *The Red Shoes* (1948), Michael Powell and Emeric Pressburger's film of an all-encompassing romantic desire to "die for art" through the world of the ballet. As the two women discuss the price of the dress, there is a cut to Maddalena in the mid-foreground, looking out of frame to her left as she continues talking to the seamstress. In the foreground is the assistant, who constantly fluffs the tulle, slightly blocking full visual access to the protagonist. A more "logical" way to frame such a shot would be to place Maddalena, with so much dialogue to utter, in the foreground, with the assistant behind her, connecting the assistant to the other women who can be seen at work behind Maddalena. At this moment, however, it is the fabric that most interests Visconti, a fabric compelling because it is being touched, moved about, and discussed but without it being shaped into specific form.

Near the end of *Time Regained*, Marcel refers to the novel he wishes to create. This novel will be the one we have almost finished reading and of which *Time Regained* is its final volume, *In Search of Lost Time*. The prospective novel will take its cue from how Marcel's housekeeper Françoise sewed. "I should construct my book," Proust writes, "I dare not say ambitiously like a cathedral, but quite simply like a dress."[9] Not the hard, masculine world of architecture as its model of creation but the soft, feminine world of the dress, an echo of Colette's cry for a cinema that flows and weaves. In Antonioni's *La signora senza camelie* (1953), cowritten by d'Amico, new film star Clara Manni (Lucia Bosé) confesses she is only good at buying fabric due to the fact that her father sold it in his shop, where she had worked as a clerk. But in *Bellissima*, the fabric of the dress is raw material for creation, offering a world of possibilities for, in this instance, the cinematic image, fabric being at once a crucial item within the mise-en-scène, a metaphor for the initial gesture of *producing* images, and (like Manni's origins in Antonioni's film) a reminder of the economic and class issues at stake.

Although much of the action of *Bellissima* is set in the world of commercial filmmaking, Visconti claimed to have no particular interest in this aspect. "The whole

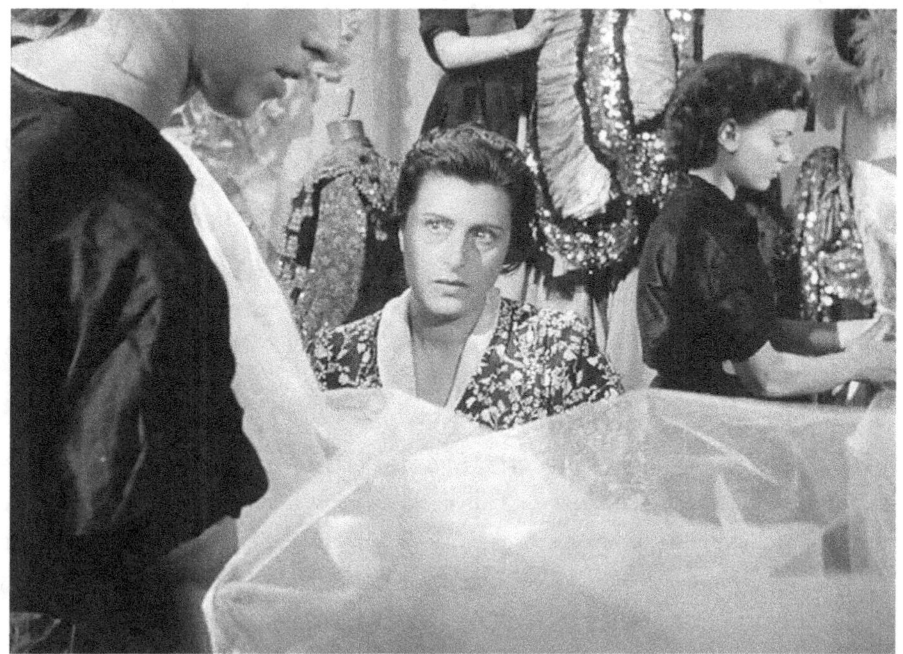

Bellissima (1951). Fabric as raw material for creation.

subject was Magnani," he insisted. "That was what interested me. Not so much the cinema *milieu*."[10] The final film does not back up this assertion. If "the whole subject was Magnani," this in itself allows *Bellissima* to become a film about the cinema or, at the very least, a film about a very particular kind of cinema at a certain moment in its history. Magnani is arguably *the* central actor of neorealism, the very embodiment of its ideals, preeminently through her work with Rossellini in *Rome, Open City* and *L'amore* (1948) and Alberto Lattuada in *Il bandito* (1946). A dedication title card in *L'amore* states that the film is intended as an homage to the art of Magnani, neorealism incorporating within its ethos the possibilities of the emotive power of the star, the diva, something in which *Bellissima* even more fully participates.

Bellissima partakes of a number of neorealist tropes even as it heightens and theatricalizes them in order to turn the film into a vehicle for Magnani. Angela Dalle Vacche has described the performance styles of the divas of Italian silent cinema as "overreactive, spectacular, and operatic instead of psychologically motivated and introspective."[11] Such a brief description of the diva's performance style is by no means antithetical to *Bellissima* or, for that matter, to *Senso*. Magnani's connections to neorealism would suggest that if she is a diva her presence constitutes a significant reimagining of the diva's ossibilities for a late wartime and immediate postwar audience. Her performance style in her most notable roles partakes of the overreactive, the spectacular, and the operatic even as it grounds them in the authentic, the (neo) real. Such emotions are appropriate for her status as a "woman of the people," in particular in *Rome, Open City*, where they are legitimate responses to the trauma and economic deprivations of war. For Magnani to be surrounded by luxury, to be extravagantly dressed and made up, is virtually antithetical to her star image. In *Teresa Venerdi* (Vittorio De Sica, 1941), made before that image had been solidified, or *Il bandito*, made in the midst of its emergence, Magnani is fashionably dressed. But the characters in both films are unsympathetic, and when seen today her physical appearance is almost disturbingly incongruous.

Bellissima does not so much dress Magnani down as create a heightened, theatricalized version of her neorealist star image. And by 1951, a star she undoubtedly was. At one moment in *Bicycle Thieves*, as the father and son go searching for the stolen bicycle, they pass a newsstand selling movie magazines in which Magnani's face is on the cover. And in *La signora senza camelie*, Magnani's portrait hangs at a bar in a movie theater, alongside those of Greta Garbo, Bette Davis, and Katharine Hepburn. The black fabric worn by the women in *La terra trema*, so strongly tied to the evocation of mourning, is in *Bellissima* transformed into a suit worn by Maddalena. Fitted at the waist and flattering Magnani's figure, it is almost chic, an outfit for a movie star who is playing a working-class character. *Bellissima* was Piero Tosi's first credit as a costume designer for Visconti and, according to Drake Stutesman, "[Tosi] famously clothed the film by stopping people in the Roman streets to ask them for the clothes they were wearing. They willingly stripped when he said three magic words: 'cinema,' the adored escape from postwar depression, and 'Anna Magnani,' the idol of millions of Italians."[12] Tosi has stated that Visconti, in using clothing in this manner, "wanted to catch the real. For *Bellissima*, I had to walk in the street looking for people who most resembled the characters and get their clothes off them. And without washing them or changing them, I had to put them on the actors."[13]

Maddalena's husband, Spartaco (Gastone Renzelli), is designing a suburban home into which he hopes to eventually move his wife and child. In his muscularity and physical attractiveness, Spartaco is a postwar, domesticated reworking of Gino from *Ossessione* whose T-shirts and other clothing items are pressed and relatively new. While the Ciccone apartment has evident signs of wear and tear, the sheets and towels look clean. The distended rhythms of *Ossessione* and *La terra trema* are replaced by speed and frantic motion, with Maddalena always in a hurry, always running out of time. Her sewing machine is tucked into a corner of the kitchen with a fabric item spread across it, as though she became distracted and had to stop. This all becomes part of a world of comic overflow, indicators of the potential for postwar economic prosperity in which even the heat and sweating bodies are less naturalist indicators than signs of comic excess, situated within an ambitious world of newly found possibilities.

Marcus has written on how the film turns Spartaco into a more maternal figure than Maddalena, so that Spartaco "embodies the nesting instinct, with all its concomitant values of stability, nurturing, and familiar order."[14] The myth of the diva, though, is one in which such conventional gender roles as the wife and mother are repeatedly challenged by the diva's grandiose presence and one that cannot be contained within domestic environments. Even as she mimics the values of the dominant social order she does so in such an emotive register that the values of that order are themselves often called into question. One aftereffect of this is the tendency to feminize the male figures or to turn them (rather than the diva) into an object of desire. In either instance, the male becomes a lesser being. Even if the dialogue may grant him moral authority, the diva's presence gives her a power overriding (or at the very least complicating) such authority.

Through Magnani in particular, *Bellissima* establishes its working-class world as a space of performance, seen with a particular clarity in the backyard of the Ciccone's apartment complex. This yard is introduced through a crane shot that begins on the stage where a rehearsal for a live performance is underway. A heavy piece of fabric is at the far right foreground of the shot, attached to the scaffolding. As the camera cranes around this yard, laundry for the various apartments is hanging out on lines to dry, in particular white bedsheets, that iconic fabric image of working-classness so central (as we have already seen) to *Bicycle Thieves*. As the sequence continues, sheets and other fabric items hang out of windows as part of the overall busyness of the frame. This is a world where the sheets no longer have to be pawned.

The use of deep focus and long takes in the film bears little relation to the extremes of duration and mobility in *La terra trema*, the protagonists of *Bellissima* most often surrounded by an active world with little time to sensuously linger over fabric. There is too much to do and money is at stake. The Ciccones cannot afford Maria's dress, and Maddalena makes use of funds designed for the house Spartaco wishes to build, destroying his dream for the sake of her own, as though Proust's distinction between architecture and clothing as a metaphor for creation is being literally enacted. Maddalena's dreams for prosperity go beyond basic material needs (such as shelter) and instead are tied to the cinema, to moving from the position of spectator, watching *Red River* (Howard Hawks, 1948) at the outdoor theater in the backyard of her apartment complex, to camera subject but at one remove: It is her daughter Maria who will become the unwitting victim of Maddalena's ambitions. Throughout Visconti, to be spellbound but awake, to move from the position of viewer to the position of subject and back again, is a central dynamic. Maddalena is enraptured by *Red River*, a film about the drive to achieve economic power within the context of history and the building of empire through the acquisition of cattle and land. In the urban world of *Bellissma*, another kind of "cattle drive" occurs, one generated by the mothers attempting to launch their little girls as movie stars and in which the new empire is the cinema.

In Rossellini and De Sica, there is an attempt to bear witness to the world and fully apprehend its reality and where the cinema may even have a negative force. In *Bicycle Thieves*, there is a cab driver who states that he doesn't like the movies, as though the movies are something still tied to, on the one hand, the period of Fascism and, on the other, Hollywood. The working class should have better things to do. In *Bellissima*, as in *Rocco and His Brothers*, there is a reference to the story of Pinocchio. Spartaco offers to buy Maria a Pinocchio doll while asking his daughter if she is familiar with this story of a boy whose nose grew longer because of all the lies he told. Immediately following this is the sequence in which Spartaco and Maddalena watch *Red River*. An implied link is occurring here in which a conception of the cinema and its ostensible world of lies and appearances has a destructive potential. While Zavattini (author of the screenplay for *Bicycle Thieves*) was responsible for the basic story situation of *Bellissima*, Visconti's aestheticism prohibits confident ironic moralism, the attraction for aesthetics able to coexist with neorealist ethics. For Visconti, the world is a spectacle to be viewed from a discreet distance, from the other side of glass, a screen, a camera, a veil, always something mediating that view, and disaster often arises when one attempts to cross over that barrier or to confuse realms. Viewing becomes both a form of surrender to the beauty of what one sees and the site of new potentialities—and this also affects the relationship between fabric and gender identity. *Red River* is another one of Hawks's self-described love stories "between two men," in this case men who are also a symbolic father and son (the oedipal dynamics setting off another atmosphere of ambivalence), and a world in which the desire for women may also be seen as a displaced desire for men. Maddalena is excited not by the film's top-billed star, John Wayne, but by the more androgynous Montgomery Clift, who is denounced by Wayne at the end of Hawks's film for being "soft. Won't anything make a man of you?"

A Constant Vision in Black

Two years after *Bellissima* and a year before he began shooting *Senso*, Visconti contributed an episode to the portmanteau film *Siamo donne* (1953). *Siamo donne* was comprised of five episodes, four of them featuring a major female star of Italian cinema, each episode with its own director. The nature of *Siamo donne* was to showcase a star but have that star reenact an everyday, but nevertheless emotional, moment in her life and in such a way that, within the film's rhetoric, she becomes deeply human. Such a strategy is not without risks, not the least of which is the potential for the star's power to override the project's neorealist ambitions. In terms of fabric, the film is not (even in the Visconti) of major interest. But the placement of the Magnani episode at the very end of the feature is, if nothing else, a testament to her star power in relation to all of the other women in the film.

Siamo donne was made during a period of uncertainty as to neorealism's future. In an episode featuring Valli (directed by Gianni Franciolini), a reporter asks her for her thoughts on neorealism, given the current scarcity of original subjects. As with a similar question that would be put to Sylvia in *La dolce vita* seven years later, the question is something she does not answer. And how could she? Unlike Magnani, Valli's stardom was not tied to the emergence of neorealism. Prior to *Senso*, her career in Italy was within the commercial mainstream, in particular its calligraphic tradition during the Fascist era, including the film that launched her as a major figure, *Piccolo mondo antico* (Mario Soldati, 1941), another melodrama about the Risorgimento. By the time of *Senso*, though, Valli was an international figure, with a brief period spent in Hollywood, and she had a gift for characterization that Magnani did not demonstrate. (*Senso* was Visconti's first international coproduction, with an American actor, Farley Granger, in the male lead.) In contrast to Magnani, with her emotive transparency, Valli was frequently positioned in her immediate postwar films as a somewhat remote figure whose thoughts were difficult to fully comprehend, most notably in her two best-known English-language films, *The Paradine Case* (Alfred Hitchcock, 1947) and *The Third Man* (Carol Reed, 1949).

Her Livia in *Senso* is partly within this tradition and partly outside of it. Livia is the film's melodramatic heroine and her subjectivity dominates: She is in every sequence (with one notable exception) and her internal diegetic narration is a prominent structuring element of the narrative. At the same time, the film's critical distance on Livia, its reliance on dramatic irony, complicates conventional attempts at empathy. This in itself would not place the film outside of a tradition of female-centered historical melodramas likewise inviting critical perspectives on their heroines, in the cinema Vivien Leigh's Scarlett O'Hara in *Gone with the Wind* (Victor Fleming, 1939) being the most famous example.[15] Like *Senso*, *Gone with the Wind* is historical fiction in which we observe the decline of one culture and its replacement with another. The criticism of the heroine typically emerging in such projects is one in which her social and sexual conduct is in excess of the historical moment being depicted, this conduct inviting criticism not only within the diegetic world of the film but also, implicitly, on the part of the audience. The women "go too far," even as historical irony emerges for the contemporary spectator made aware of the contradictions and repressions for women within that moment. Scarlett's excessive behavior is counterbalanced by her commitment to larger social good, such as her attachment to her plantation, Tara, with that in turn connected to the eventual process of rebuilding the American South in the aftermath of the Civil War. Where the cinema of fabric is manifested here is how the film (taking many of its cues from Margaret Mitchell's source novel) so often integrates, on both a large and a small scale, fabric into the drives and conflicts of its historical narrative: Scarlett and Mammy (Hattie McDaniel) arguing over the proper way for a "lady" to wear a dress at the barbeque; Rhett Butler (Clark Gable) and Scarlett having a sexually tinged discussion about pantalets; or Scarlett's seduction of her sister's suitor, Frank Kennedy (Carroll Nye), begun by placing her hand in his coat pocket as she claims to be cold, the type of gesture Nadia will employ in *Rocco and His Brothers*. But most famously there is the moment in which a financially destitute Scarlett transforms a set of drapes at Tara into a gown she will wear in the hopes of attracting the affections and financial resources of Rhett. In all instances, Scarlett is exhibiting strong drives at once masculine and feminine, combining both a resistance to and an acceptance of the social order, tying her to concepts of land, property, and nation building.

Senso inverts and amplifies this tendency by positing Livia's drives not only as in excess of the social order but as ones in which she betrays her commitment to the Risorgimento by having an affair with Granger's Austrian officer, Franz Mahler. In the final sequence of *Gone with the Wind*, Scarlett has been abandoned by her husband, Rhett, but she explicitly states her determination to win him back: "Tomorrow is another day." Livia's choice, though, is a dead end as she now also betrays Franz and turns him in to the Austrian army as a deserter. The final moments of *Senso* show Franz being executed as Livia roams the streets of Venice, dressed head to toe in black, her veil falling off of her gown as she madly cries out Franz's name. She would appear to have no literal or symbolic place to which she can now return, no tomorrow.

The intensity of *Senso* emerges through the combination of this critical distance toward its heroine and the expressive power of its musical and visual elements, culminating in Livia's performance of despair in black. In *Piccolo mondo antico*, the costumes (by Maria De Matteis and Gino Sensani, the former the costume designer on *Ossessione*) are all impressively detailed, but Soldati's framing and staging fully contain and naturalize these costumes, something that does not happen in *Senso*. "It all began that evening. It was the 27th of May," is the first moment of Livia's narration, spoken over a low-level shot of Livia moving down the hallway of the opera house, past a number of other men and women. Through this framing the gowns on Livia and the other women are visible from head to toe, the shot serving as an announcement of intent for the film to follow, in which Livia's costumes will be at once an extension of her character, a marker of her historical and class status, and a crucial sign of her downfall. Such framing is evident in *Gone with the Wind*, in the Atlanta Bazaar dance sequence, the antebellum dresses on the women becoming layered, mobile fabric as the women move across the floor with their male partners. But while Visconti has called *Senso* "a romantic film filled with the true essence of Italian opera," the epic sweep of *Senso* is far more attenuated than in *Gone with the Wind*, the lavishness of *Senso*'s fabrics suggesting possibilities beyond those of historical romance.

Livia's costumes are by Marcel Escoffier. His designs for Edwige Feuillère on Jean Cocteau's *The Eagle with Two Heads* (1948) anticipate his work on *Senso*. Cocteau's film is also about the downfall of an aristocratic woman, a widowed queen played by Feuillère, whose attraction to death finds its fulfillment in her relationship with the anarchist poet Stanislas (Jean Marais), an angel of death who will eventually murder her. *Senso* opens with a lengthy intertitle, explicitly laying out the precise moment and place in history the film will be addressing, not simply the Risorgimento but Venice in the spring of 1866 when the Italian government had forged a pact with Prussia in an attempt to expel the Austrians from the city. This intertitle is placed over an on-stage performance of *Il trovatore*, as Manrico is making his choice between his love for Leonora and his duty to the republican cause. *The Eagle with Two Heads* also opens with an intertitle. But that intertitle, written in the first person by Cocteau, informs us that the film to follow is not history but fiction tied to Cocteau's own imagination. The costumes and décor situate the film in an allegorical space, the designs grabbing from multiple sources. Such a refusal of the authentic denaturalizes the enterprise, the film trafficking in a queer play with signs in a "Kingdom of the Enigmas," as Stanislas puts it. *Senso*, on the other hand, is obsessed with the concrete historical reality of the moment, reproducing this in virtually every detail in terms of costuming and décor. Ivo Blom's research on *Senso* has demonstrated that the designs for the interior of Livia's villa were intended to involve a clash of historical periods. But such a clash goes no further than the nineteenth century in its references and could still be logical within the context of the historical setting.[16]

At the same time, as Blom has noted, Livia's costumes, with their evocation of the gowns and dresses found in the nineteenth-century paintings of such figures as Alfred Stevens and Franz Xaver Winterhalter, exhibit a fetish for historical detail while also suggesting the latest in 1950s high fashion.[17] But the muchness of these gowns suggests additional possibilities. If, for Visconti, the diva achieves her force through being rare, extravagant, and exceptional, she also exerts her fascination through evoking, if not catalyzing, sickness, and Livia's outfits are the primary markers of these ambivalent states. Geoffrey Nowell-Smith has described Franz as being "in the full sense of the word, a decadent; and it is as a study of decadence that *Senso* carries its most complete and perfect conviction."[18] And Aristarco has argued that *Senso*, like *Buddenbrooks* (1901), is "the epic of a decadent age, almost one might say the epilogue to Mann's novel itself."[19] For Livia, Franz is desirable because he opposes both aspects of her already contradictory social world. Franz speaks to a need to transcend these states into a timeless world of sexual fulfillment. Their dialogue in the Venice hotel room sequence makes this explicit, where Livia says their sexual encounters occur outside of time, the very impossibility of this sexual utopia understood by her to be a type of sickness.

For Alexander García Düttmann, Livia's love affair with Franz is "unmistakably homosexual," Franz himself becoming "a deceitful gay sex object, a preening queer."[20] But such an argument runs the risk of erasing any kind of female subjectivity from the enterprise, the film becoming a type of gay masquerade. For if Franz is a fully decadent character, then his diseased love affair with Livia is consistent with just such fascinations among the Decadents. This may be linked with the concerns of certain gay artists associated with Decadent movements, such as Oscar Wilde and Arthur Rimbaud. But it is not the sole province of the gay artist. Visconti ended his career by adapting a novel by the Italian Decadent Gabriele d'Annuzio, *L'innocente* (1892). But d'Annunzio was not "unmistakably homosexual." Boito's story is likewise an example of this Decadent sensibility. "It was the very depravity of the man that attracted," Livia states of her love in the Boito, a line not in the film.[21] Nevertheless, given the historical context for both the setting of *Senso* (preceding the emergence of the Decadents) and the moment in which the film was made (less than fifty years after the end of the Decadents), the representation of a sexual desire that is a threat to the social order could also serve as a mirror of same-sex desire. The latter would have been, by the historical definitions of the period, a sickness, whereas the relationship between Livia and Franz is a decadent option. Visconti's use of fabric intensifies the mirror-like elements of heterosexual/homosexual desire, in which "seeing" and "seeing as" or (more specifically for my purposes here) *being seen* become crucial to the dynamic.

When Livia veils herself it both hides her face and, through the specifics of the veil's construction, turns her into a spectacle. When she goes to pay a surprise visit to Franz at his barracks, she is first shown in long shot scampering through a square in Venice, passing various officers and working-class women. Tosi has described Visconti's attraction for Winterhalter as one tied to the director's love for the "outré" and for how in Winterhalter fabric becomes "chiaroscuro, movement, suggestion."[22] This world of outré movement through fabric is found here as Livia moves across this square, the back of the large veil attached to her hat flying up in relation to her frantic movements, and the veil that hangs down over her face is sheer, so that her features are still recognizable. With the outsized gown she is wearing, the outfit in several shades of gray and pale brown, she turns herself into a mobile image to be noticed, even as she appears to be attempting to furtively make her way to an adulterous encounter. Once she is alone with Franz in the quarters he shares with other officers, he lifts up her veil but only the first layer of it, exposing her mouth, as her nose and eyes remain covered. Placing his hands on her arms, he repeats a line from the Heinrich Heine poem he had earlier recited to her, "Lyrical Intermezzo" (1823), during their first extended encounter, the nighttime walk through Venice where she initially indicated succumbing to him by lifting a brown veil from her face.

The importance of the veil to Visconti has been addressed in some of the biographical and critical literature. Such a fascination with the veil has been more typically ascribed to a restaging of Visconti's own biography. According to Tosi, Visconti's adored mother frequently wore veils, this serving as an explanation for their recurrence in Visconti's films. In such a reading, the veil is an opportunity for him to return to primal moments at one remove, the veil as a displaced form of the maternal body. While such testimony may very well be accurate, this does not take us far enough in addressing the significance of veils across the body of work. Blom has offered detailed descriptions of these Visconti veils as well as provided various historical contexts within which the veil has served denotative and connotative functions: as an indication of divinity or of death and ghostliness, as a sign of mourning, as a form of protection against the weather, or as seduction.[23]

I would add still another way of thinking about these veils, at least in relation to *Senso*. We have a film about (for Visconti) a failed revolution in light of the history that followed it. The Risorgimento is initially personified by Livia's idealized cousin, Roberto Ussoni (Massimo Girotti). His world is clandestine in nature, underground, a "closeted" world, at least temporarily. In one of the film's most self-consciously melodramatic sequences, Count Serpieri (Heinz Moog) follows his wife through the streets of Venice. It has been established that Livia is disconsolate over Franz's absence. She "discreetly" looks for him in an ostentatious dark blue outfit, the hems of the dress dragged through the damp streets, wearing a hat dotted with violets around its rim and a heavy veil worn tightly around her face, the outfit becoming yet another display of her emotional state. In *The Eagle with Two Heads*, the Queen gives a ball and her guests arrive in the aftermath of a storm, requiring them to step out of their carriages and into mud before making their entrance to the palace. Such an idea establishes a comic contrast between the luxury of the costumes and the mud being splattered on them. More significantly, the mud becomes tied to degradation and death, forces larger than the precariousness of the luxurious surroundings. Such a contrast is not quite so forceful in this sequence from *Senso* (due to the absence of close views of the gown being dragged through the wet streets) but is there nonetheless. In Boito, the water in the canals of Venice is incorporated into Livia's sexual masochism: "I would trail my bare arm up to the elbow in the water, letting the lace trim on my short sleeve get wet."[24] Visconti does not explore these possibilities in relation to the canal. Instead he substitutes for them with Livia's gown being literally dragged against the wet ground in the name of an overpowering sexual desire, tying her back to the naturalist female figure of Giovanna in *Ossessione*. Of his *Beauty and the Beast* (1946), Cocteau writes of a film dominated by "silence, music, wind and trailing dresses."[25] These trailing dresses, in both Cocteau and Visconti, become a potent image of sexual desire that has been degraded, dragged along the ground, but is all the more seductive for being so.

In the midst of this, Livia's maid, Laura (Rina Morelli), relays a message brought to her by an anonymous man instructing Livia to go to Campo San Geremia. Livia misinterprets this as a message from Franz and impulsively runs off, instructing Laura to tell the Count everything. As the Count promptly follows Livia, the melodramatic rhetoric intensifies as excerpts from the first movement of Anton Bruckner's *Symphony No. 7* (1885) nondiegetically erupt. Like the Heine poem Franz recites to Livia, the Bruckner symphony becomes one of several markers of an Austro-German culture submerging Livia's Italianness at the very moment when she is devoted to expelling the Austrians from Venice. (The name Franz Mahler, clearly meant to evoke Gustav Mahler, six years old at the time of the film's setting, and possibly Franz Liszt, is another of these markers and specific to the film: In the Boito, the character is named Remigio Ruz.) As she rings the bell upon arriving at the Campo, Livia turns to the Count and emotionally confesses she is there to meet her lover. But when the door opens, Livia is greeted by Ussoni and his followers and she falls into Ussoni's arms in a false display of devotion.

What is collapsed at such a moment is a tension central to the film between what Dalle Vacche contrasts as "the body erotic and the body politic, the illusions of the senses taking over the illusions of the Risorgimento."[26] Livia is positioned as a sexually unfulfilled wife, and the film offers no backstory on how her marriage to the Count could have occurred, whereas in Boito Livia chooses to marry the Count because their age difference would give her the freedom to explore sexual possibilities outside of marriage. In the film, while it is made clear she possesses a strong will over which the Count has minimal control (concisely enacted through a gesture in the opening sequence in which she takes a black chiffon shawl and defiantly wraps it around her shoulders as she faces the Count), this will is initially enacted in a political context. Franz, on the other hand, mistakes Livia's close ties with Ussoni as romantic, not realizing Ussoni is her cousin. Such confusion is germane to the film's project since Livia's political drives emerge at least partly from frustrated sexual ones then displaced onto a commitment to the Risorgimento. The casting of Girotti intensifies this aspect of the film, the Risorgimento embodied in his leading man good looks. Indeed, if their early encounters in the film were to be extracted out of their larger context they could play as scenes between clandestine lovers. With the arrival of Franz, Livia exchanges this "secret lover," in which incestuous desire is repressed, for an actual secret lover, in which another type of forbidden desire is fully consummated.

But there is an equally strong desire, within and by the film, to turn what is sexually forbidden into a grandiose mise-en-scène, fully visible. If Maddalena insists on moving from the position of enchanted spectator to agent of the spectacle itself, Livia takes such a position even further, with even more disastrous consequences. Near the end of the film, as she leaves her villa at dawn in order to meet with Franz in Verona, Livia rocks back and forth in the carriage while the Bruckner symphony swells on the soundtrack. She is swathed in black, her head against velvet cushions of deep violet. In spite of the apparent heat, she keeps her veil on while wiping the sweat off of her face with a white handkerchief. Her discomfort is indicated by the way she pulls on the stifling veil and gown. At one point she reaches down as though to lift the veil from her face but thinks better of it, as though this image of herself covered in the veil is the one to maintain. But such agony is clearly being compensated for by the sexual pleasures she believes will await her in Verona: as a smile, visible under the veil, comes across her face, a dissolve ecstatically shows the carriage en route, the dissolve itself a type of veil. This gesture of Livia's is a variation on an idea from a passage in Boito in relation to an earlier adulterous encounter with her lover: "I did not want to remove the veil from my face. Instead I undid the top buttons of my dress and tucked the flaps inside. With the air on my breast I was able to breathe more easily."[27]

It is the same veil Livia will be wearing when Franz, in his hotel room at the end of the film, violently pulls it back and entirely removes the hat from her head. Visconti has claimed the basic idea for *Senso* came from what he called a "constant vision of a woman dressed in black who endures the insults of her lover with her face moist from too much weeping."[28] Franz's lifting of the veil is a transposition of a related gesture in Boito that occurs after Livia has run away from the encounter from Franz: "As I was going through the gate I felt the veil being torn from my face. I turned and

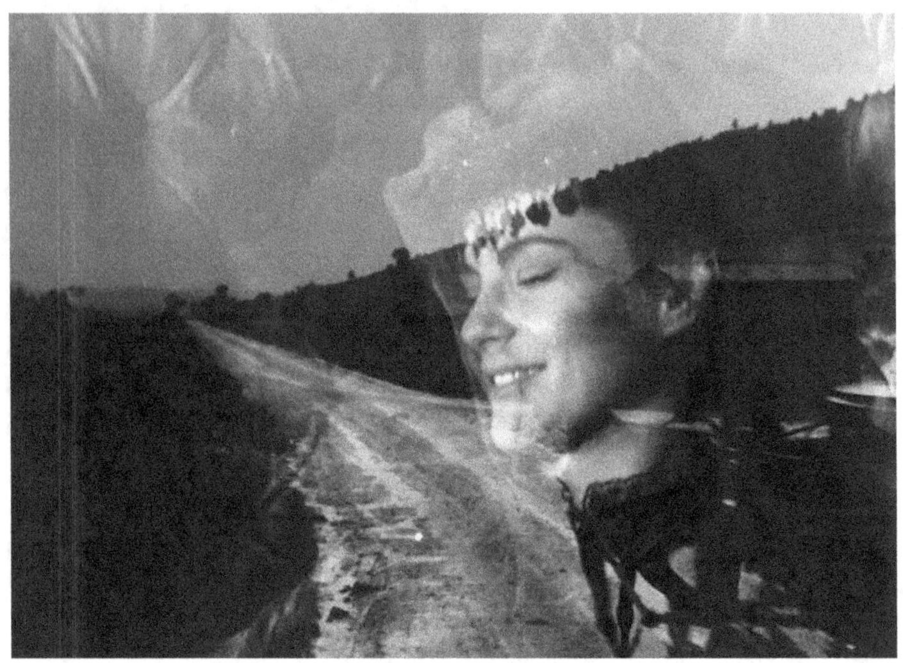

Senso (1954). The dissolve as a veil.

saw before me the unsightly features of the Bohemian officer. He removed the stem of his pipe from his huge mouth, and with his moustache coming at me, he spat on my cheek."[29] For Visconti, the cruelty of this gesture had to come directly from the source of that destructive desire. Livia enters the room for an extended humiliation, in which a prostitute (a more passive character than in the Boito) eventually emerges out of the bedroom and is forced to participate in the ritual. Franz sarcastically refers to his undesirable nature because he has not bathed or shaved in days, or only has dirty glasses for her to drink out of, knowing full well his filth is precisely what she has found attractive. His mocking laughter, combined with the sudden, offscreen sound of the prostitute's voice (Livia was previously unaware of her presence), sends Livia cowering to a corner, where she grabs ahold of the thick red velvet curtains and tassels, as though for support. Franz humiliates her here on two levels: Livia is the older "john" who has purchased her time with Franz the way a wealthy man of the period would more typically purchase his time with a prostitute; and Livia is a "sgualdrina" herself, the word specifically used by Franz as he mocks her, the words sending her scurrying out of the apartment and down the hallway. The power of the veil in *Senso* is that it becomes the ultimate image of this desire that hides and protects itself as it also cries out for recognition and visibility.

Projected

Valli's Livia is not the film's only diva. For Dalle Vacche, Franz is "a sort of diva in reverse," since it is Franz more than Livia who assumes the traditional role of the destructive woman.[30] Livia releases a "feminine side" to Franz in which their affair "acquires a tinge of sexual ambiguity." Franz's white military uniform is "too elegant for a man of war, as if the spectacle of fashion is about to undermine the Austrian military reputation."[31] No less than Livia, Franz is linked with fabric, but such a linkage has different implications. If for Visconti the appeal of using Winterhalter as a source for the designs of Livia's gowns was due to their *outré* impression of movement, with Franz it is his white cape that assumes such potential. In a mad gesture of transferring allegiance from the body politic to the body erotic, Livia gives Franz her cousin's money so he can desert the army and live comfortably. This was money with which Ussoni had entrusted her with the ultimate intention of giving it to his officers. In a self-aware statement of tragic implications, he tells Livia neither she nor any person should love him, and he runs off with the money. As he runs, the camera films Franz from behind. With his back to the camera and the white cape dominating his body from neck to ankles, the cape in movement becomes a Romantic image of destructive masculine allure, a Byronic form of vampirism in which the cape serves as an extension of the sexual hold Franz has over Livia.

Franz is a hypnotist/*metteur en scène*, his mastery tied to his capacity to engage in (to use a term of Eisenstein's) a synchronization of senses. "Man and the relations between his *gestures* and the *intonations* of his voice," writes Eisenstein, "which arise from the same emotions, are our models in determining audio-visual structures, which grow in an exactly identical way from the governing image."[32] In their Venice hotel room, Franz draws Livia's attention to the sounds and textures of their environment, such details the stock-in-trade of the *metteur en scène*. Fabric is the nucleus of an investment in detail, a "governing image," the sequence opening with Franz touching the curtains of two different windows as he discusses sound, including the rustling sounds of such curtains. Due to the sunlight coming through the windows, these curtains, moving in relation to a slight breeze, cast shadows against the wall and become a form of projected moving images.

In *Bellissima*, it is Blasetti, as the director of the film Maddelena so desperately wants her daughter to star in, who will become the literal purveyor of projected moving images. Blasetti's well-known objection to Visconti's using the charlatan theme from *L'elisir d'amore* as his character's leitmotif for the film's underscoring, and Visconti's response to Blasetti that all directors are fundamentally charlatans, is a key anecdote:

The cinema, like sexual desire itself, achieves its force through its power to simultaneously seduce and destroy.[33] In the case of Blasetti, the ironies extend into the political. A major figure of Italian cinema and a director of considerable talent, Blasetti is also linked with Fascism, producing some of his signature works during that period. Marcus notes how Visconti dresses Blasetti in African safari clothes so that he implicitly becomes a "Third World potentate."[34] As Visconti must surely have been aware, however, Blasetti's cinema is not so simple as to imply its one-to-one collusion with Fascism. Bazin refers to the irony of Blasetti making, a year after *The Iron Crown*, with its "hypertrophied mise en scene" so typical of Fascist cinema,[35] a film like *Four Steps in the Clouds* (1941), an "uninhibited and poetic comedy"[36] and one of a number of Italian films of the period anticipating neorealism. Bazin lists several negative traits of *The Iron Crown*, including a vulgar taste for décor; the glorification of the star system; an artificial approach to performance as well as "all the pomp of bel canto and opera"; and scenarios "influenced by stage drama, romantic melodrama and the medieval verse chronicle in the form of the cotemporary serial novel."[37] Many of these are the very traits Visconti will revisit in *Senso* but transform them in the process by conjoining them with his rethinking of the goals of early neorealism.

In *Bellissima*, Blasetti's authority and mythic status, while on one level very real, are also the source of affectionate parody, as when another of the stage mothers faints as she hears his voice coming out of a speaker. Moreover, the film complicates a simple opposition between the mesmerizing power of the *metteur en scène* and his subjects through the characterization of Maddalena, who is, as Marcus notes, "herself a peddler of illusions."[38] In particular, she offers her own elixir, the injections she gives to her various clients that promise the rewards of great health but whose rejuvenating ingredients (if any) are unclear. And she is also capable of masterfully staging scenes of her own, and doing so around fabric, as when she resists Spartaco's attempts to put a stop to her ambitions for Tina. This act of resistance occurs through Tina's dress for the screen test arriving in the midst of a fight between the couple over her (to Spartaco) irresponsible mothering, with the dress becoming the ultimate confirmation of her frivolous expenditures. She stages an elaborate defense of her desires for her daughter's success while standing at the kitchen table with the dress piled in front of her, hysterical tears streaming down her face as she recites a monologue for the benefit of the women in the building, all of whom have gathered in the kitchen. She will occasionally touch the dress for dramatic effect, as the women's anger toward Spartaco increases. He eventually relents, overwhelmed by her energy, leaving her alone with Tina and the other women. His exit serves as a cue for Maddalena, with Tina now sitting on her lap, to drop her mask and laugh with relief over this temporary victory. Tina's dress, while linked to class ascension and the desire to live within and for the cinema, also becomes, in this sequence, a prop for Maddalena, the diva becoming *metteur en scène*.

Livia's situation is more complex. In the rented room sequence near the end of the film, when Franz confesses to Livia it was he who turned Ussoni's name in to the authorities, an act that led to her cousin's exile, he also adds that this is something Livia has known all along but could not admit to herself. Such a line is connected to the larger sense in which Livia is not simply enacting a melodrama of her own life but at the same time watching herself do it. Where this type of self-dramatization differs from Maddalena's has to do with what is at stake in relation to the collapsing of the functions of diva and *metteur en scène*. Whereas Magnani's performance style signifies its ties to realist and comic forms, thereby leaving room for a measure of spontaneity, Valli performs more firmly within a melodramatic tradition. She repeatedly strikes poses, sometimes freezing into a gestural tableau, as though self-consciously creating an image of herself in the midst of a scenario largely of her own making. If Maddalena is capable of staging a scene of pathos in her kitchen in which her daughter's white dress becomes the central expressive object, she can also very quickly drop the mask and laugh, taking pleasure at her own skillful artifice. Livia lacks such irony and instead is enveloped by her own desires and fantasies. In virtually every instance of this, fabric is situated in a central manner.

On her second visit to Franz's quarters, Franz is not there and she is confronted with soldiers casually wearing their uniforms, jackets unbuttoned and hanging loose, or the jackets not on the men at all. Their bodies are decoratively draped in the shot, some of the men playing cards at a table, others lounging about. Blom has noted an intertextual citation in the compositions of this sequence, of Telemaco Signorini's *La toeletta del mattino* (1898). Signorini's painting is of a brothel, the human subjects female prostitutes.[39] But in *Senso*, it is the officers who assume the function of prostitutes, as men fighting on behalf of political ideals become sex workers, their uniforms less indicators of national unity than of erotic male spectacle. As she walks among the men, waiting for Franz, one officer (Christian Marquand) asks her if she likes this all-male environment. She ignores the brazenness of the question, prompting another officer to sarcastically note that Livia won't say whether she likes such an environment but she comes there nevertheless. She steps into the bedroom and paces, waiting for Franz, as we hear an off-camera voice recite a list of laundry items: two pairs of shorts, three shirts, two dress shirts, and two sheets. She soon stops pacing and walks over to the source of this voice and, in a panning movement, the camera shows us that an Austrian officer is talking to a laundress, who exits with the laundry basket as the officer smacks her on the rear end. Talking to Livia about Franz, he continually adjusts the coverings to his bed as Marquand's officer enters the room, walks behind Livia, and goes over to the window before coming to the bed and leaning against the foot rail, as though waiting for an opportunity. While he attempts to reassure Livia of Franz's eminent return, both his dialogue (with its recitation of Franz's various sexual conquests) and his body language suggest a more insidious intent. The positioning of Marquand in the frame as he leans against the bed and the arrangement of his uniform (shirt open almost down to the waist, jacket completely open, thumbs in suspenders, waist and hips thrust out and toward Livia) imply another kind of sexual opportunity for Livia and, by extension, any number of women. Livia's dreams of romantic, albeit adulterous exclusivity are temporarily shattered.

Unfurled

In reviewing *Senso*, Bazin argues that, while the film aligns itself with a naturalist literary tradition "simultaneously descriptive and critical," the film is also, like Visconti's prior films, highly theatricalized.[40] Nonetheless, the film is also one in which "Visconti seeks to impose upon this magnificent, beautifully composed, almost picturesque setting the rigor and, most importantly, the unobtrusiveness of a documentary."[41] As an example of this documentary impulse, Bazin draws attention to a moment in the Custoza battle sequence in which the Italian flag is taken out of its protective covering and unfurled. The documentary impulse here is showing this moment in long shot so the flag is "barely visible" and all of the other details in the shot are given equal weight. Visconti resists the convention of giving the flag a great symbolic importance but instead integrates it into a larger idea of a new Italian army and a new culture coming into being.[42] Contrast this with Blasetti's approach in his Risorgimento epic, *1860* (1936). While foreshadowing some aspects of neorealism, Blasetti's approach is rhetorical in a different manner. The waving of the Italian flag near the end of the film is captured in three shots, one of a soldier carrying it, filmed from behind, running up a hill; then at the top of the hill, again filmed from behind as he waves the flag to the advancing soldier; then in a striking low-angle shot, the image slightly masked and filmed from the front, as he continues to wave the flag. In this low angle, the flag looks enormous, its size here both realistically tied to the narrative moment (the flag needs to be made visible to the advancing forces) and elevated to the status of myth.

The connection of a flag to national and cultural unity—or its destruction—is a privileged cinematic trope. There is the famous crane shot of *Gone with the Wind* in which Scarlett walks past all of the injured soldiers on the ground, the camera's movement culminating with the tattered Confederate flag flying in the far left of the

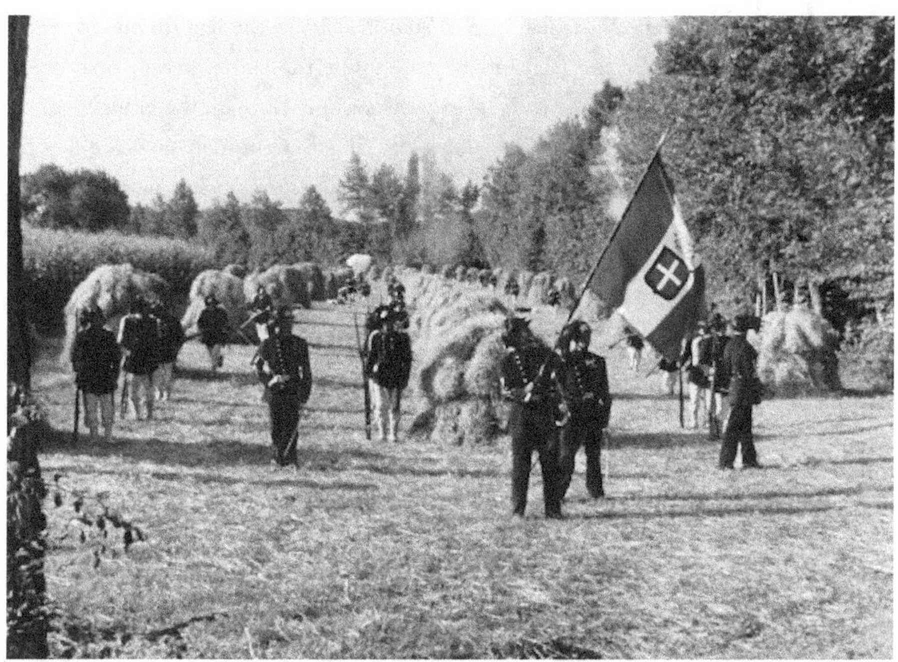

Senso. The flag in long shot, an ambivalent image of a new culture coming into being.

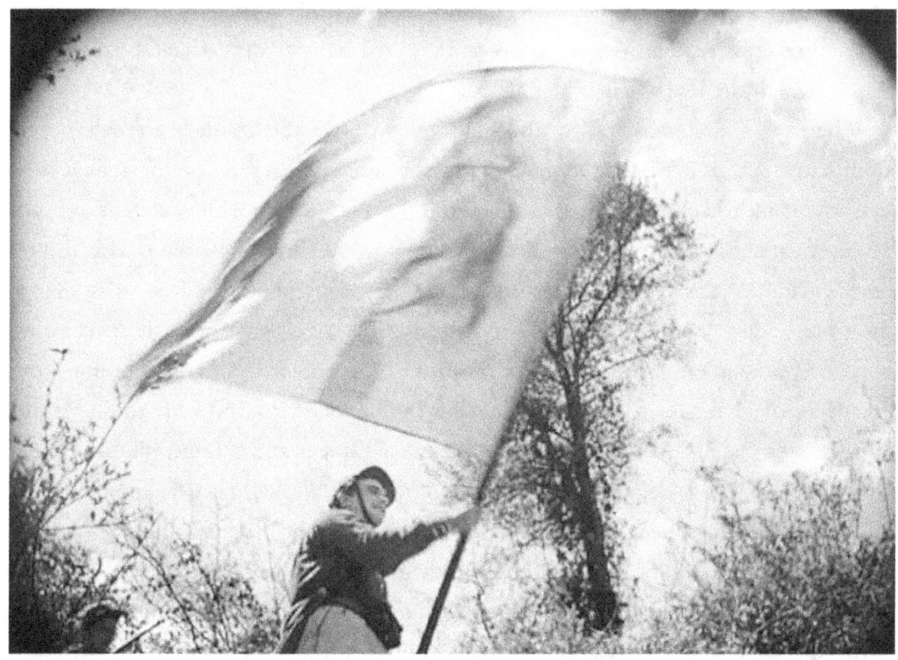

1860 (Alessandro Blasetti, 1936). The flag in low-angle frame, given mythic stature.

frame. The raising of the ship's flag in *Battleship Potemkin*, the flag tinted red, as the residents of Odessa spot the flag and happily await the ship's arrival, unaware of the massacre about to occur, achieves its impact not only through the boldness of the red erupting into an otherwise black-and-white film but through how the flag becomes part of a weaving of fabric imagery tied to the film's montage structure. The flag in *Senso* emerges out of markedly different historical contexts. It is in long shot not only because of the documentary impulse Bazin isolates but also because of the critical distance the film has on this particular "revolution," so its fabric energies are directed not toward symbols of an emerging nation but toward the personal, the sexual that will override them. The hotel room in Venice serves as one example of this kind of space, where Livia rises from her bed and wraps a sheet around her naked body in the immediate aftermath of sex with Franz. As she walks across the room, Valli uses this sheet with a diva-like expressivity. Livia's bedroom in her villa is another, even more crucial space for this articulation. Throughout *Senso*, and unlike in the montage of Eisenstein's cinema, Visconti not only employs fairly extended takes and middle- and long-distance framing but he rarely repeats a camera setup in any given sequence. The continuity editing conventions of the master shot and the rhythmic opportunities of the eyeline match/shot-reverse shot are effectively dispensed with. One general result of this is a sometimes slow pacing, particularly in the scenes between Franz and Livia, as though the film is giving credence to time standing still for the two lovers. However, the bedroom is frequently marked by its delimited nature, a theatrical, boxlike space within which the lovers stage their affair.

When Franz deserts the army and hides out in Livia's bedroom in the villa, fabric dominates. And it is here where Franz returns to exercise his gifts as a devious *metteur en scène*. Dalle Vacche has noted of this room that the "heavy, white curtains of Livia's windows and the transparent, white veils hanging over her bed rhyme with the red stage curtain of La Fenice."[43] Curtains become privileged items in *Senso*, tied as they are to two ideas: marking the division between theatrical space and the space of the spectator, and shielding the sexual act from outside observers. Franz does not create the décor of Livia's bedroom. Instead, it is lying in wait for him, ready to do his bidding. Livia's bed is thick with sheets, blankets, pillows, and drapings, the bedding an outward sign of her deepest (and, prior to Franz, unfulfilled) sexual longings. Once such longings have been given voice, however, they remain fundamentally behind closed curtains due to not simply the adultery but the unspeakable nature of the political betrayal involved. The fabric imagery throughout this long section of the film gives form to these enacted desires. But it does so only within the confines of the bedroom, never to venture outside of it. Image after image frames this encounter in such a way that its theatrical nature is foregrounded and the fabrics repeatedly frame (often literally) the dramatic action in a rhetorical fashion.

Franz's sudden arrival at the villa is handled in three sequences (or possibly two, depending on how we are to define a sequence). The first is his entrance into her bedroom, an event lasting just over five minutes and handled in six successive camera setups, each of these involving some kind of panning or tracking. This is interrupted by Livia leaving the bedroom in order to meet her husband and the servants responding to the barking dogs excited by a strange but unseen presence on the grounds (Franz). This sequence (or perhaps an interlude within one long sequence) lasts less than a minute and is covered in five different setups, most of them long shots, of Livia, the Count, and the servants attempting to investigate. This is immediately followed by Livia's return to her bedroom, this lasting for five minutes and covered in seven successive setups (some static, some mobile) culminating with a dissolve taking us to the early morning hours, still in Livia's bedroom, with a sequence lasting for approximately three minutes and covered in two mobile setups. In these three sections or sequences, fabric and the use of décor and light create a theatrical atmosphere (due to the confinement of the space in such a protracted manner, the use of offscreen or "offstage" sound, and the melodramatic nature of the dialogue and performances) while sustaining an atmosphere of seductive, unspeakable sexual desires. Livia gives a performance of wanting to resist Franz as Franz gives a performance of an almost Mephistophelean power.

In the first section, Franz is first seen by Livia standing outside the double doors of her bedroom, with only his white cape visible as he stands in profile, a double-layered curtain of red-and-white lace serving as a frame for him. As Livia moves toward him, her image is doubled and framed by a mirror to her far right. Much has been written on the use of mirrors in *Senso*, such a use beginning in the opening sequence, in the opera box where Livia and Franz have their first conversation. The large mirrors there serve to both frame and destabilize the space while also setting up the mirror as a central metaphor for the film, establishing a relation between onstage and offstage, the theatrical and the real. At the villa, this use of the mirror is incorporated into a systematic use of fabric so that mirrors and fabric frame and comment upon the relationship between Livia and Franz. As she sits on the bed and tells him she doubts his sincerity, he stands against the wall to the left of this bed, arms folded, as both he and Livia are framed by the bed's draping. While Livia's face is visible during this section, Franz's face and body are obscured by the draping as he now assumes the position of the veiled woman previously enacted by Livia. A surprising cut takes us closer to him as we see something not clearly visible in the wider shot: he is standing in front of a portion of a fresco in which a dark, bearded man pulls back a curtain and leans into another (somewhat androgynous) man. Is the man pulling back the curtain whispering a secret to the other man? Or has the bearded man caught the other man engaged in a secretive act? Visconti does not provide the original context for this fresco and clearly wants to use it for his own purposes. What such an image implies is a world of secrets, of innuendo, perhaps even teasingly evoking same-sex desire, one man leaning into another in order to say or do something scandalous. Franz then walks over to Livia and falls to his knees, the drapings of the bed again serving as a frame for the lovers but with Franz now able to position his body close to the bed of his lover. She slowly relents, putting on a lavish violet robe and telling him to wait in this room as she begins to go out. He then touches one of her clothing items hanging in a closet and briefly lifts it up. This is an echo of his gesture of touching and then raising a curtain in the Venice hotel room, but here it assumes a different kind of intimacy, a surreptitious need to touch the fabric of another person.

When Livia returns, still agonizing over her attraction to Franz, she sits at her dresser and he comes up behind her, his image again reflected in a mirror, this one a small oval as he holds up a green chiffon scarf. As she attempts to distance herself from him, saying she has lost all dignity as a result of the affair, he paces around her as the tracking

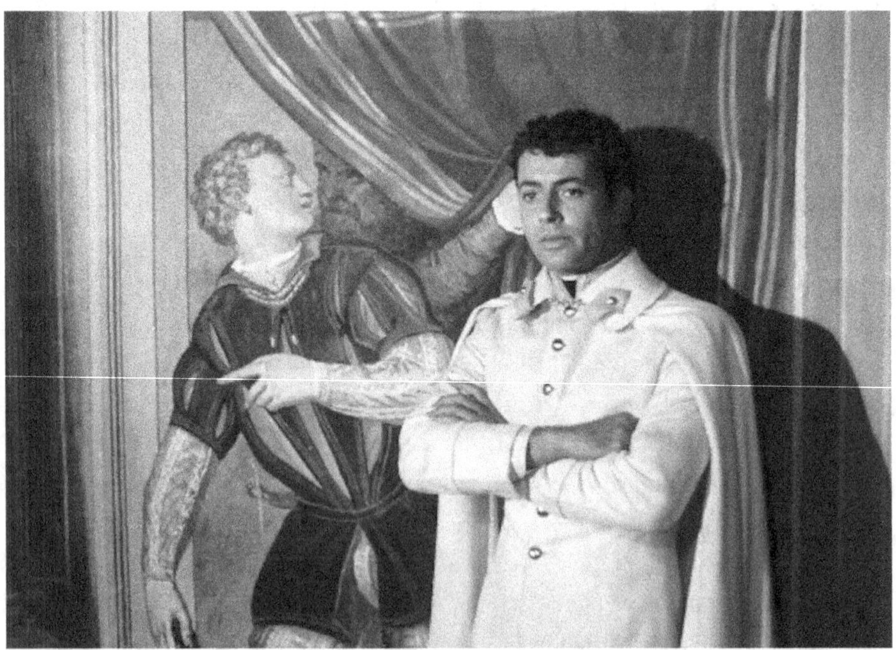

Senso. A world of innuendos behind the curtain.

camera follows his movements. As he paces, he continues to fondle her scarf as though the scarf has metonymically taken the place of her temporarily reluctant body. But this fondling of the scarf (the scarf's bright green causing it to stand out in a space otherwise devoid of such intense color) also feminizes Franz as he plays with a lady's accessory, the kind of thing a "real man" should not do. Realizing her resistance is stronger than he had imagined, he backs away and then walks behind her, takes off his cape, and lies down on a chaise lounge, returning to some of his Venice hotel room strategies of attempting to awaken Livia's senses. He rhapsodizes over the fragrance of wheat in the air, the "lazy sweetness" of the summer, all of this evocation of surrender as his own supine body creates an image of just such a surrender. The framing and editing reinforce Franz's power, the first cut to a slightly high angle of him lying languorously on the chaise, a fragment of the cape draped over the edge. This is followed by an even higher angle shot of Livia sitting in front of her makeup table, her violet robe spread out on the floor, Franz at the right of the frame, his cape now fully visible as it, too, is draped and spread out. These clothing items are giving voice to desires that are at this point still suspended while showing evidence of self-conscious control on the part of both characters, as though they are enacting and posing for the situation at hand. The camera slowly begins to crane down as she tells him repeatedly to go, but the craning movement is abruptly terminated by a cut to a closer two-shot of them as he comes to her, the camera dollying around them as they finally kiss and the Bruckner music swells. Still embracing one another, they walk across the room toward the open closet, her clothes hanging there, a mirror to their left draped in blue silk as the camera dollies backward and the image dissolves to her night table. The camera executes a dolly around the table and then moves over to the mirror by the window, the same mirror in which Livia's image was reflected upon Franz's arrival. But now both Livia and Franz are reflected in and framed by this mirror in what is presumably a postcoital embrace. A cut to a two-shot of them lying on the couch, his head in her lap, quickly develops into a mobile image as the camera tracks backward, with white curtains moving in the breeze, the sun now coming up. This movement is also reflected in the mirror, creating effects of projected movement similar to those in the Venice hotel room. They have briefly gone backward in time to the early days of their affair in Venice.

For much of this sequence, fabrics enact the push and pull between Livia and Franz, becoming forces of seduction and forces of resistance between the object of desire (Franz) and the desiring subject, as well as between two divas who have briefly found a point of happy collaboration. Fabric has become attuned, however tentatively, to their desires. Livia convinces Franz to stay one more day. She will hide him, the very prospect of this exciting her in a film in which the hidden, the closeted, are a source of both oppression and previously unimaginable ecstasy, as well as a type of foreplay for theatrical and aesthetic creation. The impossibility of sustaining such an enterprise under these conditions, however, can only culminate in the madness and death of a "constant vision in black."

Bellissima resolves its tensions in a very different manner. Maddalena does not, as in Zavattini's version, have to face Maria's screen test being rejected. Instead, Maddalena herself rejects the offer after overhearing collective laughter in the screening room directed at her daughter's technical incompetence, an incompetence that nevertheless charms Blasetti. Unaware of this latter detail, her maternal instincts rise up and she rejects the offer for her daughter to star in the film. This gives Maddalena a strong ethical choice she must make rather than simply becoming a victim of the machinery of the film industry. Such a resolution also entails a somewhat conventional restoration of the "natural" order, Maddelana giving up her fantasies and finally becoming fully committed to the domestic sphere. However, the film has already established the world within which Maddalena moves as being dominated by performance and not in opposition to but fully contained within its own (neo) realist gestures, with Magnani in the midst of the entire project, its raison d'etre for Visconti, its diva. Even if Maddalena officially forsakes her dreams of cinema, the movies are still being shown in her own apartment courtyard as she jokingly pretends to be enchanted by the voice of Burt Lancaster spilling into her bedroom. (In itself, a misrecognition since the voice is not Lancaster's own but that of an Italian actor dubbing for him.)

It is the film's final shot, though, that is most compelling for my purposes. The camera tracks toward a sleeping Maria, a sheet covering her body from the waist down, her head resting on soft pillows, as the melody from an aria in *L'elisir d'amore,* "Quanto è bella, quanto è cara," is nondiegetically heard. In the Donizetti, this aria is performed by the male lead, Nemorino, a peasant in love with the unattainable Adina and it is Adina he is singing about here, "how beautiful she is." In *Bellissima*, the beauty we are being asked to perceive is not tied to sexual desire but to a more platonic beauty attached to a female child who has gamely accepted being dragged all over Rome in order to live out her mother's fantasies. In the novel of *Gone with the Wind*, Scarlett muses about the security she once felt in her childhood home, "with the protection of a mother's love wrapped about her like an eiderdown quilt."[44] Maddalena's intensity and self-involvement preclude such maternal fabric metaphors, and Maria is in bed alone. She is wearing a sleeveless white T-shirt, a bead of sweat rolling down her face, her hair wet from the heat. If the fishermen from *La terra trema* are exhausted from relentless labor, Maria's exhaustion is no less tied to labor although of a different sort. The final shot restores her to her innocent state as a child, away from the cinema and

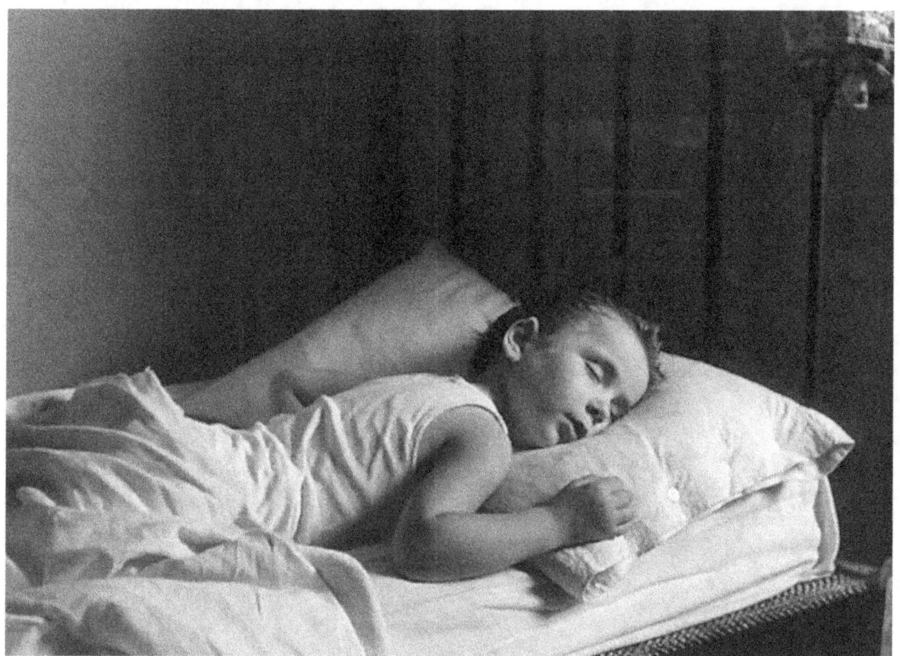

Bellissima. The bed as image of suspended possibilities.

its attendant labors and fantasy-generating mechanisms but also away (temporarily) from the exhausting diva behavior of her mother. It is a very tender image, the bedding clean and ordered, in contrast to the more disheveled beds in *Ossessione* or *La terra trema* and the erotic and theatrical intensities of the beds in *Senso*. But it is also a beautifully filmed arrangement of light and shadow and texture playing off of the flesh of the girl and the fabric surrounding her. No less than the sleeping sailors in *Battleship Potemkin*, it is an image of possibilities. But whatever possibilities might be implied through fabric and the body here are, by virtue of this being an image of a child, indefinitely suspended.

TIGHT FITS

3

Bandages

If the diva was a central figure linking the two films in the previous chapter, we now return to the male actor and a specific one, Marcello Mastroianni. But his presence in the two Viscontis in which he starred, *White Nights* (1957) and *The Stranger* (1967), is unlike that of any actor so far addressed. The films are separated by a period of ten years during which Italian cinema (and the cinema as a whole) underwent a number of major changes, preeminently brought on by the emergence of new film movements and revisions to older ones. How some of these changes affected neorealism I addressed in the first chapter in relation to *Rocco and His Brothers*. But by the time of *The Stranger* there was a significant intensification of the challenges being posed to Visconti, with his ties to both neorealism and postwar European art cinema. First, however, let us turn to Mastroianni.

Before appearing in *White Nights*, Mastroianni had been a central figure in Visconti's theater work, including appearing as Diomedes in the 1949 production of Shakespeare's *Troilus and Cressida* (1602), and as first Mitch (1949) and later Stanley Kowalski (1951) in Tennessee Williams's *A Streetcar Named Desire* (1947). But in *White Nights* and *The Stranger* are the only times Visconti cast Mastroianni in a film, and neither film has received the amount of critical attention that the other Visconti features addressed so far in this book have. Some of the neglect of *The Stranger* is due to the film being kept out of theatrical circulation for decades because of a rights issue with the estate of Albert Camus, whose novel serves as the film's source. Other factors are also central in comparatively marginalizing the two films in the critical reception, partly tied to issues arising in relation to the ambitions of the films and partly tied to Mastroianni. But *White Nights* and *The Stranger*, made under very different conditions, contain not only useful contrasts but, even apart from Mastroianni, surprising links.

In between his two Visconti films, Mastroianni became an international star, not centrally because of Visconti but because of Mastroianni's association with Fellini, beginning with *La dolce vita* and soon followed by *8½* (1963). Like *Bellissima*, *8½* is a film about filmmaking that takes us inside of Cinecittà. But unlike the Visconti, it is told from the perspective of a director, Guido (played by Mastroianni). In *8 ½*, a film of stark visual contrasts between blacks and whites, we have white fabric everywhere—sheets, scarves, handkerchiefs, veils—tied to intersecting notions of cleanliness, innocence, and childhood, to the world of sleep and dreams, and to the maternal body. But Fellini also connects these fabrics to the aesthetic impulse itself, to the white blank page or screen as well as to the modernist idea of nothingness, of silence. Mastroianni functions for Fellini as both a double for the *auteur* (essentially playing a version of Fellini himself in the autobiographical *8 ½*) and an embodiment of the values of the films, a masculine figure who is also the source of comic befuddlement in an atmosphere of sexual and creative chaos.

Mastroianni's physical attractiveness, however, is different from that of the male figures discussed so far. His face and body are too rugged, too masculine for Visconti, in contrast to Alain Delon, Massimo Girotti, or Farley Granger. Delon was, in fact, Visconti's first choice for the role of Meursault in *The Stranger*. There is in these Visconti/Mastroianni films a slight element of strain in terms of expressive effects, partly due to a leading man who is a tight fit for the issues at stake. In other respects, though, Mastroianni's presence is by no means antithetical to these projects and is consistent with the tendency in his career of being cast in roles in which he is both agent and observer of events, a function he assumes in such other major roles of the period as the novelist Giovanni Pontano in Antonioni's *La notte* (1961) or the journalist Enrico in Valerio Zurlini's *Cronaca familiare* (1962), the latter adapted from a novel by Vasco Pratolini. Pratolini also contributed to the script of *Rocco and His Brothers*, and both that film and the Zurlini contain moments of startling physical intimacy between brothers, including, in the case of the Zurlini, an intimacy tied to the absent, long-deceased seamstress mother of the two men. That Visconti would cast Mastroianni as the romantic Mitch and then the brutal Stanley (the latter a key ambivalent image of desire) in two different productions of *Streetcar* is one indication of Mastroianni's capacity to imaginatively act out contradictory states. His later success in portraying a homosexual in Ettore Scola's *A Special Day* (1977) was partly tied to the provocation in casting him in this manner but could also be seen as a function of a role bringing forth latent potential evident in earlier films. In *Il bell'antonio* (Mauro Bolognini, 1960), for example, he portrays a sexually impotent man whose impotence is unknown to virtually everyone in his community, all of whom take him to be a womanizer. Women find him to be intensely desirable, but his desirability is tied to his barely understood feminine appearance. Throughout the film, Bolognini returns to an image crucial to Mastroianni's unstable sexual presence: curtains sensuously moving in the breeze from open windows.[1]

White Nights and *The Stranger* are linked as well as adaptations of literary works by canonical writers, in the case of *White Nights*, a story of the same title by Dostoevsky. In the years since the Visconti, that story has served as the source for over a dozen films, including Robert Bresson's *Four Nights of a Dreamer* (1971) and James Gray's *Two Lovers* (2008). "White Nights" (1848) is an early work of Dostoevsky's, far more romantic in style than what would come later, and it does not strongly exhibit the elements of literary naturalism found in *Crime and Punishment*, *The Idiot*, or *The Brothers Karamazov*, whose imagistic descriptions much more readily lend themselves to Visconti. Nevertheless, "White Nights" offers another kind of literary language and form no less capable of being translated into matters central to the cinema. The title of Bresson's adaptation more clearly points in this direction than does Dostoevsky's own. The unnamed male protagonist in the story (called Mario in the Visconti, the female protagonist's named changed from Nastenka to Natalia) is fundamentally a dreamer, the story itself written in the first person from his perspective, within which Nastenka's own is embedded. "'A dreamer," Dostoevsky's narrator declares, "—if you must know its exact definition—is not a man but a sort of creature of the neuter gender. He settles mostly in some inaccessible place, as though anxious to hide in it even from the light of day.'"[2] To be a dreamer is to be neither fully male nor female, neither masculine nor feminine, experiencing desire in a hidden manner. This narrator calls himself a "voluptuous sluggard" who "desires nothing, for he is above all desire, for he is sated, for he is the artist of his own life, which he recreates in himself to suit whatever fancy he pleases."[3]

The story was transposed from the nineteenth century to the twentieth, the setting changed from Russia to an unnamed town in Italy, modeled on Livorno. Such transpositions of Dostoevsky are hardly unprecedented. Dostoevsky, like Zola, is often adapted in this manner—and both Bresson and Gray likewise set their films in the present day and transpose their settings, to Paris in the Bresson, New York in the Gray. But Visconti's boldest strategy was the decision to shoot the entire film on sets at Cinecittà. Unlike *Bellissima* or *Senso*, *White Nights* appeared to be forsaking virtually any claims to rethinking the early goals of neorealism, opting instead for a wholly stylized universe. Moreover, this stylization is connected to a strongly theatrical impulse, the film most obviously achieving this through the set design, which makes no attempt to conceal its artifice. Even someone as committed to Visconti's work as Guido Aristarco was puzzled by *White Nights*, seeing in the film the absence of a dialectic crucial to Visconti: a concern with corruption and decadence coupled with a "belief in an eventual transformation" of these states into a "sympathy and solidarity with the new man born of a society in crisis."[4] Accusations against Visconti for betraying neorealism scarcely originated with *White Nights*. In fact, in his theater work prior to this the element of provocation against neorealism's early tenets had already begun, as in the controversy generated by the 1948 production *As You Like It* (1623), with its sets and costumes by Salvador Dali and with Mastroianni playing a small role. Noa Steimatsky has noted the links between the theatrical nature of the set design for *Troilus and Cressida* and Visconti's contemporaneous use of location work in *La terra trema*. For the former, a three-dimensional model of Troy was created for outdoor staging at the Boboli Gardens in Florence, thus becoming "a bold intervention in an era of humble postwar production and defying any conception of neorealist culture. This 'stretching' of the theatrical set towards the continuous, open, penetrable space available in principle for a film shot on location reflects, in reverse, *La terra trema*'s landscape grasped as a theater."[5] After this, the streets of Venice in *Senso* demonstrated "the workings of theatrical space in the actual location grasped as historical stage" and the stylized studio sets of *White Nights* disclosed their "material reality" through camera movement.[6]

The cinematographer of *White Nights*, Giuseppe Rotunno (who performed the same duties on *The Stranger*), discussed the strategy he and Visconti employed in the film, in which "'everything looked artificial, false, but when you get the impression it's false, it should begin to look as if it were real.'"[7] What Rotunno is describing is consistent with the paradox at the heart of aesthetic realism. If the operatic and melodramatic elements to *Senso* represent one possible development for neorealism after its mid- to late-1940s heyday, *White Nights* represents another, if more isolated, one, and one that partly takes its cue from the source material wherein Dostoevsky's narrator exclaims: "And how easily, how naturally, is this imaginary, fantastic world created! As though it were not a dream at all! Indeed, he is sometimes ready to believe that all this life is not a vision conjured up by his overwrought mind, not a mirage, not a figment of the imagination, but something real, something that actually exists!"[8] In the previous chapter, and in spite of the clear literary forms and discourses that were apparent in *Senso*, my emphasis was on exploring the theatrical possibilities of Visconti's cinema of fabric. In this chapter, I want to return to literature, unavoidable given the source material for both films. But in doing so, I wish to retain an emphasis on fabric in relation to the theatrical while incorporating issues relating to the literary from the first chapter.

Visconti first read *The Stranger* in 1942, and it is there where he claims Camus "indicated that it is possible to live outside ordered society, avoid its laws, to lock oneself up into indifference, to confine oneself into absurdity."[9] The form and atmosphere of Camus's novel, and the example it sets, take us in at least two directions useful in terms of Visconti. One is the importance of Camus's admiration for Cain's *The*

Postman Always Rings Twice and of its influence on *The Stranger*. The other is the centrality of Dostoevsky for Camus, a subject too vast for my own project here. In terms of its bearing on Visconti, though, an aspect of Dostoevsky that fascinates Camus is its theatrical dimension. "Dostoevsky," Camus writes, "uses a theater technique in his novels: he works through dialogues with few indications as to place and action. A man of the theater–whether actor, director, or author—always finds in him all the suggestions he needs."[10] Camus himself was also, as both playwright and director, a "man of the theater," and this quote is taken from the introduction to his published play based on Dostoevsky's *Demons* (1873) and staged by Camus in 1959 as *Les Possédés*. Camus finds in Dostoevsky a theatrical language through dialogue virtually ready-made for the playwright, stripped of extraneous details in terms of environment but concise in its dramatic conception of character.

Visconti's challenges in adapting the Dostoevsky and Camus sources are, in many respects, different from what Camus is describing in transforming *Demons* into a play. The difficulties Visconti faced with *The Stranger* are well known. Camus's widow would not permit Visconti to make any major changes, causing Visconti to jettison his original conception for the film. In this first conception, the film would have been set in the recent Algerian War of Independence, thereby allowing him to again address the world of fading civilizations with a protagonist ambivalently situated between the old world and the new. It is also possible that Visconti, doubtless aware of the huge success of Gillo Pontecorvo's own film on that war, *The Battle of Algiers* (1966), with its elements of documentary pastiche, was creating a different political and formalist climate within Italian cinema, although Pontecorvo's subject, like Visconti's, was French, so he could sidestep political issues literally closer to home. (Brahim Hadjadj, who had a central role in Pontecorvo's film, would play the Arab murdered by Meursault in *The Stranger*.) Rather than jettison the entire project, Visconti proceeded with an essentially faithful rendering of the novel, the story set in Algeria in the late 1930s, also making it the first Visconti film to have a non-Italian setting. The dubbing of the voices for the international casts of *Senso*, *Rocco and His Brothers*, and *The Leopard* managed, for those who heard the "preferred" Italian soundtracks to the films, to create the experience of a homogeneous Italian universe. But Mastroianni's presence in *The Stranger* and the Italian dub as the favored release version (due to hearing Mastroianni's voice only in this version) create a sense of cultural dislocation and a slightly synthetic atmosphere. *The Stranger* has a more conventional form than any of the Visconti films preceding and following it, contrasting it as well with those films being made by the other central Italian filmmakers of the period: Antonioni with *Red Desert* (1964) and *Blow-Up* (1966), for example, and Pasolini with *Edipo re* (1968), as well as with the work of newly emerging figures such as Bernardo Bertolucci with *Before the Revolution* (1964) and Marco Bellocchio with *Fists in the Pocket* (1965).

Undoubtedly in response to contemporaneous innovations in cinema, *The Stranger* makes use of a fragmented editing style, elliptical narrative organization, and persistent use of zoom lenses, unlike any of the Visconti films addressed here so far. However, this change in style had already begun with *Vaghe stelle dell'orsa* (1965), a film to be addressed in the next chapter, although *The Stranger* is otherwise constrained by the scenario's obligation to be faithful to Camus. The limitations of such fidelity, however, do not preclude *The Stranger* from having an interest beyond a mechanical transcription of its prestigious source. In adapting *The Postman Always Rings Twice*, the cryptic prose of Cain's short novel is transformed in *Ossessione*, as we have already seen, through a process of amplification and embellishment, as well as through a transposition in setting. Such an approach is not possible for *The Stranger*. What Alexander García Düttmann sees in the film is an attempt by Visconti to create a "purely factual film, a study in yellow and blue."[11]

Early in the film, Meursault is visiting the casket containing his just-deceased mother. Düttmann draws attention to the shot of an Arab nurse walking past Meursault, the nurse wearing a blue headscarf, a white bandage covering her nose: "The gaze [of Meursault] bounces off the unmediated hardness of facticity."[12] The nurse sits in a chair, framed at the far left of a medium long shot, wearing a white smock and turned three quarters away from the camera. She can be clearly seen knitting. Camus does not write that the woman knits while she is sitting next to the mother's casket. This is taken from a slightly later passage in the novel, when the nurse returns that evening and Meursault observes her from across the room and "the way her arms were moving made me think she was knitting."[13] Moving this forward gives the woman something to do and is typical of Visconti's general need for an active frame. But as we have seen in relation to *Ossessione* and *La terra trema*, images of women knitting do not simply evoke the domestic sphere but draw upon knitting in relation to the perishability of that sphere, as though knitting is among the final gestures holding these worlds together. To the nurse's right is the mother's casket, perched on a black sawhorse, dismantled sawhorses and another chair also visible in the shot. The white of the walls has been worn down through years of grime so that the white of the woman's robe stands out. A door opens and light from the opposite side of the frame spills into the room as the cast shadow of a man appears. A reverse-angle cut identifies Meursault as the source of this as he nervously looks around and then up as there is a cut to his point-of-view shot of the glass ceiling before there is a return to the prior shot of him, the caretaker now entering the frame. When Meursault is invited by the caretaker to sit

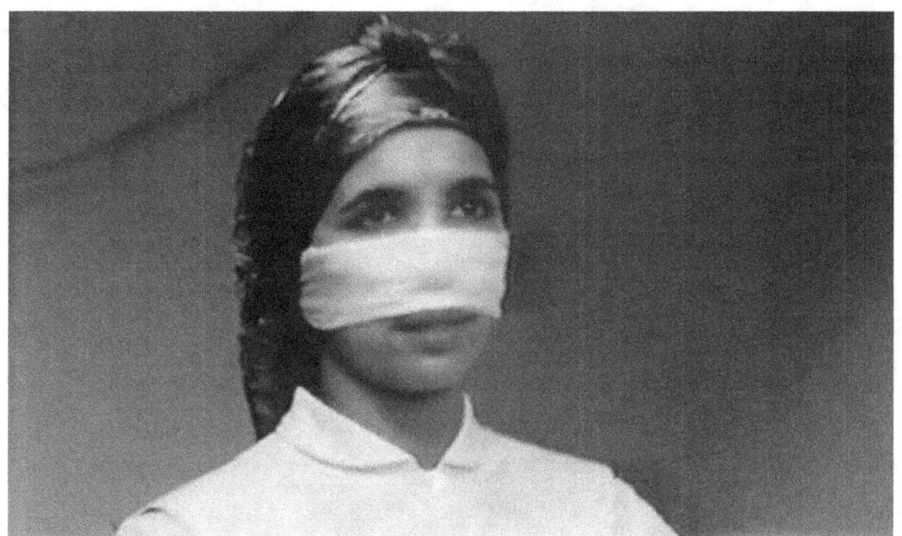

The Stranger (1967). The white bandage as fabric.

down, the woman gets up and walks toward the camera, and it is here where we see her from the front, the white bandage covering her nose and the middle of her face, eyes, and mouth visible. After the woman leaves, the caretaker explains that the bandage is the result of a tumor.

In the novel, the caretaker refers to the bandage before Meursault even notices it, generating his look toward her. In the film, as the woman walks toward him he first sees the bandaged face and then the caretaker offers the explanation. For Visconti, the woman's bandaged face precedes an explanation and becomes close to an irrational sight. "All you could see of her face," Meursault states, "was the whiteness of the bandage."[14] With this sentence, Camus subtly shifts the nature of the cryptic prose he has more immediately employed in describing this setting to a more subjective realm in which "all he could see was the white bandage." Barring any blatantly expressionist devices for rendering this subjectivity, Visconti creates an indelible image of a white bandage and red-and-green scarf covering a face, as though imprinting this image in the mind of the spectator as much as in Meursault. But I would also insist on seeing this bandage as a type of fabric, partly because it is not entirely clear what material this bandage is made from but also because it essentially functions in the way fabric does in Visconti. Such implicit transformation occurs in, for example, *Ossessione*, when Gino frantically unwraps the bandages from his torso, the unwrapping becoming yet another unveiling of his body. In a manner not inconsistent with the neorealist need to connect phenomena to their surrounding totality, Visconti wants the strangeness of the bandage on the woman's face to be felt in relation to all that surrounds it. At the same time, such a moment partakes of the neorealist trope of the sight that is miraculous, terrifying, or inexplicable *because* it has its origins in the real. And it is not so much yellow and blue as whiteness that dominates here, permeating from the bandage down to the smock and out to the walls. White is central to both *The Stranger* and (as the title already implies) *White Nights*, the white often having its origins in fabric, a whiteness that then circulates through the films, manifesting itself in other forms.

Fabric and Fog

Dostoevsky's white nights are those of a summer, when the sky of Petersburg "was so bright and starry."[15] The arrival of spring causes Petersburg to become comparable to a female body as she "reveals herself in all her might and glory" and as "she blossoms out, dresses up, decks herself out with flowers."[16] For the narrator, this happy atmosphere gives him the sensation of having "suddenly found myself in Italy."[17] For Visconti, though, the white nights are those of winter, with the electric lights of the film's urban setting creating one manifestation of white, as do the final moments of the film when snow falls.

But there is another layer of white central to the film: fog. This was created not from mechanically controlled condensed vapors pumped onto the set but out of tulle hung from rafters. Rotunno explains: "These veils, invisible when unlit, became visible as fog when my lights, which I positioned where I could . . . were powered up by a control panel."[18] We are seeing here a variation on a technique with its origins in silent cinema, in which the placing of gauze over the lens becomes a form of diffusion, or in which a softening of the background of a shot occurs through fine netting being placed on the set, often behind the camera subject.[19] Fog becomes fabric, but fog itself is capable of evoking fabric's enveloping capacities. Unlike Dostoevsky, Visconti offers a twilight world of the demimonde in which sexual desires emerge and recede from the fog, hiding in darkened alleyways and doorways, the town itself veiled. As Mario walks about in the opening sequence, he comes across a shadowed passageway where a man is standing. He and Mario exchange greetings but without our ever seeing the man's face. Who is this man who stands in passageways at night? Is he looking for a sexual pickup? If so, with a man or a woman? He is another of the recurring male figures in Visconti creating a strong image for being on the edges of an environment, in shadow, leaning against the décor, convincing young men to journey off with them to greater adventures. These men, bundled up in trench coats or (like Spagnolo in *Ossessione*) with their clothing in tatters, give a muted voice to partially articulated desires.

As in *Rocco and His Brothers*, the weather in *White Nights* is cold, with the coat again becoming a crucial item of both covering and exchange, not white coats now but dark ones serving as a visual contrast with the possibilities of white that are elsewhere. Throughout the film, a character not in the Dostoevsky, a prostitute (Clara Calamai), prowls the streets hoping Mario will eventually succumb to her. She wears the blackest of coats, its deep black also made prominent by the white scarf tucked in at the collar. The coat, combined with her black hair, becomes one limit point of options for sexual desire, the other being the man in the passageway. Mario, though, is able to resist both figures, not even remotely tempted by what is being offered. He is attracted to something more pure, something that implies, however provisionally, a relationship to light: Natalia.

In Dostoevsky, Nastenka is first spotted by the narrator "engrossed in looking at the muddy water of the canal" and wearing "a most enchanting yellow hat and a very charming black cloak."[20] *Two Lovers* reverses genders and protagonists for this same moment. In the opening sequence, the dark-haired and Jewish Leonard (Joaquin Phoenix), effectively assuming the role of Nastenka, will plunge into a bay, making explicit the atmosphere of suicide surrounding this moment in Dostoevsky. Just prior to this, as Leonard walks toward the water, we see in a low-level, slow-motion image various dry-cleaned shirts covered in plastic and paper that he will abandon, dropping them to the ground. We soon discover that Leonard works with his father in a dry-cleaning business, one of several evocations in the film of *Rocco and His Brothers*. The dry-cleaning business becomes the source of conformity, as one shirt after another rolls along the assembly belt. All of this is nevertheless tied to the kind of organic world, via family and culture, that Dostoevsky and Visconti avoid. Leonard's options are embodied in two women, the blonde, gentile Michelle (Gwyneth Paltrow) and the dark-haired, Jewish Sandra (Vinessa Shaw). It is Sandra's father who has plans to purchase the dry-cleaning business from Leonard's father, the marriage between Sandra and Leonard becoming the continuation of Leonard's preexistent social situation. When Michelle walks into Leonard's apartment for the first time, she notices the smell of mothballs, reminding her of her grandmother's home, as Leonard ironically tells her the mothballs are due to his parents trying to protect all their designer clothes. The image (and odor) of mothballs, aging, and deadness through clothing becomes a crucial site of stagnation, with Leonard seeing in the non-Jewish Michelle an avenue of escape. In *White Nights*, Mario's desire is focused solely on Natalia and it is she who is torn between two lovers, although this is handled in a very different register from the Gray film.

Nastenka is described by Dostoevsky as having dark features. But Visconti cast the pale, blonde-haired, and blue-eyed Swiss Austrian Maria Schell, and with Mastroianni beside her they form another white/black, dark/light contrast. Although Schell speaks

Italian in the film, her national origins are not specified and her accent adds another layer of otherness to her character. Visconti had served as the head of the jury of the Venice Film Festival in 1956 where the Best Actress prize was given to Schell for her performance in the title role of the laundress in René Clément's *Gervaise* (1956), an adaptation of Zola's *L'Assommoir* (1877). As in much of Clément's work, *Gervaise* builds its image structures around water and fabric, frequently linking the two phenomena. A year after *White Nights*, Schell would go to Hollywood and appear as Grushenka in Richard Brooks's adaptation of *The Brothers Karamazov* (1958). In her first important shot in the Brooks film, she is sitting in the back of a carriage, a white lace veil covering her head, and the beatific lighting she is given serves as an ironic contrast to the character she is portraying. Schell's blondness led to her frequently being cast in roles in which she is either an innocent who is destroyed by the cruelty of the world around her, as in Alexandre Astruc's Maupassant adaptation *Une Vie* (1958), or whose innocence is itself relative, unstable, hiding other potentials.[21]

If in "White Nights" both our protagonists are dreamers, this status has a somewhat different emphasis than in the Visconti. In Dostoevsky, the male protagonist's status as a dreamer is also tied to him being an avid reader of literature who is often placing the events around him in relation to works of fiction, someone who transforms the reality in front of him into aesthetic matter. The dreamer protagonist as artist is literalized in *Four Nights of a Dreamer*, where Bresson gives this character (named Jacques) the profession of painter. In *Two Lovers*, the aesthetic dreamer is an amateur still photographer and a cinephile. Visconti dispenses with such possibilities. Neither Mario nor Natalia have any interest in the arts, and instead the film emphasizes their isolation as a simple form of romantic pathos.

In our first close view of Mario, he is standing in front of a film poster. Tucking his scarf into his coat, he looks off, not noticing the poster itself. The film being advertised is *Vestire gli ignudi/Clothing the Naked* (Marcello Pagliero, 1953), an adaptation of Luigi Pirandello's 1922 play of the same title. The implications of that title are tied to Pirandello's concern with symbolically clothing oneself in order to hold on to one's illusions. The heroine Ersilia's monologue at the end of the play, spoken as she is dying, engages in shifts between clothing as material item and clothing as metaphor. She speaks of only wanting to "make myself a decent dress to die in" and also of a wedding dress she once dreamed of but which has since been metaphorically torn off of her.[22] Visconti never staged a Pirandello play, but *White Nights* distantly contains a Pirandellian idea of characters caught "in the act of creating themselves in the other's eyes."[23] This is also found in the Dostoevsky, where the narrator declares of Natalia, "Can it be that he has only seen her in ravishing visions, and that his passion has been nothing but an illusion?"[24]

Nevertheless, the modernist play with masks, surfaces, and appearances in Pirandello is not a primary concern of Visconti's and he remains attached to a certain literary conception of the detail charged with potential meanings and a world in which the dream, even if exposed as a form of self-deception, is rendered in its full imaginative capacity.[25]

While waiting for Mario, Natalia stands in front of a shop window, staring at a white gown laid out on a long pedestal, the pedestal draped in dark fabric. Mario walks up behind her, his reflection caught in the glass as he eats a candy cane. She spots him through the reflection and happily turns around but he is gone. Mario briefly becomes something he otherwise fails at being for Natalia, a romantic vision appearing and disappearing at will. It is as though the gown in the window briefly creates an atmosphere for Natalia's desires. Mario walks away while also looking back, as though hoping to reverse a defining feature of their relationship. He stands in front of a café window, the glass covered with steam generated by the heat inside. Several women inside walk over to the window as Mario stands on the other side, the women smoking and adjusting their makeup. One woman spots Mario and, clearly attracted to him, writes "ciao!" backward on the glass, her hands covered in gloves. The woman is attractive and well dressed, a coat draped over her shoulders. Mario distantly returns her smile but he remains connected to Natalia and walks away. These two windows are central to the film's conception of sexual and romantic desire (and have no counterpart in the Dostoevsky.) We are in a world in which desires are placed in the midst of not simply cold but fog and mist, windows covered in steam, objects of desire just out of reach.

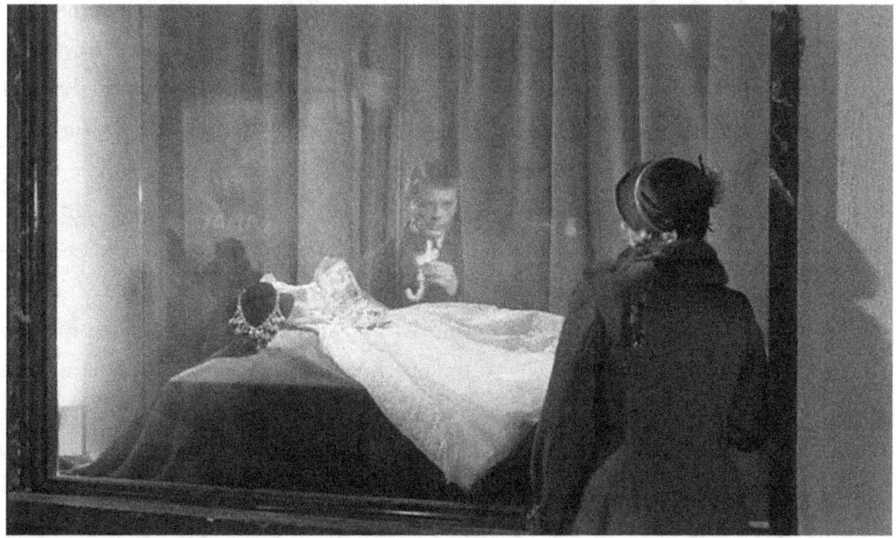

White Nights (1957). The gown in the window creating an atmosphere of desire.

Tied Together

A central idea *White Nights* retains from Dostoevsky is of Natalia being tied to her grandmother by a safety pin, this pin evoking both an umbilical cord and a diaper. In Dostoevsky, Nastenka explains that, due to an indiscretion when she was fifteen, her grandmother pinned Nastenka to her, and it is here where she spends much of her time, as the grandmother knits. In the story, Nastenka is seventeen, the narrator twenty-two. Schell was thirty when she played Natalia, Mastroianni thirty-three, and neither character's age is specified in the film. The romantic, youthful behavior of the protagonists in Dostoevsky becomes in Visconti a delayed passage into adult sexuality. The reason given for the safety pin in the film is that Natalia's parents ran off when she was very young and her grandmother has pinned Natalia to her for fear that she, too, will run away.

The protagonists of *The Stranger* are comparatively "adult" but no less adrift or innocent in their social world. Whereas *White Nights* is dominated by cold, *The Stranger* is dominated by intense heat. Also unlike *White Nights*, and consistent with its source novel, much of *The Stranger* takes place in bright daylight. As with *Ossessione*, *The Stranger* opens (following a fast-paced prologue of Meursault's arrest for murder) with a sweating man arriving at a new, disorienting location. But, unlike Gino, Meursault is fundamentally bourgeois, thus setting him apart from the protagonists who otherwise dominate Visconti's cinema who are either aristocrats or of the proletariat, the approach to clothing likewise deriving its force from the stark differences between these worlds. Meursault is tied to white-collar labor and to family, albeit a family that is, via his mother, literally dead. At his mother's funeral, Meursault states, "It was hot in my dark clothes."[26] Visconti substitutes the dark suit for a light gray one, perhaps all the better to establish the whiteness of things, the pale colors also making sweat more visible. (Meursault will wear this suit again, at his murder trial.) Also unlike Gino, this atmosphere of overheated bodies does not translate into Meursault becoming a naturalist object of desire, either for the camera or for any of the male and female protagonists within the film itself. In terms of the former, it is entirely possible to imagine a film in which such a strategy could have occurred, and had Delon assumed the role the emphases might have been very different. But Visconti films Mastroianni in a straightforward manner. The opposite of Livia, Mastroianni's Meursault is indifferent to giving a performance.

In a sequence set in his apartment, his girlfriend, Marie (Anna Karina), is happily wearing his pajamas, laughing, the morning after they have had sex. This detail of the pajamas is from the novel. But in Camus, her laughter arouses Meursault and they again have sex. In the film, they have sex again as well but there is no implication that the sex arises from Meursault's response to her laughter. Instead, he walks over to where she is standing, unbuttons the top of the pajamas, and pulls them down to her shoulders as they then move to a double bed. The state of arousal implicitly occurs through her being dressed like him. While such gender reversals through sleepwear are virtually a convention of romantic comedy, thus barely constituting a radical gesture, this does indicate a slight (even queer) deviation from the function of the pajamas in Camus.

By contrast, in *White Nights* the bed in which Mario sleeps is a twin bed with not a hint that sexual activity could ever occur on it. At one point he wakes up sneezing, a long scarf comically functioning as a nightcap and absurdly placed atop his head, a desexualized image. Unlike the male protagonist of the Dostoevsky, Mario is given an exhausted demeanor, thus anticipating Meursault. But his sleepiness is tied to his activity as a romantic dreamer. The major bed of the film belongs not to Mario or to Natalia but to the boarder (Jean Marais). For her first visit to his room, Natalia ascends the stairs to his room, the design of the stairs exaggerated in its height and length, as though to indicate that she is moving into an enchanted realm. Dressed in a dark shirt and blouse, she is holding a large white rag as a pretense for an intention to clean his room. Once in the room, she is first shown sniffing his hair gel. The sequence evokes Gino's exploration of Anita's room in *Ossessione* but with crucial differences. In both sequences, fabric and other items of décor become an extension of the desired body. As already noted in relation to *Ossessione*, the desire is also one for an entire world represented by Anita, contrasting with the world of Giovanna. What we have in *White Nights* is an inversion of this in which the boarder represents not, as with Anita, domestic stability but an escape from this, a breaking of the safety pin in order to attach oneself to a wandering male figure. Whereas Anita has personalized her room, the boarder makes little attempt to engage in a similar strategy, and fabric items are minor, such as lace coverings over tables or dressers, hanging towels or washcloths, all of this preceding him staying there.

Four Nights of a Dreamer offers a more intense experience of fabric in relation to the same moment. The first impression Marthe (Isabelle Weingarten) has of the new tenant as she enters his room is of his open suitcase on the bed, with his shirts on top, the shirts and other displayed contents becoming the substitute for the body of the man she has not yet seen. Throughout the film, Bresson's camera will move closely to the texture of a woman's sweater, to the way a dress clings to a woman's body as she walks, or to the brown corduroy jacket and pants on Jacques (Guillaume des Forêts), even calling attention to the sounds the corduroy makes as he moves. Fabric takes on

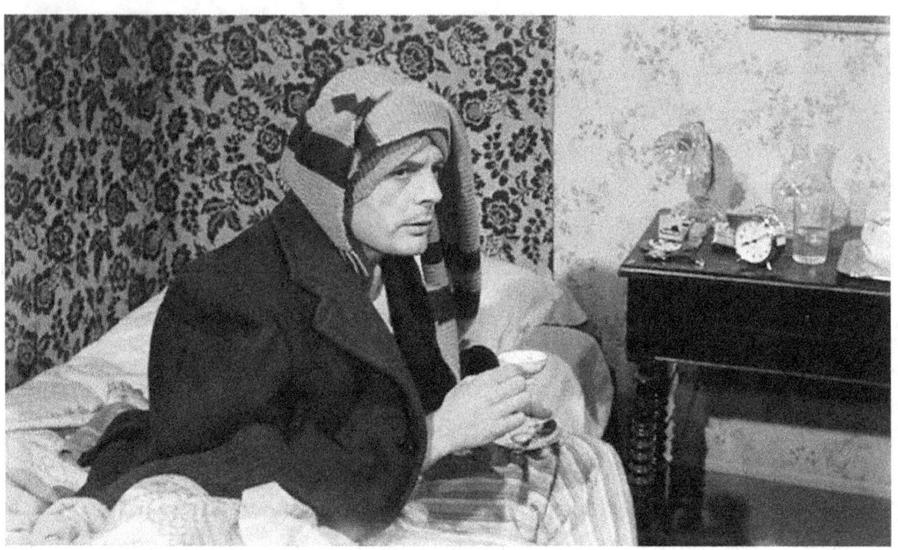

White Nights. Oversized nightcap as desexualized male image.

a directly erotic charge, as seen in the astonishing close-up of Jacques's crotch on the bus so we see the thickness and protrusions of the corduroy. *White Nights*, a film of erotic frustrations, keeps such strategies in check. Like Mario, the boarder sleeps on a small twin bed. When he tells Natalia he is going away, she throws herself on this bed, illustrating Dostoevsky's prose: "Shame, love, pride seemed to speak in me all at once, and I fell on the bed almost in convulsions."[27] In a striking shot with no correspondence in Dostoevsky, she is facedown, one pillow neatly piled on top of another, with a white washrag visible at the top right of the frame. In *The Stranger*, on the morning after Meursault's first sexual encounter with Marie, he sniffs the white pillow where she has slept and, as Camus writes, tries "to find the salty smell Marie's hair had left on the pillow."[28] Natalia has no such option, and these stacked pillows in their clean, white cases on this small bed that can barely hold two people at once (he will soon join her on the bed as they embrace) represent the body to be taken from her.

A significant addition to the film is the occupation given to Natalia and her grandmother: they repair rugs. In the first section of the story she narrates to Mario, Natalia is sitting amidst the ruins of a building. She describes her first encounter with the new boarder, a foreigner. This reference to him as a foreigner engenders a literal movement by the camera into the past, panning and then reverse tracking, revealing the room in which Natalia and her grandmother repair rugs. This movement is handled without a cut, the space clearly one large set. The effect is at once theatrical, as though the lights have gone up on a previously obscured stage set, and cinematic in the surprising reveal, in a single camera movement, of the two distinct parts of the set. What is revealed are rugs everywhere: on the floor, rolled up against the wall, hanging on the wall, and covering the table for repairs, along with rolls of yarn. Once this movement is completed, the new boarder, dressed in a tweed coat and hat, enters the room. A reverse angle shows what would have been, in the studio set from the previous shot, the ruins in which Natalia had been sitting but which now is the other side of the room with Natalia. In this new angle, the grandmother is knitting (as she does in Dostoevsky), an embroidered blanket covering her chair as Natalia works on a rug. Surrounding these women are still more rugs, great piles of them, hanging or rolled up behind them. As the grandmother, responding to the new boarder's request, tells Natalia to get the rent ledger, Natalia excitedly jumps up but with a safety pin still attached and, in a forward tracking shot as she attempts to pull away, the grandmother's needlepoint is visible in her lap as we also see yarn draped around her arm. Knitting women have been central to other Visconti films addressed so far. But *White Nights* takes this to another level. This space where Natalia and her grandmother knit is one of abundance due to the rugs. But such abundance remains tied to not only labor but the declining social status of the women since Natalia's grandfather had been a rug merchant, with Natalia and the grandmother now reduced to repairing rugs for others. Moreover, the implications of Natalia being tied to her grandmother as she is otherwise surrounded, if not engulfed, by rugs and other old women working with her implies a space of both ruin and sexual potential, even the possibility of being transported out of this world, the rugs becoming, with the entrance of the new boarder, a magic carpet.

Dressed for the Weather

Natalia is also a teller of tales, endowed with a greater imaginative capacity than Mario. Her storytelling involves not so much conventional flashbacks as visual projections. Small wonder she and Mario have little time for, or interest in, going to the movies and are unable to concentrate on literature. When the boarder takes her and her grandmother to see Rossini's *The Barber of Seville* (1816), the experience is less aesthetic for Natalie than romantic, further strengthening her attraction to the boarder. Natalia creates her own mise-en-scènes, partly theatrical and partly cinematic. In reference to her letter to the boarder, for which Natalia enlists Mario's help, Nowell-Smith notes that she has, by this point, "imposed her vision completely."[29] The rugs she repairs make Natalia not so much a weaver of original, magic stories but a naive artist of things patched together, worn-out romantic dreams that nevertheless retain a certain potency.

In Dostoevsky, the physical characteristics of the new boarder are not described, and in the Bresson film, the man cast in this role is unremarkable in appearance. But

Visconti's casting of Marais adds two distinct dimensions. One is that Marais's physical beauty creates a strong image of desire. The other is that Marais is not simply an actor but one whose mythology is intimately tied with Jean Cocteau. Marais, regardless of the conventional romantic leading man roles he often played, always carries with him an aura of sexual ambiguity, at its most indelible in the three roles he assumed for Cocteau in *Beauty and the Beast*: the Prince, Avenant, and the Beast. Susan Hayward has argued that *Beauty and the Beast* is a film of "homo-erotic love" that is "also about attempting to discover a different, non-phallic, perception of human relationships."[30] She notes that the potentially phallic nature of Marais's Beast is called into question in various ways, including through his clothing. While some of the clothing details are consistent with masculine attire of the sixteenth century in which the story is set, the enormous collar and the lace adorning his boots would have been more traditionally worn by women.[31] (Marcel Escoffier is among the film's credited designers.) In his scenes with Natalia in *White Nights*, Marais's boarder represents a sexual and romantic otherness, a male figure unlike any she has ever encountered. Natalia is given a choice between two very different potentials in terms of sexual desire, between Mario's transparent and almost adolescent love for her and the mysterious realm of the unnamed boarder.

Near the end of the film, these issues reach a moment of culmination when it snows. In the cold of *White Nights*, the snow (literalizing the film's title) becomes a transformative sight for Mario and Natalia. Earlier in the film, when they are caught in a downpour, they duck into a doorway as a balding man wearing glasses ducks into the same space. The man takes a handkerchief out of his coat pocket and wipes his face and glasses, then folds the handkerchief into a kerchief he places on top of his head before dashing back out in the rain. Then, discouraged, he quickly returns as he pulls his impromptu kerchief off. Like the sweater Mario wears on his head while in bed, the wet kerchief is a comic sign of failed masculinity, the sort of object a housewife or cleaning woman might wear as she dusts a room.

With the falling snow the film gives itself the task of another kind of evocation. When they were standing in the doorway protecting them from the rain, Mario told Natalia he was unaware women like her existed outside of fairy tales, and during the snow sequence the fairy tale references return. The emphasis on drowsing protagonists reaches a romantic apotheosis with the falling snow as he tells her the rest of the city is asleep as the two of them are surrounded by white, as though the city is made to the measure of their desire for one another. She is, he states, a sleeping princess who will one day awaken and have all she desires. Moreover, he explicitly compares the snow here to fabric and states that the snow falls on Natalia as though it were a bridal veil. Her wedding gown, he later adds, will be all in white, like the snow itself. If the fabric-created fog central to much of the first half of the film becomes an extension of this world in which desires drift in and out of this decor, snow transforms this same décor into that of a fairy tale. As this romantic interlude comes to a conclusion, he wraps his coat around her, the desiring male protagonist's final gesture toward the desired woman. Mario's hoped-for finality through such a gesture is abruptly terminated when Natalia spots the boarder, the moment of this discovery filmed in long shot, the boarder's back to the camera.

When we are given the reverse angle of the boarder, it is difficult to come to an exact interpretation of him. He is wearing a raincoat, made of either vinyl or leather, and the expression on his face is somber, the lighting on his face low key. We know very little about this man, and the shot of him here distantly suggests she is making a mistake or, at the very least, she may discover things about him that will destroy her romantic ideals. When Natalia spots the boarder, she screams in excitement and runs to him, her rejection of Mario enacted through his coat falling off of her and onto the ground. Mario's tears over the cruel turn of events are supplemented by the way he pulls his sport jacket closer to him, hugging himself for comfort in the face of Natalia's abandonment. After Natalia and the boarder happily walk off together, Mario goes over to the coat Natalia has dropped, dusts the snow off of it, and puts it back on, displaying resignation in the face of his defeat as he walks alone through the streets. The film does not attempt to dramatize Dostoevsky's coda, in which the male protagonist receives a letter from Nastenka expressing her love for both men but saying that she must now think of the protagonist as only a brother and friend. After he finishes the letter, the protagonist projects upon the environment surrounding him, turning it into a space of the future dominated by ruin within which he will live alone for the remainder of his life. Visconti offers something that condenses and simplifies this life of perpetual loneliness. Mario walks down an empty street, petting the same stray dog that had followed him in the opening sequence, as man and dog, in a Chaplinesque image, go off together in the final shot.

Still, what is to be made of Natalia's choice, as she leaves a defeated and heartbroken Mario behind? Strictly within the domain of fictional characters, pathos more firmly resides with Mario than with the reunited couple. But reading *White Nights* within the mythology of film stardom, her choice is between the more masculine (if not heterosexual) Marcello Mastroianni and the sexually ambiguous (if not homosexual) Jean Marais. Natalia, the heroine out of a fairy tale of her own design, walks off with her prince and with an actor whose relationship to fairy tales is indelible due to *Beauty and the Beast*. The controversial ending to the Cocteau, in which the Beast dies from a broken heart and becomes merged into the Prince, is at the core of Cocteau's own ambivalent treatment of sexual desire. Beauty gets her conventional Prince but by now both she and the spectator have adjusted to the more transgressive potential of the Beast. In *White Nights*, Natalia has chosen a prince of more uncertain potential, and the film does not address Marais's complex sexual identity in the manner in which it was treated in Cocteau. Residual effects remain, however. Natalia has also chosen, over that passive dreamer of the "neuter gender," a nameless male beauty who makes a more striking appearance in a coat, a man (unlike the slightly disheveled Mario) whose sexual potential for the desiring woman is uncertain, even as that man is otherwise thoroughly prepared and dressed for the weather.

Overall

In *The Stranger*, there is a sequence set on the beach that could be aptly described as a set piece. Here we have, as with so much of the film, an approximate rendering of Camus's prose. But interest arises in the small deviations, in certain inflections brought to the material not present in the novel. This is particularly acute in the treatment of the Arab men, including the murder victim. Camus barely describes the physical characteristics of the Arabs, creating instead a dominant image of them through their blue overalls. The representational nature of Visconti's cinema, however, demands specificity. In using the Arabs, Visconti is not only specific but he adds an element of the erotic through the casting of the men, who are physically beautiful. In the sequence immediately prior to the visit to the beach, Meursault, Marie, and Meursault's friend Raymond (Georges Géret) spot these Arab men leaning against a storefront, one of them specifically stalking Raymond. Raymond points to this stalking Arab. A cut and a quick pan to first one Arab and then the man in question immediately follows. This man, with his perfectly proportioned features, is wearing a white turban, a detail not present in the novel but which gives him an almost ceremonial stature, foreshadowing the violent ritual to come. The turban is, along with the white bandage on the face of the nurse earlier in the film, one of the film's two primary points of whiteness. Following Camus, it is Meursault and not Raymond who will turn around and give these men one more look before all three board the bus to the beach. When Meursault does look back we see, in a wider shot, two additional men. The one on the far right of the shot has his shirt open, and all of them either have their hands in their pockets or their arms folded. Camus's preoccupation here is with the detachment on these faces, "staring at us in silence, but in that way of theirs, as if we were nothing but stones or dead trees."[32] Visconti reproduces this cold stare, but the casting of the men, the posing of them in the frame, the open shirt, all of this equally suggests a latent sexual violence.

In Camus, the handling of the murder involves the cryptic prose now becoming relentlessly figurative as it documents Meursault's delirium building up to the murder, much of this figuration involving references to the sea, the heat, the sun, and the clothing. In the film's imagery and voice-over narration Visconti does not violate the general intent of this language. But again, we find various shifts in the descriptions as well as additions. In the film, most likely as a point of visual contrast with the dark overalls of the Arabs, Meursault, Raymond, and Raymond's friend Masson (Mimmo Palmero) are clothed in various degrees of white: a sleeveless T-shirt on Raymond, along with a gray hat and dark pants; a white shirt with a T-shirt and beige shorts on Masson; and a white shirt, no T-shirt, and oatmeal-colored long pants on Meursault.

After an initial knife fight on the beach between the Arabs and Raymond (from which Meursault remains somewhat detached), Raymond and Meursault return to the same location and find the Arabs there. "They were lying down, in their greasy overalls," Camus writes. "They seemed perfectly calm and almost content."[33] One of these men is described as playing the same three notes over and over again on a reed, as both men remain largely still, staring. The outlines of this encounter are reproduced in the film. But the shots of the two Arabs are of interest beyond Camus. When Meursault and Raymond first encounter the Arabs, there is a cut to the first of these men. The "greasy overalls" are pants, but the man is now shirtless as he rests his body on his shirt and lies against a rock. As he plays the reed, the camera zooms into his face. He is wearing a yellow-striped turban, an echo of the white turban on his friend from the earlier sequence on the street, but also an eroticized, masculine version of the improvised kerchief worn by the man standing next to Mario and Natalia in the rain in *White Nights*. This shot is followed by a cut to his friend, the camera again executing a forward zoom, the friend's overalls more clearly visible, white T-shirt underneath, both arms behind his head as they rest against his jacket, armpit hair (as with Rocco lying in bed, as he looks into the camera) seductively visible as he stares. A cut returns us to Meursault and Raymond looking at the men, now hesitant as to whether to shoot the Arabs.

It is possible to read these two shots of the Arabs as being Meursault and Raymond's shared point of view. But the framing is not quite tight or forceful enough in terms of their eyelines to make this explicit. There is something overdetermined in the presentation of the Arabs. The man with the reed does not, as in Camus, monotonously play the same three notes over and over again but varies these notes, giving him a Pan-like quality, as though luring men to their doom. And the eroticism occurs not simply through the attractiveness of the two men, with their "bruised, swollen lips that recall Caravaggio paintings,"[34] but through the arrangement of fabric on their bodies and the slightly teasing element of seduction emerging through this arrangement.

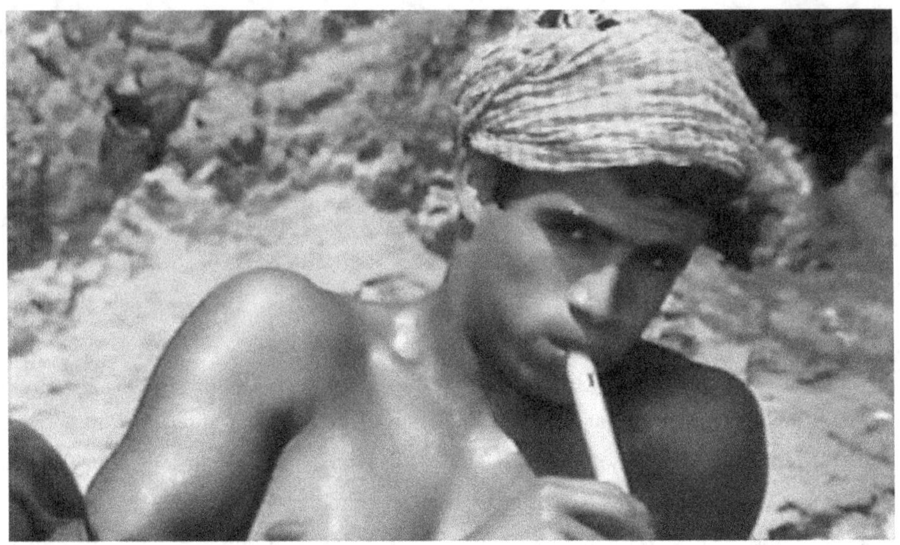

The Stranger. Turban tied to erotic allure.

Laurence Schifano has referred to "magical moments reminiscent of Tennessee Williams" in the early sections of the film, but she does not specify any shots or sequences.[35] In the film version of Williams's one-act play *Suddenly, Last Summer* (Joseph L. Mankiewicz, 1959), the homosexual poet Sebastian is murdered and devoured by a group of starving and impoverished male Spanish youths, among them men whom he has paid for sex. The character's name makes obvious the sense of a closeted homosexual martyrdom through his death, a culminating event in the film's weaving together of this death through fabric. He is murdered on a "blazing hot white day" while wearing a white silk suit that is torn off of him, a color of negation, of death, but also of a desire for purity, for making clean that which is "dirty"—that is, his sexual desires. It is a blazing hot white day when Meursault murders the Arab. But why does he kill? What is suggested in Visconti's handling of these images? The possibilities are far less clear than with the murder of Sebastian in the Mankiewicz film, much of this traceable to the asynchronous sensibilities between Visconti and Camus. Even so, fascinating discordances arise.

Referring to Camus's early obsession with Ivan Karamazov's "attack against procreation," Anthony Rizzuto has written that Camus will increasingly be drawn to the possibilities of a chaste, all-male society as "an essential feature of his social contract" and of his desire to escape from conventional forms of manhood.[36] But this fantasy of a nonprocreative society does not lead to a direct confrontation with the possibilities of male homosexuality. When Meursault returns alone to the beach in order to eventually perform the murder, he finds the Arab who had been stalking Raymond, alone: "He was lying on his back, with his hands behind his head, his forehead in the shade of the rock, the rest of his body in the sun. His blue overalls seemed to be steaming in the heat."[37] Visconti transposes this description of the positioning of the Arab's body from a slightly later passage in the novel to a slightly earlier section of the film, giving the camera more time to linger. Now, though, the top portion of the Arab's overalls has been removed and, from the waist up, he is in a sleeveless T-shirt. In contrast to the earlier presentation of him, the shots do not linger and instead everything unfolds at a rapid pace, with the Arab quickly sitting up when he spots Meursault. The sequence is otherwise preoccupied with capturing the almost irrational intensity leading to Meursault becoming a murderer. The film dutifully reproduces from the novel the intensity of the heat and the sun burning into Meursault's eyes, causing him to fire the gun. But whereas Camus is preoccupied with the sweat dripping off of Meursault's face and falling into his eyes, causing him to be "blinded by the curtain of tears and salt,"[38] the film, while reproducing this as well, complete with Mastroianni supplying illustrative gestures, adds details of his shirt becoming soaked in sweat on both the back and the front. We have a reversal of the death revealed at the end of *Suddenly, Last Summer*. It is now the figure in white who is the murderer and not the victim. Within the context of the novel, Meursault is shooting at the stillness and silence of the afternoon (the film reproduces this self-awareness in the narration), at his own passivity, even at his own failure to properly mourn his mother's death. He draws a link with the intensity of the sun on the beach "as being the same as it had been the day I'd buried Maman."[39] But the film eliminates the reference to his mother, opting for his more immediate response to the terrifying whiteness of things. The fetishistic handling of the Arab men, though, significantly building upon (if not subverting) the "dirty overalls" of Camus, points to other possibilities.

Within the context of Visconti's cinema, the murder becomes another example of the passage his protagonists typically undergo from spectator to spectacle. With Meursault, the irony of such a transition is doubly inscribed. During the trial, as he notes the reporters looking at him, he suddenly has "the odd impression of being watched by myself."[40] Meursault, then, never entirely loses his status as an observer, his reluctant position as spectacle the source of the novel's famous final sentence (reproduced in the narration in the final seconds of the film), in which Meursault states, "I had only to wish that there be a large crowd of spectators the day of my execution and that they greet me with cries of hate."[41]

There is one striking detail in the second half of the film with no correspondence in the novel. When Meursault is in prison, he takes a blanket and wraps it around the bottom half of his face, covering his nose and mouth. After having murdered an Arab, Meursault uses the blanket in such a way as to evoke a desert headdress, Meursault briefly becoming an Arab. Even more specifically, this shot evokes the bandaged face of the Arab nurse, Meursault becoming not just an Arab but an Arab woman. In contrasting Camus and Franz Kafka with that writer so central to Visconti, Marcel Proust, Roger Shattuck writes that in Camus and Kafka, "experience generates very little motivation to undertake anything, to oppose the world or to affirm oneself. They act out of gratuitous impulse or yield to mere circumstance. In Proust, the opposite is true. Multiple desires and motivations converge on every action and often impede its execution."[42] In *The Stranger*, these stray images of male flesh and fabric are, as with so many images of eroticized males in Visconti, offered to the viewer as much as to the characters within the fiction, as though demanding a response. And throughout the film, the shots of men and women in connection with fabric point to another kind of film, perhaps the one Visconti wanted to make, in which cinema and politics, flesh and fabric set into play a more complex convergence of "multiple desires and motivations" than what we have in this film to which Visconti so reluctantly signed his name.

CLASSICAL FORMS

4

Behind the Curtain

In *Il lavoro*, three books may be spotted in the apartment of Pupe and Ottavio: Alain Robbe-Grillet's *The Erasers* (1953), J. B. Priestley's *Saturn over the Water* (1961), and Giuseppe Tomasi di Lampedusa's *The Leopard* (1958). The last of these would, three years later, be the source of one of Visconti's major successes, notwithstanding its commercial disappointment in the United States, where the film was heavily cut. *The Leopard* was another international coproduction for Visconti, the most expensive of all of his films, and it featured the biggest star with whom Visconti would ever work, Burt Lancaster, as the nineteenth-century Sicilian aristocrat Don Fabrizio Corbera, Prince of Salina. 20th Century-Fox attempted to sell the film to American audiences as though it were a traditional epic, the posters emphasizing romantic grandeur, violence, and spectacle. Even in its cut form, however, and released in English (with Lancaster's own voice used, in contrast to his dubbing in the Italian version), the film does not have the structure and rhythm of a film that would appeal to audiences more accustomed to the Hollywood roadshow epics of the period. The stunning credit sequence, accompanied by Nino Rota's romantic main theme, is, in some ways, deceptive. Through a series of shots, many of them with the camera mounted on a crane, we gradually move closer to the Prince's estate of Villa Salina, the imagery imparting a mythic grandeur to this world of the past. All of this promises a historical epic comparable to *Gone with the Wind*, a film to which *The Leopard* was sometimes disparagingly compared on its initial release and a comparison made explicit in the trailer for American audiences. (Both films open in 1860 and place their concerns in relation to wartime conflicts that would transform their respective cultures). However, this credit sequence is equally preparing us for a different approach to historical narratives.

The Robbe-Grillet visible in *Il lavoro* is an example of the *nouveau roman*, thus part of the forefront of European literary modernism. The Priestley, on the other hand, is an English detective thriller, although it does engage in a self-conscious play with its genre that is also a modernist gesture. The form of the Tomasi di Lampedusa (his only novel and published posthumously) sits somewhere in between. *The Leopard* was a phenomenal best seller but the source of a sharply divided critical reception, with criticism coming from both the political Left and the political Right. The appeal of the project to Visconti, though, is obvious. Its Sicilian setting returns him to the world of *La terra trema* but with the focus now on the aristocracy. The Risorgimento era addressed in *The Leopard* revisits the historical and political issues in *Senso* but now staged on a broader scale. Its love story, unlike the one in *Senso*, is on a slightly secondary level of importance and, following the novel, the film focalizes much of its vast panorama through the perspective of the Prince. This scale also results in the film's extended length (current versions run 185 minutes), allowing it to achieve epic status similar to *Rocco and His Brothers*.

Tomasi di Lampedusa's novel, while employing a form central to its widespread success, is also an example of what Edward Said has identified as late style, in which an artist, approaching death, creates works of "vulnerable maturity, a platform for alternative and unregimented modes of subjectivity" as these works "play off the great totalizing codes of twentieth-century Western culture and cultural diffusion."[1] Visconti, though, was not approaching death in 1963, and his film (contrary to Said's argument on this issue) is tempered by other concerns. As with *Rocco*, the appeal for Visconti in such a project (and unlike the struggles he would later face in adapting *The Stranger*) is partly a cinematic revitalization of a nineteenth-century literature no longer in the vanguard but, with the appearance of Tomasi di Lampedusa's novel, returning as a ready-made contemporary object. Even more specifically, it is the influence of Marcel Proust on Tomasi di Lampedusa that becomes generative for Visconti for engaging in an essentially harmonious implied aesthetic exchange with Tomasi di Lampedusa over the notion of the Proustian. But Visconti's own stated intent for the adaptation at once confirms and complicates matters: "I adopted a reading closer to Proust than to Verga," he said while also adding that the film was a continuation of *La terra trema* and *Rocco and His Brothers*.[2] "He can contemplate yesterday hung out to dry with the wettest August bank holiday on record a little further down the clothes-line," Samuel Beckett has written of Proust. "Because his memory is a clothes-line and the images of his past dirty linen redeemed and the infallibly complacent servants of his reminiscential needs."[3] Unlike Proust in relation to the narrative world of *In Search of Lost Time*, Visconti and Tomasi di Lampedusa were born too late to have had any firsthand experience of the period covered in *The Leopard*, and the question of affective memory so central to Proust is not a driving force. With Visconti, this remove is also cultural, in that, unlike Tomasi di Lampedusa, he was not Sicilian but Milanese. What both men share are their ties to their (very different) aristocratic backgrounds. In adapting *The Leopard*, what Visconti creates is less a film of Proustian involuntary memory than a film whose images, so detailed in their historical recreation, often imply a literal and metaphoric death in which fabric is less "dirty linen redeemed" than the very embodiment of the end.

Also linking *Rocco* with *The Leopard* are two actors, Alain Delon and Claudia Cardinale, playing the lovers Tancredi Falconeri and Angelica Sedara. In *Rocco*, the function of Cardinale's character was minor. Not so with Angelica. Visconti's interest in Cardinale would be extended to his next film, *Vaghe stelle dell'Orsa*, a film different in crucial respects from *The Leopard* and seemingly made against it, in which Cardinale would have the leading role. "*Vaghe stelle dell'Orsa* is a short swift film," Jean Collet would write in his review for *Cahiers du cinéma*.[4] *Vaghe stelle* was conceived with Cardinale in mind, in response to the producer Franco Cristaldi's invitation to Visconti to make such a film (although Cardinale had played leading roles in a number of films in the early 1960s). What resulted from the invitation, however, is less a star vehicle than a work aligning itself with certain immediate strains of European film modernism in a way that cannot be claimed for *The Leopard*. The prologue, a party set in Geneva hosted by Sandra (Cardinale) and her American husband, Andrew (Michael Craig), is filled with a multilingual, jet-set crowd, briefly tipping the film in the direction of *La dolce vita* and *La notte*. Such an evocation is brief. The credit sequence that directly follows is one that, as in *The Leopard*, literally moves us closer and closer to the home of a wealthy family. But in *Vaghe stelle*, the movements (taken from inside of Sandra and Andrew's sports car) are "short" and "swift," as the car and the camera gain momentum on the highway from Geneva to Volterra. The speed of the movements alternates, slowing down when moving through small towns but becoming faster, almost manic on the highway, as though the car is drawn by something larger than itself, foreshadowing the tumult to come. Thomas Elsaesser has argued that *Vaghe stelle* "begins where *The Leopard* ended."[5]

The source material for *Vaghe stelle* is not a novel, nor does the film employ the self-conscious hybridity of nineteenth- and twentieth-century literary forms as in *Rocco and His Brothers*. Instead, the screenplay by Visconti, Suso Cecchi d'Amico, and Enrico Medioli bases its central situation on the myth of Electra and, implicitly, its various dramatic manifestations. Sandra becomes a new incarnation of Electra, the story transposed to not only a contemporary setting but one in which past actions are tied to guilt, betrayal, and complicity: Sandra and her brother Gianni (Jean Sorel) blame their pianist mother, Corinna (Marie Bell), and her lover and, later, husband, Antonio Gilardini (Renzo Ricci), for betraying their scientist father, a betrayal resulting in the father's death. At the time of the film's release, Visconti addressed the film's ties to the *Oresteia* while distancing himself from them, claiming the *Oresteia* was "nothing but a convenient reference," the analogies at best approximate.[6] And, in fact, the film changes many aspects of the myth and of its various theatrical incarnations. Unlike the Sophocles and Euripides Electra plays, the language of the *Orestia* is dominated by fabric imagery and metaphors, in particular robes and nets in relation to the exchange of power as well as in relation to death. In justifying her murder of Agamemnon, Clytemnestra declares that "as fishermen cast their huge circling nets, I spread/deadly abundance of rich robes, and caught him fast."[7] But in *Vaghe stelle*'s conception of the mother, she is mentally incapacitated, incapable of poetic lucidity and tragic self-awareness. Fabric is crucial to *Vaghe stelle* but the focus shifts from robes and nettings to other phenomena as the contemporary setting generates other issues.

Moving outside of Greek tragedy, Visconti discussed the film's "relative unity of time and of place, the strongly emphasized dramatic conflict, [and] the frequent use of close-ups," linking his approach with the *kammerspiel* tradition of Weimar silent cinema.[8] The film also draws upon or explicitly references historical and cultural forms of the Middle Ages and nineteenth-century Romanticism. The title of the film is taken from a poem by Leopardi, *La ricordanze* (1829), and Gianni quotes from its opening lines near the end of the film: "Shimmering stars of the Bear, I never thought that I'd be back again to see you shine over my father's garden, and talk with you from the windows of this house I lived in as a child, where I saw my happiness come to an end."[9] This citation resonates on several levels, including one of tying aesthetic forms to ancient and medieval worlds in order to give birth to new forms. In Leopardi's early work, these forms are often placed in relation to the immediate moment, tied to his commitment to the goals of the Risorgimento. In *All'Italia* (1819) he writes of a disgraced Italy in allegorical language in which the veil is central: "[H]air undone, without her veil,/she sits alone and hopeless on the ground, her face between her knees, and weeps."[10] In this regard, Leopardi's sensibility is of some interest in relation to *The Leopard*, where Leopardi is evoked but never directly cited.

The Leopard was shot by Giuseppe Rotunno in color and seventy-millimeter film. By contrast, *Vaghe stelle* is in thirty-five-millimeter, black-and-white, nonanamorphic widescreen. Rotunno is replaced by Armando Nannuzi, a gifted but less lyrical artist who was mainly associated up to this point with Mauro Bolognini. (Nannuzi would later shoot *The Damned*, in collaboration with Pasqualino De Santis, and *Ludwig*.) Rota underscoring is absent and instead we hear one recurring piece of music, used both diegetically and nondiegetically, César Franck's *Prélude, Chorale and Fugue* (1884), a solo piano work serving as an audio analog to the *kammerspiel* while also signaling a connection to late Romanticism. But the piece is also connected to Corinna, who is later shown playing it, and it becomes associated with her character. When Sandra hears a pianist playing the Franck at her party in the prologue, her mood abruptly darkens, as though this music is capable of pulling her toward her mother and into aspects of her own past. Geoffrey Nowell-Smith has described the Franck as "a tense piece of music whose romantic turbulence is kept in check by an iron vest of classical form,"[11] an apt description of the entire film, in which tensions between the modern and the classical are given different emphases than what is found in *The Leopard*. But the cyclic form of the Franck serves as another analogue to the film's form, in which time itself becomes cyclic rather than linear.[12] And while for a few years prior to this Visconti had begun to make tentative use of the zoom, on *Vaghe stelle* it dominates, giving the film a more aggressive rhythm and unsettling sense of space than any of his prior films. Like the Italian pop songs heard here in scattered form, the zoom feels contemporary, part of a structure of contrast between past and present, ancient and modern. In what follows, I wish to place these two different Visconti films alongside of one another, not to collapse them in terms of intent but to create a dialogue between them.

Let us begin with curtains. As the credits to *The Leopard* conclude, the camera has reached Villa Salina. Behind the credit for Rotunno, the windows of the villa are visible, the two windows on the left side not only open but with white awnings hanging over them, as white curtains move in the breeze. Visconti's name in the credits then replaces Rotunno's and the credits come to an end as Rota's music fades out, the nondiegetic music replaced by the offscreen, diegetic sound of voices praying in Latin. A cut takes us slightly closer to the castle, with a continuity error suddenly apparent, the awnings now rolled up but the curtains continuing to move. Another cut gives us a tracking shot, moving left to right across several curtained windows on the front of the villa before the camera reaches its destination. This destination is a window in which, on the other side, is Don Fabrizio and his family. The splendor of the family is announced not only through the elaborate tracking shot toward them but through the white lace curtains of the window that move in a more elaborate and almost ostentatious manner than the curtains in the other windows shown here. These curtains move inward, as though directing us toward this family and this world. The camera stops as it frames the window on a slight left diagonal, which is then followed by a forceful cut taking us inside the room as the curtains now dominate the left third of the frame, continuing to move. The cut from outside to inside, and the movement within both frames, forces our eyes to shift from right to left, largely guided by the curtains. Once inside, the camera executes a slow pan, showing the size of the room and the number of people in it and eventually making its way to the Prince and his immediately family. In this slow pan, the curtains periodically move into and out of the frame, as though their presence must be continually announced. Even once the panning moves to a point where the curtains can no longer be seen, their lace construction, in combination with the sunlight spilling into the space, will cause their mobile presence to be projected as shadows across the room, as with the curtains in the Venice hotel room in *Senso*. The offscreen sound of praying with which the sequence began is now replaced by another offscreen sound, of agitated voices, as the family continues its prayers even as a few family members begin to notice the sound. The following cut appears to be responding to this agitation from the outside world, yet does not take us to the source of the noise but to the room directly behind the family, a room visible in the background of the previous setup. This cut rhymes with the first image in the preceding shot, as lace curtains are once again moving, flowing into the house. But the framing reverses the position of the curtains from the previous shot and they are now placed at the far right, sometimes filling up as much as half of the frame before receding and then moving out again. This new setup also gives us a view of the altar where the family is praying, with Father Pirrone (Romolo Valli) leading the prayers.[13]

As we return to the original room, the succeeding shots are ones in which fabric continues to be central: the heavy draping surrounding a set of doors through which a servant enters; the large white handkerchief the Prince has been kneeling on and, as he stands once the service has concluded, precisely begins folding as the Princess (Rina Morelli) watches him, the gesture and the size of the handkerchief but one indication of his stature; and the curtains of the two windows that continue to move in and out of the rooms. In the adjacent room one of the Prince's sons looks out the window through a gap in the curtains, his back to the camera, as the Prince continues to sit with one of his daughters by his side. Windows will continue to be important throughout much of the film as indicators of a particular way of seeing beyond the immediate world of a declining aristocracy. But these windows are always framed in such a way that the curtains achieve as much visual power as the window itself, as though every look beyond must be mediated or veiled in some way by curtains.

As in *Senso*, fabric in *The Leopard* is at the center of historical change, tied, in turn, to questions of stasis and movement. But whereas costuming assumed a privileged function in the earlier film, in *The Leopard* it is comparatively muted, even showing a certain restraint when Tomasi di Lampedusa's prose would indicate other possibilities. For example, the opening of the novel and the opening of the film address the same situation. Tomasi di Lampedusa writes in relation to the service coming to end, "The women rose slowly to their feet, their oscillating skirts as they withdrew baring bit by bit the naked figures from mythology painted all over the milky depths of the tiles."[14] The film, though, does not pursue the possibilities of oscillating fabric but integrates the shots of the rising women into larger framing and staging ideas that do not draw

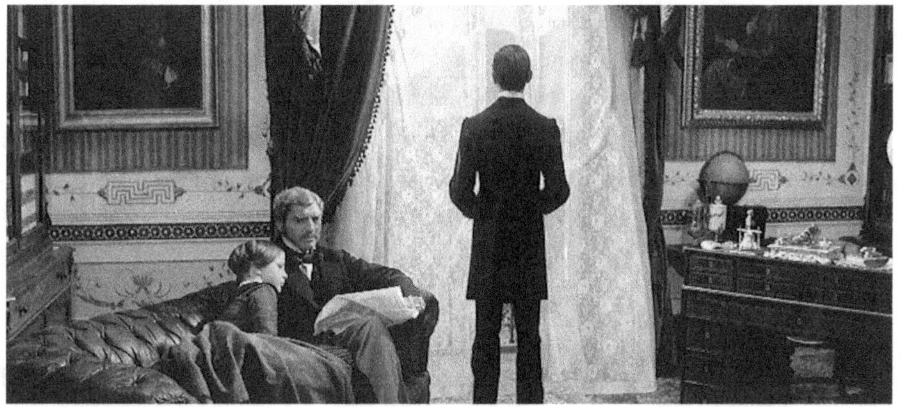

The Leopard (1963). The curtained window as a look beyond immediate social environment.

marked attention to moving fabric. Nor is there any dramatic reveal of mythological figures painted on the tiles initially hidden by the skirts. Instead, curtains are the dominant image of mobile fabric. And yet Tomasi di Lampedusa makes no reference to curtains in his opening pages, the film's added detail supplying another type of expressivity, implying the beauty but also the fragility of this world whose values are now shifting due to conditions beyond the control of its inhabitants.

The political situation in *Vaghe stelle dell'Orsa* is no longer tied to the resigned melancholia of the "revolution" of *The Leopard.* Instead, the film concerns itself with the aftermath of the Italian wartime situation via the death of Sandra's father in a concentration camp. As with so much of Italian cinema in the two decades after the war, Italian complicity in relation to this history, itself the culmination of over twenty years of Fascist rule, is not directly acknowledged. It would even be possible to read *Vaghe stelle* as a film that uses this history as a pretext for a subject increasingly of interest to Visconti: the decline into decadence of an aristocratic culture. This still begs the question as to why use this particular moment as the historical referent. And, in particular, why make use of a subject as potentially loaded as a Jewish father exterminated at Auschwitz because of a (possible) betrayal from his wife and her lover, a clear reworking here, from the Electra myth, of the relationship between King Agamemnon, Clytemnestra, and her lover, Aegisthus. Visconti had already dealt with aspects of this mythic history in *Troilus and Cressida* (which focuses on the Trojan War, where Agamemnon features prominently) and in his staging, with Callas, of Gluck's *Iphigénie in Aulis* (1774), both of these projects involving narrative material that precedes and incites the conflicts to come in the *Orestia*. But *Vaghe stelle dell'Orsa* stands out for the number of things it does *not* do in its treatment of this kind of material. For example, the film does not engage in a simple transposition of an ancient source to the modern world. But neither does the film attempt, as Pasolini would later do in *Edipo Re* and (with Callas in the title role) *Medea* (1969), to create a meta-historical sense of the ancient through a clash of incongruous visual and aural elements. Nor, in placing its concerns within a modern framework, does the film attempt, as Cocteau does in his film *Orpheus* (1950) or in his play *The Infernal Machine* (1934), the latter his reworking of Sophocles's *Oedipus the King*, to treat their side-by-side ancient and modern elements in an ironic (and sometimes camp) tone, in which mythical women from the ancient world dress in *haute couture* or speak in an arch, contemporary manner. In *Vaghe stelle*, the ancient, the medieval, and the modern are each given an equal weight, treated with the same seriousness of purpose.

Virtually anyone who writes on *Vaghe stelle* will face the problem of the film's ambiguity, if not obscurity, in terms of its narrative content and character motivations, a claim that could not be made for any Visconti film prior to this. Visconti himself described the film as "a detective story in which everything is clear at the beginning and obscure at the end."[15] Visconti specifically refers to *Oedipus the King* as "one of the first detective stories," of interest here because "the guilty person is the character least open to suspicion."[16] If we return to a topic from the first chapter, drawing upon Freud's argument that ambivalence has its origins in man's relationship to his father, and given the centrality of the Sophocles play to Freud's thought, the ambiguities of *Vaghe stelle* are tied to this question of ambivalence, here manifested on a scale of unprecedented intensity. This leads to not only a narrative dominated by unresolved questions but expressive effects that do not fully "uncover" the mysteries. Eisenstein has written of the detective novel being "built entirely upon a double meaning," a contrast between a "spontaneous perception" of phenomena and a perception that "penetrates to the essence." The first is a "'physiognomical' interpretation, perceived in images" and the second an interpretation "revealed conceptually."[17] In *Vaghe stelle*, fabric is tied to this desire to know, to reveal, to apprehend. But it is equally tied to covering up, to hiding. In *Vaghe stelle*, curtains are primarily associated with beds. In *The Leopard*, the marital bed of the Prince and Princess is one of passionless sex. In *Vaghe stelle*, the bed is tied not simply to sex but to activity of a scandalous nature, possibly having its origins (if Sandra and Gianni's accusations are correct) in the adultery that took place between their mother and Gilardini and (if Corinna and Gilardini's accusations are correct) the incestuous relations between Sandra and Gianni. That the film never confirms either of these accusations becomes a crucial method for its formal strategies.

There are two major sequences involving curtains framing a bed, the first of these occurring not long after Sandra and Andrew arrive at her family estate. The housekeeper,

Fosca (Amalia Troiani), has prepared the guest bedroom for the couple rather than Sandra's original bedroom. Once the three of them are in the bedroom, the curtains framing the bed are, like those of Livia's bed in *Senso*, immediate signifiers of wealth, as Andrew cannot stop remarking upon the museum-like splendors of what he is seeing. He hands her two letters from Gianni given to him by Fosca, and Sandra walks over to the bed, sits on it, and tears the envelopes open. As she does so, Andrew steps over to the bed. What follows involves the use of the bed curtains as a way of both situating Andrew within this space and excluding him. Framed from the neck down, he places his left hand on the bedpost, his right hand gingerly running up the curtain as he watches his wife. All of this activity is framed in a tight panning master shot, showing only the entrance to the room, a dresser with a mirror, and a portion of the bed. The first cut, to a close-up of Andrew, is of his face three quarters turned away from the camera as the curtains are framed just behind him. Another cut moves us somewhat farther away from him, but the setup reverses the angle of the preceding shot so we now see his face as the curtains dominate the right half of the frame. Andrew is on the left as he announces, across the two setups, that he will attend to their luggage. From this second setup, a pan follows Andrew as he moves toward the door, Fosca pressed against this door, where he hesitates for a moment and turns back to look at Sandra. The reframing that occurs through this movement now places the bed curtains at the far right and far left of the shot, framing Andrew, as Sandra, engrossed in the letters, is barely conscious of his departure. Andrew never sits on the bed. At the beginning of the sequence he sits on the floor and leans against the bed, but it is only Sandra who sits and even then not until she is given the letter.

In her first two films with Visconti, Cardinale's characters represent the transition from a world of the past to a world of the present and future. In *The Leopard*, Cardinale not only plays Angelica but, in a brief flashback narrated by the church organist Don Ciccio (Serge Reggiani), her mother, the illiterate Donna Bastiana. Don Ciccio's language in describing Donna Bastiana is Tomasi di Lampedusa at his most naturalist. She is "a kind of animal . . . just a beautiful mare, voluptuous and uncouth; she's incapable even of affection for her own daughter! Good for bed and that's all."[18] In the film, Donna Bastiana is dressed in an ornate black gown, most of her face covered in veils, only her eyes visible. In order to sneak a look at her, Don Ciccio must pull aside violet curtains in the church. Donna Bastiana becomes a major image of ambivalent desire for *The Leopard*, a woman of stunning beauty and voracious sexuality whose husband keeps her out of public view, as though the very sight of her will cause the men of Donnafugata to be driven to sexual frenzy. In *Vaghe stelle*, the modern Sandra is now being drawn into the past of her own family history but also that of the potentially irrational power of the ancient world in which the values of the modern, of logical forms of detection and uncovering, are outstripped by a confrontation with an "old Etruscan riddle" that cannot be answered.[19] Laurence Schifano writes of Visconti's desire to sculpt Cardinale's face and body in such a way that Sandra simultaneously reverts to her childhood while also evoking the "mysteries" of Etruria.[20] Cardinale's modern presence equally evokes the ancient, signaled most obviously in this film by how the style of her hair increasingly begins to resemble the hair worn by Etruscan women.

As an extension of Andrew's status as detective, he playfully films Sandra with a super eight-millimeter camera on their first night in her family home. But Sandra does not wish to be filmed, as though already being pulled back into a history preceding the modern, preceding the cinema. Andrew, on the other hand, is tied to American pragmatic and rational modes of thought. He needs to film in order to know, even if such strategies are finally unable to grasp what they see and hear. The contrast between white and dark fabrics in the film is an extension of the contrast between light (the desire to know) and shadow (the surrendering to obscurity) in a film in which electric lights are frequently being turned off and on. But the "double meaning" of detective fiction does not give way to an essence.

After Andrew's departure, Sandra asks Fosca about Gilardini in the second major sequence involving the bed curtains. Fosca walks over to the bed, pulls back the curtains, and adjusts the sheets and pillows as she talks about Corinna, recently moved by Gilardini from a sanitarium into the Gilardini home. It is the last shot of the sequence that demands the most attention. It begins as a middle-distance shot of Sandra sitting on the bed, talking to an offscreen Fosca. The curtains are behind Sandra, suggesting less containment than a brief moment of suspension in relation to the upheavals to come, while the diegetic sound of a ticking clock, persistent since the beginning of the sequence, grows louder, as though complicating the relative calm of what we see. We are moving toward and away from something, the precise nature of which is both as expressive and as impassive as the curtains adorning this bed.

Red

The offscreen sound interrupting the service in the opening of *The Leopard* is related to activity occurring on the grounds of the villa. A soldier of the Fifth Regiment has been found dead in the garden. In the novel, the discovery of the soldier had occurred a month earlier than it does in the film, and in the novel the incident functions as a memory of the Prince's. In the film, the discovery becomes a melodramatic eruption, drawing immediate attention to the threat of Garibaldi and the proximity of his army. The novel describes the solider lying facedown, his body covered in blood and crawling with ants, his intestines spilling onto the ground, these intestines likened to a "puppet's stuffing."[21] Visconti does something else with this soldier. As in the novel, the soldier has been shot in the stomach. But the detail of the intestines is absent and instead the more restrained sight of red blood is offered. Moreover, he is not facedown but faceup, one hand covering the wound, the other hand on the ground in a claw-like gesture, his right leg partly raised up and decorously resting against his other leg. And the actor cast in the role is beautiful, an aspect Tomasi di Lampedusa does not address. Tomasi di Lampedusa's naturalist language not only puts descriptive pressure to bear on the realistic details of the soldier's decaying body, it also makes reference to the soldier having crawled to this spot under the tree, like an animal returning to its home. The red handkerchief used to cover his face in the novel appears in the film as well, but now it becomes the culminating moment and the description of his wound being covered by the tails of his coat is eliminated. And finally, all of this is shown through the implied point of view of the Prince, in a forward tracking shot as he approaches the body. The indication that this is the Prince's point of view occurs not through a reverse-angle cut to him but through the dialogue of the other men in the sequence acknowledging the Prince.

It is the cut to the sequence directly following this that becomes a surrogate for the "missing" reverse angle, as the Prince and Father Pirrone are in a carriage and the Prince is contemplatively looking off, as though still thinking about the soldier. The carriage's interior is dominated by deep blue fabric with green curtains at the windows. The discretion implied in these colors and the darkness within the carriage are tied to where the Prince is headed: sex with a prostitute. When Bourbon soldiers, on the lookout for the Garibaldini, stop the carriage, there is a cut to the Prince from the side as he talks to them through the window. When the conversation closes and the Prince and Pirrone are free to move on, a dissolve returns us to the two-shot with which the sequence began. But the dissolve itself occurs over the preceding shot of the green curtains, as though linking the gentle movement of these curtains with the dissolving of a film image. The tight, enclosed world of the carriage is a space between the expansive, aristocratic world of the villa, with its large open windows and white curtains, and the dead Bourbon soldier, the end of his life ceremonially marked by the red handkerchief placed over his face. With this soldier, Visconti has chosen an agonized image of death, deeply romantic in nature (like Goethe's Werther), in which a subject who has died is also an object of desire for the spectator precisely *because* he is beautifully dead. The red handkerchief, one detail among several for Tomasi di Lampedusa is, in the film, more fully charged with meaning, a way of discreetly covering up that which the camera would appear to desire. However, that this is filmed from the Prince's point of view without our actually seeing him within the space complicates matters even further.

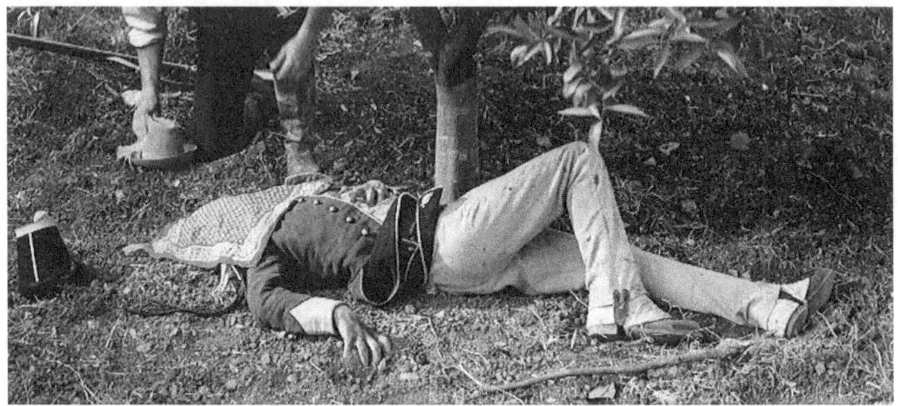

The Leopard. The handkerchief covering the source of desire.

For all of its visual splendor, *The Leopard* is, in its filming of male and female bodies, less erotic than any other Visconti film, with the exception of *The Stranger*. There is a restraint here, as the camera transfers its fascination to other forms and atmospheres. Some of this has its basis in the novel, where descriptions of interiors, exteriors, animals, and human beings form a continuum of personification and anthropomorphism. The presence of Delon in relation to the film's sensual reticence is particularly striking, given how central his face and body are to *Rocco and His Brothers*. In *The Leopard*, Visconti employs little intertwining of flesh and fabric from the earlier film, and Delon is given no scenes of dressing and undressing. Instead, his clothing announces the various opportunistic changes occurring in Tancredi, a man easily stimulated but, unlike the Prince, lacking a sensual morality. The black eye patch he wears after being injured in battle stands in contrast to the adhesive patch he periodically wears as Rocco. In the earlier film, that adhesive above his eyebrow reinforces his status as a saintly beauty, suffering for the sins of his own world. The eye patch on Tancredi, though, worn proudly by him, reinforces his ruthless opportunism, like a pirate, with the covered single eye a metaphor for the character's focused but limited vision. In fact, his injury is the result of a gnat flying into his eye, the black covering nothing more than an affectation.

There has been a tendency, largely anecdotal in nature, to see in the Prince a double for Visconti himself, with Lancaster reportedly basing his performance on the director's own personality and mannerisms. Relentlessly exploring one-to-one correspondences on this matter would most likely produce limited results. But the precise nature of the Prince's point of view in the sequence of the dead soldier implies a conjoining of the camera's look at the soldier with that of the Prince. Visconti stated that he had a "love-hate relationship" with the world of *The Leopard*, "a world fated to perish amid dazzling splendours."[22] The novel's characterization of the Prince allows for such ambivalences to be presented to Visconti with little need of adjustment, as when the Prince describes himself (a line repeated in the film) as belonging to "an unlucky generation, swung between the old and the new," finding himself ill at ease in both.[23]

There is one sequence in which the issues of Visconti's relationship to the Prince are clarified but also complicated, echoing and contrasting with the sequence of the dead soldier. It occurs as part of a flashback situated in the midst of a picnic the family enjoys while traveling from the Villa to their palace at Donnafugata. As in the sequence with the dead solider, the Prince's point of view occurs without the Prince being visible. The Prince narrates an event (described in the third person in the novel, where it does not arise in the midst of the picnic) that had occurred months earlier, soon after Garibaldi's entry into Palermo, when Tancredi brings home a Tuscan general (Giuliano Gemma). A slow dissolve takes us from the picnic to an entrance to the villa through which Tancredi, the general, and another officer, Count Cavriaghi (Mario Girotti/Terence Hill) pass. While the shot initially implies a view untethered to any character, as the men move forward, headed by the general, they soon notice an offscreen presence as they step up, look into the camera, and salute as the Prince's offscreen voice is heard welcoming the general to his home. Tomasi di Lampedusa describes "a general in a red tunic with black froggings" and Tancredi as "red-shirted and irresistible," the caps on all three men "as floppy and faded as those of any Bourbon officer."[24] From these scattered details, Visconti creates the shot in the film that is now the subject of discussion. Red is used selectively in the film, preeminently associated with the uniforms of Garibaldi's soldiers and, by extension, with historical change.

The first extensive use of red in the film occurs in the first Tancredi sequence, in which he visits the Prince. The Prince, a white silk towel over his shoulders, is shaving, red curtains draped around the windows with these curtains being particularly prominent in the shots of Tancredi alone. Mirrors dominate, Tancredi's image repeatedly captured in them, either with the Prince or alone, clearly indicating their symbolic father/son ties while also creating an image of Tancredi's facile nature. Tancredi promises to return with the tricolor Italian flag, but the Prince is horrified by the clash of colors such a moment promises, preferring the purity of the white Sicilian flag. Unlike the newness of the tricolor flag being unfurled in the battle sequence of *Senso*, in *The Leopard* this flag dominates the extended battle sequence. Multiple versions of the flag are visible in many of the shots, their movements through the frame, in tandem with the red shirts of the Garibaldini, creating an indelible impression of the flag's mythic stature even as the long-distance framing encourages critical distance.

As the three soldiers line up before the camera, the red handkerchief on the dead soldier's face is echoed in and amplified by the uniforms of three living soldiers fighting on the opposite side of history. By being so red, all three men become "irresistible" but not equally so. The general is on the far right, in sharp focus, and receives slightly more light than the other two men; Cavriaghi is in the middle, a bit out of focus, and Tancredi is on the far left, eye patch on, his right shoulder cut off by the frame, and he is about a step behind Cavriaghi. The framing attests to Cavriaghi's importance. But all three have clearly been cast in relation to physical attractiveness.

Seeing this in the film through the point of view of the Prince adds still another implication. Unlike the single mobile shot of the dead soldier, this brief sequence of the general's arrival breaks down into eight separate shots. The first two are unambiguously aligned with the Prince; the second begins with the general stepping into the next room by pulling aside the deep red curtains framing the entrance, followed by Tancredi turning around and looking into the camera and at the Prince, Tancredi ironically drawing attention to the fact that the general has addressed the Prince as "excellency" in violation of Garibaldi's edict, a foreshadowing of larger political betrayals to come. The shots that follow are less explicit in their alignment, with two successive shots of the men introducing themselves to others in the room. If we are to read these as still from the Prince's point of view, the continuity from the first shot to the second would give him an impossible physical domination, miraculously able to move from one area of the room to another. The Prince's voice continues to be heard in these two shots as he addresses the general's desire to look at the frescoes. Another cut takes us closer to the general, looking up at the ceiling, as the Prince begins to narrate what is being represented in the frescoes. A tracking shot across the ceiling follows this look, as we see mythical Roman figures draped in layers of fabric, testifying to the glory of Salina. The tracking shot of the ceiling implies point of view. But is it the Prince's as he narrates or the general's as he looks or a combination of the two? However, when there is a cut back to the general, as the Prince is about to narrate what is on another side of the ceiling, he has not moved from his earlier position and the cut to the second tracking shot, in which the Prince discusses the fresco of Apollo surrounded by clouds, would then appear to shift point of view so that we retroactively read the prior tracking shot as belonging to the Prince. (These shots of mythological figures will later be ironically rhymed with a pan and tilt down from the area above the altar in the church in Donnafugata where Catholic iconic figures are similarly draped.) The cut that directly follows, though, is a dissolve returning us to the picnic, and the Prince is no longer seated in the narrating space that initiated the flashback. Instead, the picnic has come to an end and everyone is packing up. This drifting in and out of subjectivity, this ambiguous use of point of view, testifies, on the one hand, to the Prince's power, with him being a godlike figure able to manifest himself at any given moment. On the other hand, this slippage between his presence and absence equally testifies to his own eventual death and to the death of the world whose values he embodies, absorbed into the floating clouds and drifting fabric covering his ceilings.

But does the Prince also *desire* these men in red who have come into his home, in particular the aesthete general interested in the frescoes? I would argue that the Prince himself is not meant to have these kinds of desires but that Visconti's aestheticizing of the three male figures creates an erotic surplus. It is pointing to a type of desire that is outside the world being represented, a desire that can give voice to itself as it moves along with the Prince due to the Prince's own ambivalent relationship to that world. More than any character in the film, the Prince is associated with the act of looking. This is epitomized by his status as an amateur astronomer and by the sequence in his study with Father Pirrone in which the Prince is framed in relation to his telescopes. In this room, the curtains to the enormous windows that look out upon the landscape are pulled back to such an extent that they barely register in the shots. We now simply look out at this magnificent view with no mediating or obscuring fabric. It is a look beyond the social and an explicit rejection of Pirrone, who gently polishes one of the telescopes but does not look through it, as the sounds of battle from the following sequence bleed into the final shot, the Prince looking out, Pirrone walking away with his back to the windows. For Iris Origo, Leopardi was "the greatest poet of the skies"[25] and there is in this aspect of the Prince a Leopardian idea of the stars and the skies as a space of transcendence. In Leopardi, this is tied to a pervasive sense of otherness, of one's desires and body being outside of the social structures of the surrounding world even as one remains, by virtue of one's class status, within it. The Prince's otherness here, though, is tied to his increasingly tragic sense of the end of the world that defined him.

In the novel, the Prince dies in 1883, with a separate chapter devoted to this, and the novel concludes in 1910, with the unhappy marriage of Angelica and Tancredi and eventually Tancredi's own death. The film ends in 1862, turning the chapter devoted to a ball attended by the Prince and most of the major characters into the film's conclusion. The final sequence shows the Prince walking home alone, after the ball. The novel explains the Prince's desire to walk home alone is because "he wanted to draw a little comfort from gazing at the stars." The film retains the Prince's connection to the stars but otherwise changes some important aspects of this moment. The opening shot of the sequence is a tilt down from the decaying rooftops of the houses of the underclass of Donnafugata, the drabness of the shot broken by two fabric images: the Prince's white scarf and gloves (he is otherwise dressed in black coat and top hat) and, visible at a diagonal behind him, an orange curtain marking the entrance to one of the homes. The light coming from inside this building causes the curtain to emit a somber glow, the reason for the use of this expressive device made clear in the next shot. Before there is a cut to this shot, we hear an offscreen sound of a ringing bell as the Prince falls to his knees. A cut to a wider shot shows a priest following a young boy who is ringing that bell. The priest, we surmise, is going to perform last rites. A cut returns us to the prior setup as the priest and boy pass the Prince and step into the home where this ritual will be performed. A woman greets the priest and pulls the curtain back as these two male figures disappear inside. The Prince, however, remains on his knees and, in close-up, he looks up at the sky and says, "O faithful star, when will you give me an appointment less ephemeral, far from all of this, in your own region of perennial certitude?" The film does not cut to the star he is addressing and instead we are taken to the inside of a carriage transporting Angelica, sleeping on Tancredi's shoulder, and, across from them, her father, Don Calogero (Paolo Stoppa). There is a slight movement in the green curtains in their carriage, the lining of the carriage not in the muted blue of the Prince's vehicle but a more vulgar red, particularly prominent in the reverse-angle shots of Calogero, the central figure representing the rise of the new social order. A sound of gunfire from the army awakens Angelica as her father praises what such a sound implies for the new Sicily, and Angelica then happily drifts back to sleep. Their carriage moves through an underpass, the windows on the various homes at this early morning hour covered in drapings, their proletarian inhabitants about to awaken, as the emerging ruling class will now go home to sleep.

The final shot of the film returns us to the Prince, at last rising from his knees and walking down a narrow street, disappearing into the darkness, church bells announcing the beginning of the next day. At the top left of the frame as he walks down this street are awnings that are, like the window drapings in the previous shot, moving in the breeze. The novel supplies a vivid, naturalist idea of death for this moment as a cart filled with bulls that have just been killed at a slaughterhouse is taken through the otherwise empty streets, blood occasionally dripping on the ground. The film replaces this with the melancholia and slight indeterminacy of these images and sounds. If *The Leopard* begins with the white, delicate curtains of the aristocracy moving in the breeze as one embodiment of the fragility of the Prince's aristocratic world, the films ends with thick awnings, the window coverings of the underclass, that are now central to the sense of both mourning and new awakenings.

Soiled

The sequence in which the Prince looks at Jean-Baptiste Greuze's *Le fils puni* (1778) in the midst of the extended set piece at the ball is the central moment in relation to his melancholic status as observer. As Blom has noted, both Tomasi di Lampedusa and Visconti have shifted the emphasis in the painting from the disgraced son returning home, only to find that his father has just died, to the father himself and to the reactions of his grandchildren immediately surrounding him.[26] While the film follows the general outline of the novel's description of the Prince's response to the painting, Visconti's staging considerably draws out the ways in which the Prince looks at this work of art. Whereas Tomasi di Lampedusa straightforwardly writes that the Prince steps into the room due to his weariness and then notices the Greuze, Lancaster makes use of telegraphic gestures, wiping his forehead, shaking his head, smacking his hand on the arm of the sofa, before suddenly stopping and noticing the painting. The cut that follows as he finally looks at the painting is not his point-of-view shot but a setup taken from the side, the painting shown at a slight diagonal. He then walks over and looks in a sustained fashion, putting his glasses on, looking further, and then taking them off as he lights a cigar and continues to contemplatively look before walking back toward the sofa. He does not yet sit down, though, but stops and turns to look at the painting again, now from a distance.

We have here another instance of the neorealist trope of the look overwhelmed by the enormity of what it is beholding. This contrasts with the relatively calm and resigned nature with which he looks at the painting in the novel. In the novel, the painting is one in which "the old man was expiring on his bed amid welters of clean linen. . . . The girls were pretty, and provoking: and the disorder of their clothes suggested sex more than sorrow; they, it was obvious at once, were the real subject of the picture."[27] Through the Prince's subjectivity, the novel shifts the emphasis away from the overt content of the painted scene and instead focuses on details within it in such a way that these details take on a different implication. The Prince does not so much see a family in mourning as see eroticism in the disorder of the girls' clothing, this becoming the painting's "real subject." Death is confronted but in a tranquil manner. He wonders about his own death as he speculates on the linen being "less impeccable" and that "the sheets of the dying are always so filthy" while hoping the girls surrounding him will be better dressed than in the painting.[28] In the film, the Prince's projecting of the erotic onto the women's clothing is avoided. Once Angelica and Tancredi enter the library in the film, the free indirect discourse of the prose becomes dialogue for the Prince, including his thoughts on death calming rather than disturbing him. The direction of the sequence, however, complicates such calm resignation. Instead, the sustained act of looking, to the point where looking becomes a virtual beholding of one's own immenent mortality, replaces this sense of resignation and in which, as Sam Rohdie argues, "he is looking at his own future, that is when he will become the past."[29] Fabric is now tied exclusively to the decaying body, to death.

Near the end of the chapter on the ball, Tomasi di Lampedusa writes of a "disordered little room, filled with chamber pots spilling over with urine."[30] The Prince is not present in this space. In the film, on the other hand, he is not only present but stares fixedly at his face in a mirror. Tears begin to fall and he closes his eyes and opens them again. When there is a cut to a wider view of the room, white towels are draped on various pieces of furniture. The Prince takes out a white handkerchief and wipes his face as he walks toward a room holding the various chamber pots. Throughout this chapter, the Prince's sense of alienation and melancholia is also tied to his mounting sense of his own biological death, of the end of those around him (including Angelica and Tancredi), and of the death of his own aristocratic order. Unlike the reliance on dialogue for the sequence involving the Greuze painting, this sequence works entirely through mise-en-scène, conveying through Lancaster's performance and the décor the Prince's sense of mortality. The shot of the Prince looking at himself in the mirror not only echoes an earlier shot of him at the party looking into another mirror as he feels faint but more evocatively it echoes the shot of him looking at the Greuze, as though that painting has been the precondition for how he is able to now fully look at himself. Central to the image of a dying world are the white towels, neglected by the now-exhausted servants, the towels soiled (echoes here as well of the soiled linen in the Greuze) as the Prince, removing his own clean white handkerchief from his pocket, evokes similar gestures from the opening sequences: the Prince removing his handkerchief from his jacket pocket at the end of the Catholic service and the covering of the face of the Bourbon soldier with a red handkerchief.

When we look at this soiled white fabric here or in the Greuze we may be reminded of other moments in the film when white fabrics are prominently used. I am thinking in particular of a transition from two panning movements of the family in bed at a roadside inn, one moving right to left as we pass the Prince and Princess asleep and another from left to right that reaches its end point as the two sisters lie in bed, the eldest daughter, Concetta (Lucille Morlacchi), wide awake, to an astonishing cut to a white tablecloth being unfurled the next day as the servants help to set up a picnic for the family. It is as though the cut (in tandem with Rota's lyrical music) is reacting against Concetta's agitated state, briefly transporting us to an idyllic dimension. The presumably musty sheets of the tavern now give way to the clean, extreme whiteness of the tablecloth at the picnic. The white and the lightness of the fabric in the tablecloth also evoke a sheet, one briefly covering the frame before its fluttering movements soon cause it to be controlled, folded, and set down on the earth in a shaded area. What gives this shot its magic?

In Fellini's *Intervista* (1987), Fellini and Mastroianni (along with a camera crew), playing versions of themselves, pay an impromptu visit to Anita Ekberg's home. Mastroianni, in costume as a magician for a TV commercial, takes his magic wand and makes a white sheet appear in Ekberg's living room. As the sheet hangs, he and Ekberg dance behind it, recreating in shadow form their nightclub dance from *La dolce vita*. Such moments evoke precinematic shadow plays while simultaneously allowing for the creators of *La dolce vita* to make an impossible journey into their own professional past. But a cut suddenly arrives as Ekberg and Mastroianni in 1987 disappear and their 1960 selves replace them, *La dolce vita* now magically projected onto the white sheet, despite there being no projector visible in the room. We are shown the famous sequence of them in the Trevi Fountain, wearing formal attire, water pouring down as Mastroianni addresses his hypothetical questions to Ekberg as to her status as a goddess or as the first woman on Earth. A cut back to Ekberg and Mastroianni in 1987 shows them watching their younger selves and smiling. The extreme simplicity and whiteness of the sheet become a primal source of the cinema's magic, containing within itself possibilities for the play with light and shadow, with movement, the sheet as the very screen onto which moving images are projected. The fluttering sheet at the picnic in *The Leopard* is, like the curtains in the opening sequence, tied to something at once transportive, even transcendent but also precious, fragile. But sheets are also something else in *The Leopard*.

In the novel, Don Ciccio (who boasts of his own peasant status by referring to the holes in his pants and then proudly smacks his rear end) tells the Prince that Angelica's sheets "must smell like paradise," a line repeated in the film.[31] Such a paradise stands in contrast to the manure (both as literal odor and as metaphor) stubbornly clinging to her family's peasant history and that even her father, in spite of his recently acquired wealth and property, cannot entirely erase. When Cologero (now mayor) arrives for a dinner hosted by the Salinas at Donnafugata, he is overdressed in white tie and tails. For the Prince, before he has actually set eyes on Cologero making an entrance, it is not a red shirt or an Italian flag that becomes the central image in his mind for the "revolution" to come but rather this former peasant now in white tails. But once the Prince sees Cologero, his anxiety is temporarily allayed due to the "disastrous failure" of the tailoring. Tomasi di Lampedusa writes: "The wings of his cravat pointed straight to heaven in mute supplication, his huge collar was shapeless, and, what is more, it is our painful but necessary duty to add that the mayor's feet were shod in buttoned shoes."[32] The film faithfully reproduces this description but with Cologero given a top hat he awkwardly carries as a more visible sign of his social awkwardness. Angelica, on the other hand, and in spite of some rough edges, becomes the embodiment of this transformation of the proletariat, the manure now gone from her clean sheets of paradise. However, Angelica is also desirable at this transitional moment *because* of these connections to filth, giving off at once the appearance of the aristocrat in dress and manners even as stray aspects of her proletarian background continue to emerge. She reinvigorates this dying class as she is also the sign of its degradation. The chamber pots and soiled towels at the party, on the other hand, while metaphors for the death of the Prince and of his culture, also refer to the aristocracy's repression of its own "filth," its bodily functions and ties to the animal world.

With the relationship between Angelica and Tancredi, the film does not attempt to follow the novel in its references to the inevitability of the doomed, sexless nature of their marriage. The star power of Cardinale and Delon, at the height of their youthful beauty, overwhelms whatever need the film might have initially had in replicating the novel's pessimism on this matter. But when the couple visits the Prince while he is looking at the Greuze, pulling off their white gloves as they enter the library, they are sweating, Angelica fanning herself. In the novel, she asks Tancredi for his handkerchief but it is the Prince who gives his to her. In the film, Tancredi will perform the honor but not before wiping his own face with it first, a gesture at once erotic (through their shared sweat) and self-centered (me first) in a manner consistent with Tancredi's character. In a bit of staging in the library not described in the novel, she wipes her face with delicate pats of Tancredi's handkerchief, gestures indicative of the aristocratic lady she is now becoming. Still, sweat is sweat. The sweat at the ball is, on one level, simply a realistic notation for a social event being held in the heat of a Sicilian summer—and the heat would have undoubtedly been even more intense in the windowless library. But sweat also becomes yet another metaphor for a world dissolving, melting, as well as a reminder of another reality, that of bodily functions no amount of aristocratic clothing and delicate lace handkerchiefs can cover up or wipe away. In fact, the tuxedos and evening gowns being worn here intensify rather than alleviate the experience of heat, as expensive fabrics become increasingly soiled and intertwined with the brute reality of the body. While Tomasi di Lampedusa writes of Angelica and Tancredi showing a "complete lack of interest" in the Greuze painting and, in general, being oblivious to the melancholia affecting the Prince,[33] Visconti handles this situation another way. Angelica and Tancredi notice the intensity with which this painting takes hold of the Prince and exchange worried glances. There is, then, a double register of witnessing in this sequence: the Prince's toward the painting and Angelica and Tancredi's toward the Prince, the three of them at once united and separated through a comingling of death and eroticism. For about four minutes, "impossible" sexual desires circulate among these three individuals, sweating in their expensive evening attire in a room outside the collective spaces of the ball.

There is another possibility for why the sequence in the library has its erotic dimension. At the end of the picnic sequence, when the flashback generated by the Prince's memory begins to conclude, a dissolve takes us from the ceiling of the Prince's villa, showing the mythological figures and cherubim draped in blue, green, and red, to the white tablecloth being folded up. The Prince is at the picnic in the rear of the shot, looking marginalized in contrast to the earlier, closer view of him when his memory initially generated that flashback. The actor portraying the Prince is another mythical being central to *The Leopard*, Burt Lancaster, movie star. In the library, two young, rising stars encounter a firmly established one from a previous generation as another kind of historical passage is implied, tied to the history of cinema. In his debut film, *The Killers* (Robert Siodmak, 1946), Lancaster's Pete Lund is fundamentally passive, eroticized by the camera, and fabric becomes crucial in emphasizing close ties to the desired and desiring bodies of the film. The film's fundamental image of Lund after his death is the pile of clothes surviving him, examined in the police station. The central item of the film, found in his possessions, is a green silk handkerchief with harps and shamrocks on it serving as the clue in the mystery of his death, the handkerchief ultimately tied to the woman to whom he is destructively attracted, Kitty Collins (Ava Gardner). Both in the opening and in a later sequence in a hotel room, Siodmak films Lund's moments of surrender in an erotic manner, Lancaster in a white, sleeveless T-shirt, writhing on a bed. As in *Rocco and His Brothers*, the image of the sweating, injured male boxer (boxing is Lund's profession) becomes central, and both films have important sequences in which the male protagonists are observed by another male in the shower. In *The Killers*, however, the man observing Lund is a childhood friend, a police officer, Sam Lubinsky (Sam Levene), and the look he gives Lund has no sexual implication. In prison, however, Lund's cell mate is a petty criminal, Charleston (Vince Barnett), and the sequence of them in the cell is played as a situation of unrequited love Charleston has for Lund. Charleston will later describe their relationship as one in which they were "as close as two guys can get." At the center of the prison sequence is a Leopardian romantic idea of the stars as a space of transcendence. Charleston identifies Jupiter and Mars and refers to "the constellation of Orion, otherwise known as the Big Bear." Lund, though, is entirely preoccupied with Kitty and twirls the green handkerchief, oblivious to the extent of Charleston's feelings for him. Lancaster's presence in *The Killers* sets into motion a world of uncertain, destabilized sexual desires.

The possibilities for these destabilizations are present in *The Leopard*, although in a different manner. Tomasi di Lampedusa writes of the Prince stepping out of his bath as Father Pirrone accidentally walks in on him, "at the very moment when, no longer veiled by soapy water, not yet shrouded by his bath-sheet, he was emerging quite naked, like the Farnese Hercules."[34] A completely naked Prince, unembarrassed, asks Pirrone to bring him a towel and Pirrone obeys, rubbing the Prince's back, the towel's enormity a sign of its own aristocratic nature. The film essentially reproduces what is described in the novel although it alters the description of a "humiliated" Pirrone forced to rub the Prince's feet. Instead, Pirrone sits in front of the Prince as the Prince continues to dry himself. But this positioning of the priest causes his head to directly face the Prince's crotch, which is periodically exposed to him and then concealed by the ways the Prince adjusts the towel. The priest's embarrassment, however, does not (in either novel or film) imply a repressed homosexual desire. Instead, this interchange between the two men is played for comedy, taking its cue from the irony evident in Tomasi di Lampedusa's prose, which does not fully give itself over to an erotic description of the naked Prince.

Is this reticence in the film tied to how the Prince himself is a double for Visconti, the auteur having difficulty in turning his gaze on himself? The Prince is forty-five at the start of the novel, Lancaster was almost fifty while the film was being made, and Visconti was fifty-seven. The object of desire in Visconti, male or female, must be young—although the aesthetic articulations of such desires for the young are so universal this alone is scarcely unique to Visconti. But in Visconti, the desirability of the young is present if for no other reason than to simultaneously point toward its eventual disintegration, to the death of desire if not of literal death itself.

Covering Up

In *Vaghe stelle dell'Orsa*, ideals of beauty are embodied not only in Cardinale's Sandra but also in Sorel's Gianni. The film reproduces, from the Electra plays and from the neo-Freudian notion of the Electra complex, the daughter's hostile relationship with her mother and her desire to replace (if not murder) her mother in the name of the idolized father. But there is now the crucial addition of implied incestuous attractions, if not relations, between brother and sister, relations present in Eugene O'Neill's American version of the myth, *Mourning Becomes Electra* (1931), set during the immediate post–Civil War period. Two other contemporaneous Italian films, *Before the Revolution* and *Fists in the Pocket*, likewise draw upon incest as part of their respective agendas. With these two films, incest is tied the desire to create new forms of cinema as well as to examine postwar Italian history and culture in relation to it. "For both Bertolucci and

Bellocchio," Schifano writes, "incest was the supremely subversive act, the rebel's final gesture before he subsides into the tomb of family life and middle-class order."[35] In 1965, Visconti had both less and more to prove, less in relation to his by-then central status as an artist but more in terms of a desire to go head-to-head with newly emerging figures. Incest, claimed Visconti, was "contemporary society's last taboo," even as he also acknowledged it was at that time "a theme that's in the air."[36] The subject was already present in his production of *'Tis Pity She's a Whore*. But the incestuous past of the siblings in *Vaghe stelle* is never confirmed, in contrast to the Jacobean tragedy of the Ford play, in which desire between male and female siblings is explicitly enacted.[37]

In *Before the Revolution* and *Fists in the Pocket*, incest occurs within a predominantly heterosexual framework, tied to the repressive nature of the Italian bourgeois family and the Catholic Church. In *Vaghe stelle*, incest is tied to the upper classes, with loose analogies drawn between the Gilardinis and aristocratic familial structures from the ancient world. The question of dynasties is important here, as it also is in *The Leopard* and, later, *The Damned* and *Ludwig*. In Euripides, Electra describes herself as being "like a beast in stable rags" and says that "I weave my clothes myself and slavelike at the loom/Must work or else walk naked through the world in nothing."[38] But Sandra wears fashionable attire, and her exile (such as it is) is entirely self-induced. The arrival of Gianni brings with it the specter of incest. But the specific presence of Sorel creates additional intensities.

Schifano writes of Gianni having an "extravagant, feminine, morbid sensitivity."[39] Sorel's beauty allows the film to treat him as an object of ambivalent desire and, more than Cardinale/Sandra's own beauty, it sets into motion the film's "unstable" sexual energies. Sorel had played Rodolpho in the film version of *A View from the Bridge* (Sidney Lumet, 1962). The Miller play that is the film's source material (already discussed in the first chapter in relation to *Rocco and His Brothers*) evokes Greek tragedy, and the entrance of Rodolpho catalyzes the incestuous tensions between Eddie (Raf Vallone) and his young niece Catherine (Carol Lawrence). But Eddie's hysteria over losing Catherine to Rodolpho causes a split in Eddie's sexual identity in which his jealousy also gives rise to his implied homosexual attraction to Rodolpho, culminating in the kiss on the mouth, shot in close-up, that Eddie gives to him. As Parker Tyler has noted, even if this kiss was intended by Eddie as a way of mocking and humiliating Rodolpho, "the plain assumption was that the accuser, not the accused, harbored the homosexual nature."[40]

In *Vaghe stelle*, Gianni's entrance into the film occurs in the villa's garden, at night. The garden had been a childhood space of play for Gianni and Sandra but they are now turning it into a park memorializing their father. A plaque commemorating his death at the hands of the Nazis has already been placed on a wall in the garden and a bust in honor of him is covered with a white sheet, awaiting the ceremony where the sheet will be removed. During her first night in the villa, Sandra is drawn to the garden and, more specifically, to the covered bust. The wind in this sequence (and throughout much of the film) partly ties the film to the romantic turbulence of gothic melodrama, as does the way the villa immediately takes possession of Sandra. When Sandra steps into the garden, we see, through her point-of-view shot, the covered bust of her father, its sheet fluttering in the wind. It resembles a clichéd image of a ghost, even as Sandra jokingly denies to Andrew that the villa, to his disappointment, has any ghosts. Sandra is wearing a knitted white shawl, its whiteness matching the sheet on her father's bust. Across several different camera setups, she quite passionately embraces the bust, this moment captured indelibly in a shot in which she and the bust are framed on the left with the placard in the middle background. This is interrupted by the entrance of Gianni, announced through a cut to him standing behind the iron bars of a gate leading to the garden, the image heavily shadowed. He opens the gate and steps out, this moment followed by his point-of-view shot as he looks at Sandra embracing the covered bust. He calls out her name and she abruptly turns her head in his direction as there is a cut to a reverse-angle fast zoom into his face, Gianni slightly smiling, an expression of potential seduction.

The intensity of her embrace of the bust invites at least two interpretations: the first, following the psychoanalytic reading of the Electra complex, as an indication of her sexual desire for the father; the second, following a reading of the film in terms of history, and one that does not negate the first interpretation, as an indication of Sandra's need to embrace her Jewish roots. While the shawl she is wearing is not designed as a prayer shawl, at the very least it evokes one here, as though Sandra and her father briefly achieve a symbiosis through two different pieces of white fabric. It is these Jewish roots that her mother will, in a sequence occurring the next day, cite as fundamental to the corrupt nature of Sandra and Gianni. As with virtually everything the mother says or does in the film, though, her mental instability renders such anti-Semitic declarations unreliable, this anti-Semitism tied, in turn, to the fascism that can now barely mask its own irrational nature. Schifano writes, "Visconti wanted the mother to be theatrical, unbearable and pathetic, all at once."[41] That he first offered the role to Francesca Bertini would suggest he saw this character as a diva in a state of degradation. Bell's most notable stage role was in Jean Racine's neoclassical tragedy *Phèdre* (1677), the play that galvanized the young narrator of *In Search of Lost Time*—in particular for his experiencing the title role as played by the subject of his own diva obsession, La Berma—making Bell's casting an especially apt dividend. But

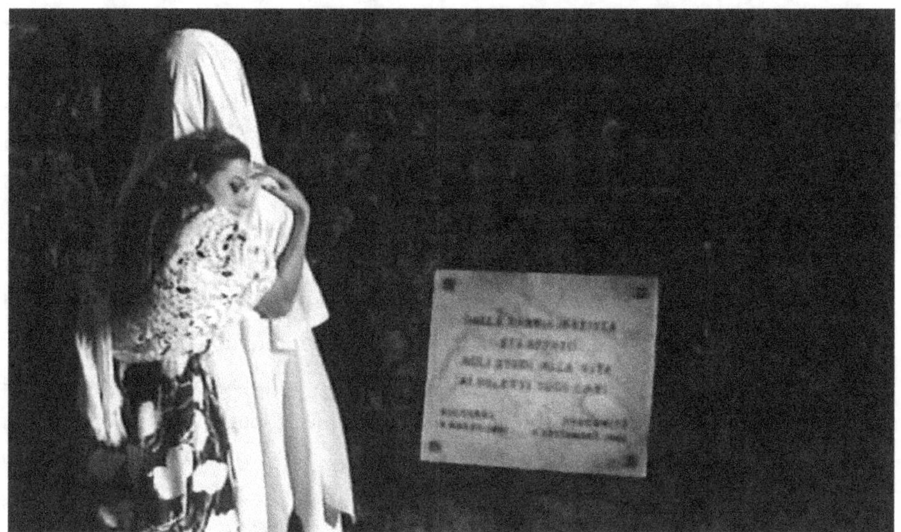

Vaghe stelle dell'orsa (1965). White sheet and shawl tied to a scandalous past.

in the sequences involving Bell as Corinna, Visconti frames her tightly and uses long lenses so that her gestures and body movements and the surrounding décor (including her clothing) are attenuated.

Gianni's entrance into the film brings additional complications. The aggressive zoom into his face as Sandra notices him introduces a discord reinforced by the rock music playing on the soundtrack. Elsaesser has compared Rocco and Gianni, "for both are animated by a desire to return to their origins, to regress to primitive affective bonds."[42] But Gianni has none of Rocco's saintliness. The dilettantish Gianni brings romantic disorder, exemplified in this sequence by the strong winds. Fosca has earlier described Gianni as someone who comes and goes, like the wind, even as the presence of the wind here evokes the trope of wind in Leopardi.[43] As with Livia and Franz in *Senso* and Natalia in *White Nights*, Gianni is a partial creator of the situations unfolding, although at the heart of the film is a struggle for control of the writing and staging of this family history, divided between Gianni, Sandra, Gilardini, and Corinna.

At the dinner party near the end of the film, also attended by Sandra, Andrew, and Gilardini, Gianni quotes the opening lines from the Leopardi poem from which the film derives its title. The parallels between these lines and the situation of Sandra and Gianni wishing to return to the happiness of their childhood home are very clear. But the Leopardi citation invites further parallels: Leopardi's status as an aristocrat, his unhappy provincial and repressive upbringing, his agonized sexual identity, and his fascination with Ancient Greece for its sensuality that stands in opposition to the dominant social order of Leopardi's day. Mauro Giori has argued that the well-known male homosexual fascination with Ancient Greece is tied to a view of this culture as a way of avoiding bourgeois ethos through a cult of beauty and classical ideals. He notes that Visconti's papers are filled with an ongoing interest in Greek theater and its scenic practices, even though Visconti rarely staged works of that era.[44] One could then see in the Leopardi reference not only Gianni projecting his own personal history onto Leopardi but Visconti, the homosexual aesthete, doing the same. At the dinner party, Gianni declares that in the aftermath of all he has experienced since the reunion with Sandra a day earlier, he plans to call his forthcoming novel *Vaghe stelle dell'Orsa*, Gianni's novel and Visconti's film doubling for one another. The novel is autobiographical and, among other things, describes an incestuous relationship between a brother and sister. But has incest ever occurred between these two? Even when alone in the film, they deny any such activities have taken place. But what we see complicates the reassurances they offer one another. Let us return to the garden.

During the garden sequence, Sandra keeps holding her shawl close to her chest, understandable given the high winds. But such a gesture also implies she may be hiding something. During the dinner party, and typical of the film's shifts between white and black, she covers herself with a black shawl and holds it against her in the same way she did with the white shawl in the garden. When she and Gianni reunite in that garden, they embrace one another in a sustained manner, closer to that of lovers than of siblings. Coming inside, she drapes her shawl on a chair and Gianni picks up this shawl and begins to make use of it for his dialogue that follows. With Andrew in the room, he discusses his passage from dilettante to journalist to novelist. As he describes this novel, he covers the bottom half of his face, an echo (as Blom has noted) of Franz using Livia's green scarf in her bedroom.[45] In both films, the body of the woman is indirectly touched through the man's seductive use of fabric, even as such gestures feminize both men as they make use of "ladies' things."[46] In *Vaghe stelle*, this idea is even stronger than the one in *Senso*, in that the woman whose body is being indirectly touched is the man's sister and, moreover, he does this in the presence of her husband. Gianni's transformation of the shawl into a veil implies that what is being described in his novel is itself in need of veiling.

As he finishes this gesture, a reverse zoom follows his abrupt rise from the chair. He exits the room and walks down a hallway, talking while pulling off his sweater, as Sandra and Andrew follow him. In his bedroom, he walks about shirtless, confesses to having stolen items from the villa, washes his face, and then rubs it dry with a white towel before tossing the towel away. Upon his suggestion to Sandra that they sell more furnishings of the house and perhaps rent the house out, she angrily leaves as he follows her, still shirtless, all of this watched by Andrew, in shadow. In the hallway, as Gianni attempts to placate her, he places both hands on her shoulders, a gesture of intimacy she rebuffs while telling him she does not approve of him undressing in front of her. Apologetic, he goes back into the bedroom, changes into a white shirt, and pulls off his pants but Sandra and Andrew remain outside, as she encourages Andrew to go out with her brother so she will be alone for the night.

Suzanne Liandrat-Guiges has written that this sequence "is in effect entirely consecrated to a celebration of Gianni's body."[47] The images of Gianni are, in a manner typical of the choreography of dressing and undressing in Visconti, offered to the spectator in excess of the dramatic logic of the sequence. But within the dramatic logic of the moment, he is sexually taunting Sandra and Andrew. For Sandra, this undressing recreates the atmosphere of incest dominating the rumors surrounding their childhood. Such rumors are something Sandra attempts to repress but Gianni now wishes to make visible, albeit through a work of "fiction." For Andrew, the undressing is a display by Gianni of a physical attractiveness with which Andrew cannot compete and in which the "prize" is Gianni's sister. At the same time, in the sequence that directly follows, in which Gianni shows Andrew the decaying landscape and architecture of Volterra, the two men are dressed in almost identical trench coats. In long shots it is sometimes difficult to tell these men apart, the forbidden male object of desire and the socially sanctioned one becoming indistinguishable.

Given how many years Sandra and Gianni have been separated from one another, if any sexual acts had ever occurred between them it would most likely have been when they were children, their activities confined to a "simple" form of genital sexuality. This makes the uncertainty surrounding their relationship both more innocent and more of an affront to prevailing norms, a doubling up of sexual scandal in relation to both incest and prepubescent sexuality. But the film discourages too much of a literal interpretation, and incest in the film invites a reading in terms of metaphor as much as it does in relation to the real. Visconti wrote that one of the central aspects of the film that interested him was the "superiority complex of the Jews."[48] He does not explicitly elucidate, though, so we are left to infer his intentions in terms of the nature of this "complex." Given what we see in the film, we may read incest as a metaphor for the sense of a closed world between Sandra and Gianni, both Jewish-identified. During the sequence of Gianni undressing, a Star of David necklace is visible around his neck. When Sandra, hugging the covered bust of her father, is interrupted by the appearance of Gianni, she silently goes over to him and they embrace in the intimate manner already described, as though a transmission from father to children is implied, the fluttering of the white sheet in the wind giving that piece of fabric an animating force.

Like homosexuality, incest stands outside of the social order and refuses or "perverts" the perpetuation of the family and the maintaining of that social order. Gianni promises that his novel will explain everything, as though such transparency will be for the social good. But the novel *Vaghe stelle dell'Orsa* is not given a chance to do so because the film *Vaghe stelle dell'Orsa* is driven by other needs.

Tightening

Sandra is walking around her bedroom, a towel partially covering her body, like Pupe in *Il lavoro*. She is explaining to Andrew the roots of her hostility toward Gilardini. In Visconti, confessions and explanations are always ironically framed, raising additional problems or questions. In this sequence of ostensible clarification, the blinds are drawn on a window framed by a set of curtains, with a sheer white curtain overlaying the blinds. As with the drawn curtains of Nadia's bedroom in *Rocco*, there is no looking out, no looking beyond, but for different reasons than in the earlier film. As Sandra lies facedown on the bed, the Franck music begins to be heard nondiegetically, but her gestures do not easily correspond to the expository nature of what she is saying. Her body language has an erotic component, as though she is offering herself to Andrew even as she recoils from his touch, the towel becoming a prop of deception. When she confesses that she encouraged Gianni to commit suicide, her direct looks into the camera and, presumably, at Andrew do not match where we eventually see Andrew standing. She and Gianni, she claims, agreed to not speak to one another in Gilardini's presence, communicating instead through notes tucked away in secret places, one of them behind a clock in the mother's bedroom atop of which sits a reproduction of an erotic figurine, *Psyche Revived by Cupid's Kiss* (Antonio Canova, 1787). When Andrew and Sandra enter the mother's bedroom, it is Andrew who finds a note tucked away in this figurine. The note is Sandra's invitation to meet its author at the water tower. As she reads, there are two pieces of black chiffon draped across the wide shot, with a small opening in the middle to allow the figurine to be seen. These curtains presumably surround the mother's bed but the absence of a master shot of the room does not create certainty. We are simply looking at a large piece of sheer black fabric. "The lace curtain through which she returns to read the note," writes Elsaesser, "marks a diaphanous fusion of present, memory and anticipation. . . . The curtain incidentally also indicates the double nature of Sandra's relation to her husband: like a veil the present interferes as deception."[49] Sandra tells Andrew that the note is from Pietro (Fred Williams), her childhood boyfriend, who was forbidden from romancing Sandra because of his class status. (He is now a doctor in Volterra.) This is soon revealed to the viewer as a lie, however, when she dashes off to secretly meet Gianni, the true author, who is waiting for her in the tower.

Near the end of the film, Gianni assaults Sandra, a sequence with ties to the two assaults on Nadia in *Rocco and His Brothers*. In *Vaghe stelle*, though, Sandra survives and it is ultimately Gianni who assumes the female function from the earlier film. Gianni has just destroyed his novel, romantically throwing its pages into the fire, and will commit suicide after his bungled attack on Sandra. In a film in which fabric has been so central in simultaneously pointing toward and obscuring the truth, Sandra's own clothing here must be ripped by Gianni, as an indication less of rape than of Gianni's need to reveal, a revelation especially important to him since he has just destroyed his novel because of Sandra's reaction to it. But Gianni's attempts at clarity do not escape a sense of the disingenuous, of seeing himself as a romantic hero, in particular since his preferred mode of public confession is an autobiographical novel that will only perpetuate the blurring of truth and reality surrounding this family drama. The assault on Sandra is one final self-dramatizing attempt at controlling the situation and giving it an aesthetic shape, of taking control away from Sandra, who has just sent Andrew back to America. In *Rocco and His Brothers*, almost immediately after offering her body to Simone so that he may stab it, Nadia changes her mind but it is too late. Gianni likewise changes his mind after attempting suicide, and that reversal is likewise too late. His suicide is, in fact, no less of an aestheticizing of his life than the novel, another game of one-upmanship with his sister but one in which he goes too far and is, possibly, defeated.

The film offers us agonized images of Gianni's death, his shirt open (torn by Sandra in trying to get away from him) and pulled down to below his shoulders, his back arched while he lies on the bed. But this is an erotic image of a beautiful, suffering male. He rises from the bed, framed by its curtains, an echo of the earlier shot of the curtains framing the Cupid and Psyche clock. The bed he is rising from is, in fact, his mother's and he will soon pass the Cupid and Psyche, which had assumed a crucial function during his encounter in this room with Sandra. In a violent gesture, he turns toward an end table, the shirt moving with him. This is followed by a graphic match from the white shirt to a white towel, in close-up, as Sandra dries off her face, a reverse zoom revealing other white towels behind her, hanging on racks, the sound of church bells prominent on the soundtrack. A cut returns us to the bedroom, where Gianni continues his agonizing. In a high-angle shot, he crawls across the floor, pulling on a rug and calling out his sister's name. But Sandra is now clearly lost to him.

The tension between white and black central to the film continues to play itself out in the final sequence in which the unveiling of the father's bust occurs. The mother arrives, accompanied by Gilardini, her memory, according to Gilardini at the dinner the night before, miraculously restored. But the evidence for it here is inconclusive. She is dressed in black, her hat a larger version of the hat Sandra wore when she visited her mother the day before. This mirroring of the two women through their clothing does not work to clarify matters, though, and merely invites further speculation. If, as Gilardini claims, Corinna now remembers, is the fact that she is dressed in a way similar to her daughter mean she is now moving toward an acceptance of her own complicity in relation to her husband's death?

A cut takes us back to Sandra in her room, getting ready for the unveiling. She opens the window curtains and tightly wraps a white scarf around her head, the camera zooming in on her face as she twice looks off at something. A cut soon reveals the object of her gaze, a letter she has written to Andrew, her voice-over reading its contents in which she promises to come to him in New York, "free from phantoms and remorse." Surrounding her in the frame are even more draped white fabrics. All of this white could imply a cleansing of her past, free from its "phantoms." (The white scarf contrasts with the black scarf she wears when she arrives in Volterra.) But this whiteness, while a rejection of Gianni's airing of "dirty laundry," is a whitening out, a form of repression in this "drama of non-existence," underlined by Sandra not simply wrapping but tightening the scarf around her head, the pervasive sense of white indicating the persistence of ghosts, of phantoms, rather than their disappearance. The discovery of Gianni's corpse by Fosca and Pietro is intercut with Sandra, unaware of her brother's death, arriving at the ceremony and soon to pull off the white sheet. When this reveal occurs, Corinna puts her hand up to face, the hand covered in a black glove. What is implied by this gesture? At first she covers her mouth and slightly turns her head in Gilardini's direction, as though she is about to say something. But she remains mute. The hand now moves farther up her face, covering mouth and nose. Then, just as it is about to cover her eyes, as though she can look no longer, there is a cut. Her gestures are as far from the telegraphic ones of a grand diva as one could imagine and are almost impossible to read.

When we return to the ceremony, after cutting away to Pietro *en route* to announce Gianni's death, the rabbi is reciting from the Book of Isaiah. As Pietro arrives, the rabbi's recitation concludes with the words, "Let us say thank you and goodbye. Amen," and it is on these words that there is a cut to a long shot of the ceremony, filmed with a very wide angle lens, as the final bars of the Franck (which had been playing throughout this final sequence) conclude and the film itself concludes. Visconti has said of the film, "Sandra and her victims (or her persecutors) find a place in the framework of contemporary society, or else discover that for them there is no longer a place. And, through their tragedy, they contribute toward

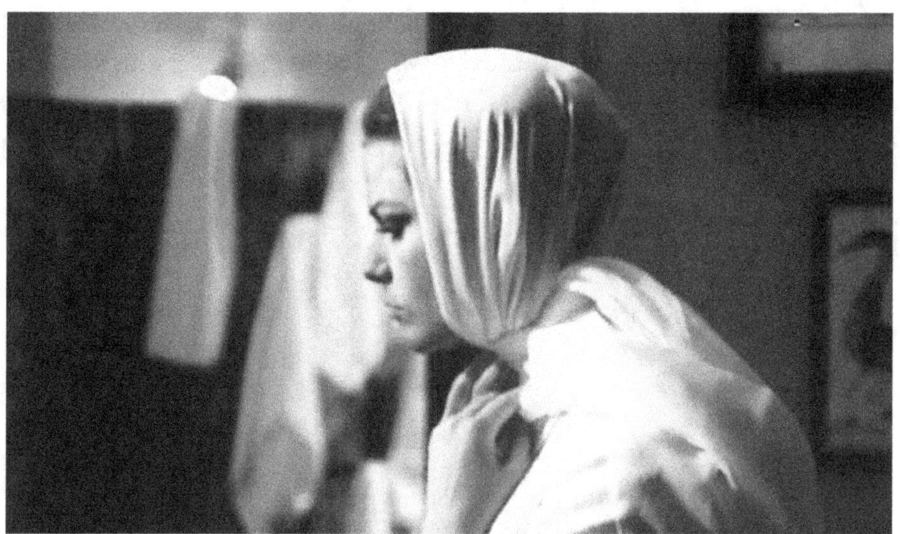

Vaghe stelle dell'orsa. A tightening of the scarf, a repressing of past events.

a better understanding of our historical situation in its reality, of its meaning."[50] Such "understanding" is presumably transmitted to the spectator, since within the film itself any revelations the protagonists experience are complicated by competing realities and subjectivities. Even as it would appear to gesture toward some kind of tentative closure, the film continues to raise implied questions. What will the response be to Pietro's news? Will this constitute a final victory of Sandra over her brother, as she soon leaves for America? Or will this death pull her back into the world she is both drawn toward and repulsed by? In this modernist tragedy that is also a film of ghosts and phantoms is Gianni now another ghost soon to rise from the dead, to challenge once again? There are high, Leopardian winds throughout this ceremony, also linked, as we have seen, with Gianni's rapid comings and goings to Volterra. It is possible that the battle for control of this decaying world will continue in somewhat different variations.

As a fabric film, *Vaghe stelle dell'Orsa* is the antithesis of *Senso*. In *Senso*, the veil becomes an emblem of the need to be seen and noticed for one's transgressions even (or especially) when giving a performance stating the very opposite of this. In *Vaghe stelle dell'Orsa*, fabric is contained within a world refusing to offer solutions to its own riddles. That these two films situate fabric in their own specific ways has very much to do not only with the historical moment in which they were made but also in relation to the history they are attempting to document. *Senso* is able to look at the period of the Risorgimento from a historical distance of a hundred years, concisely balancing its irony and melodrama. *Vaghe stelle* is dealing with a more recent history, one still insufficiently clear in its implications and for which artists are searching for the proper forms. What Visconti and his collaborators have done is find a form that in itself is an exploratory one. In *Vaghe stelle dell'orsa*, truth, revelation, and resolution are things refusing to be unveiled.

DECADENT THREADS

5

Prelude: The Witch Burned Alive

Between *Vaghe stelle dell'Orsa* and *The Stranger*, Visconti contributed an episode to the portmanteau *Le Streghe*. Unlike the other portmanteaus on which he worked, every episode of *Le Streghe* featured the same star, Silvana Mangano. Mangano is a central presence in two other films discussed in this chapter, *Death in Venice* and *Ludwig*, as well as in a film to be discussed in the final chapter, *Conversation Piece* (1974). The first episode of *Le Streghe* is the Visconti, *The Witch Burned Alive*, and the "witch" is a movie star named Gloria, played by Mangano. In *Siamo donne*, Magnani is both neorealist heroine and glamorous film star, playing herself in a reenacted scenario officially taken from her own life where she is recognized by "ordinary" people and adored wherever she goes. In *The Witch Burned Alive*, Gloria is largely removed from any connection to an organic, realistically detailed world. Instead, the film takes place at a ski lodge. The wealthy guests there make a great fuss about the star but their fawning coexists with a desire to almost literally tear the "witch" apart, a sadism unimaginable fifteen years earlier in relation to Magnani. The pacing is fast, the film dominated by an aggressive use of the zoom underlining various grotesque effects but with none of its speed tied to the stylized authenticity and controlled theatrical realism of *Bellissima*. Several actors from Visconti's earlier films appear in supporting roles: Clara Calamai, Massimo Girotti, Annie Girardot, and Nora Ricci. But Visconti does not use them in order to evoke those earlier films. Instead, it is as though everything is being done in order to negate a nostalgic relationship with this past. We are moving into the final phase of Visconti's career, where fabric will be situated in some new contexts and assume some new forms, although ties to the earlier films remain.

The naturalist world of Visconti's earlier films emerges in *Witch* less through a direct apprehension of the environment than through a contrast between the extremely constructed nature of these images and what the characters give voice to in dialogue. According to one woman at the party, Gloria is originally from the lowest element of society, a woman of the mud. But it is artificial fibers that dominate, Gloria's outfits often having a metallic look. She is also wrapped in furs and feathers and her artificial eyelashes are made out of mink, her status as a "beautiful animal" corseted by industrial production. At one point in the film she plays a parlor game that will aid her in deciding which two men at the party she prefers. The white blindfold she wears in order to play this game anticipates the bandage worn across the Arab woman's face in *The Stranger*, both women "wounded" as they attempt to navigate their way through their respective environments, senses dulled. Alexander García Düttmann has described *The Witch Burned Alive* as a film "which unexpectedly tears the mask off the film diva and then returns it to her."[1]

Historical Tapestries

Also in *The Witch Burned Alive* is a young actor in a small role as a servant, the Austrian-born Helmut Berger. In contrast to his contribution to *Witch*, Berger has leading roles in *The Damned* and *Ludwig* (as well as in *Conversation Piece*). Typical of all of Visconti's films beginning with *Senso*, *The Damned* and *Ludwig* were, along with *Death in Venice*, comprised of international casts for the possibilities of dubbing in various European and North American markets. All of these more recent features, though, were filmed primarily in English. But in the earlier Visconti films, the settings and subject matter remained Italian even when the source material was not. With *The Stranger*, shot primarily in French and Italian, this began to change, roughly coinciding with Visconti's increased importance as an international cultural figure. By the late 1960s he had begun to detach himself from contemporary political and social concerns in Italy and elsewhere, as well as from issues of Italian history with which younger Italian filmmakers were beginning to actively engage. Guido Aristarco would later write of the "moral crisis" Visconti began to undergo after *Rocco and His Brothers*, "a retreat into inwardness" in which "the threads of decadence were no longer woven within the fabric of the imperatives of a great historical/moral tapestry."[2] With the move away from Italian subject matter this inwardness is further manifested. But Visconti was not unique among major Italian filmmakers in this regard. Pasolini, for example, engaged in a similar "retreat" through his *Trilogy of Life*: *The Decameron* (1971), *The Canterbury Tales* (1972), and *Arabian Nights* (1974). *The Damned*, *Death in Venice*, and *Ludwig* have likewise been seen as a trilogy, although their predetermined status as such is less clear than in the Pasolinis.

The Damned, while over two and a half hours long, is rapidly paced, with much frantic movement within the frame as the camera nervously pans and zooms. The screenplay is technically an original one but, typical of Visconti, there are numerous evocations of literary and theatrical texts. Thomas Mann's novel of the downfall of a wealthy, mercantile nineteenth-century German family, *Buddenbrooks*, is often referred to in the literature on the film, particularly in relation to the opening sequence of the wealthy von Essenbeck family assembling for a formal dinner, this sequence evoking Part One of Mann's novel. But Henry Bacon sees a film Shakespearean in tone, "dramatic rather than novel-like."[3] The most frequently cited of Shakespeare's plays in relation to this, and a play particularly marked by its fabric imagery, is *Macbeth* (1623). The connections between *The Damned* and *Macbeth* are most evident in the characterization of the scheming Essenbeck daughter-in-law, Sophie (Ingrid Thulin), and her lover, Friedrich Bruckmann (Dirk Bogarde), this couple loosely paralleling Macbeth and Lady Macbeth. Sophie and Friedrich are attempting to take over the Essenbeck steelworks in order to align the family business with the Nazis. Their first major strategy is to have Friedrich murder the elderly patriarch, Joachim (Albrecht Schoenhals), who is reluctant to connect the steelworks with the National Socialists.

Death in Venice is self-evidently based on Mann's canonical work of literature but Visconti and his co-screenwriter Nicola Badalucco have made important changes, including turning Aschenbach from a writer into a Gustav Mahler–like composer. As with the adaptation of *The Postman Always Rings Twice* in *Ossessione*, *Death in Venice* takes a short but, in contrast to the Cain, extremely dense and intertextual literary work and considerably inflates its scale, with flashbacks showing Aschenbach with his wife (Marisa Berenson) and young daughter that have no parallels in the novella. In Mann, Aschenbach's wife died at a young age and his daughter is an adult and married. In the film, the daughter dies while still a child, and her funeral is shown. Aschenbach's intense discussions in the flashbacks with close friend and colleague Alfred (Mark Burns) over art and music are not from the novella but are based on similar discussions scattered throughout Mann's *Doctor Faustus* (1947) and occur between its composer protagonist, Adrian Leverkün, and other artist and musician figures. The running time of *Death in Venice* is about twenty minutes less than that of *The Damned* but the pacing is considerably slower. Whereas in *The Damned* the zoom and editing structure are predominantly rhetorical, untethered to individual subjectivities, the panning and zooming camera in *Death in Venice* is aligned with ambiguous shifting points of view between Aschenbach and a camera given an autonomous power to look without that look being tied to a specific character.

With *Ludwig*, the slow pacing of *Death in Venice* continues but, in tandem with the use of the zoom, now acquires a stateliness in a film almost four hours long. In Italy, *The Damned* was released under Visconti's preferred title of *La caduta degli dei*, the Italian translation of *Götterdämmerung*, or *The Twilight of the Gods*, a reference to the last of Richard Wagner's operas of *The Ring of the Nibelungen*. But it is in *Ludwig* where Wagner himself materializes as a character, although, unlike *Senso*, there are no opera sequences and the film's epic scale is paradoxically tied to its intimacy. And if tragic form is central to *The Damned*, it is no less central here. As Geoffrey Nowell-Smith has noted, the struggle over control of dynasties in *Ludwig* is not typically a theme of the novel but of tragedy. Borrowing a term from Eisenstein, Nowell-Smith argues that the "dominant" of *Ludwig* is "kingship and the destructive pairing of this with Ludwig's homosexuality," in which a "tragic ending is the only one possible."[4] But neither *The Damned* nor *Ludwig* attempt to recreate the poetic forms of verse central to tragedy, although they each make use of dialogue in a different way. In *The Damned*, the dialogue assumes straightforward functions and often has a melodramatic explicitness. With *Ludwig*, Visconti returns to collaborating with Enrico Medioli and Suso Cecchi d'Amico and the script has a literary density absent from *The Damned*. One example of this is how it uses sleep as a motif (so central as well to *Macbeth*), extending the implications of Ludwig as an indecisive and withdrawn leader, so that sleeping, lethargy, and insomnia infect the entire narrative world and the bed becomes, again for Visconti, central.

The references critics have made to Shakespeare in relation to *The Damned* suggest the film is offering an experience of dramatic fullness while also giving itself figurative if not allegorical ambitions. As Visconti admitted, his original intent was to make a film close to historical reality but this began to change, leading to something that "did not remain historical" and where the characters gradually became symbols.[5] But *The Damned* was also made during a period when postwar German cinema was at last addressing the origins of Nazism, as Italian cinema was also gradually beginning to come to terms with the origins and social climate of Fascism, with Bernardo Bertolucci's *The Conformist* (1970), adapted from Alberto Moravia's 1947 novel, perhaps the most popular and critically acclaimed of these. Visconti had already addressed the issue of Fascism in a 1956 dance version of Mann's story "Mario and the Magician" (1930), staged in Milan, in which the hypnotic powers of the phenomenally popular but sinister magician Cipolla serve as a parallel to Mussolini. But with the cinema, and in a manner not atypical of other Italian neorealist filmmakers, Visconti avoids directly confronting the subject, even in *Vaghe stelle dell'orsa*.

Of the Visconti works being addressed in this chapter, only *Death in Venice* has an Italian setting. Otherwise, it is German history and culture that now concerns Visconti, a concern no less evident in *Death in Venice*. However, the films are not unrelated to Italian neorealist concerns. Simply within the logic of his own career there should have been nothing surprising in a shift for Visconti from Italian subject matter to Austro-German. In *Senso*, the political tensions between Austrian and Italian forces are at the center of not only its love story but also its citations, so a kind of culture war is also implicitly occurring. Visconti's interest in Romy Schneider, beginning in 1961, while never as extensively realized as he initially hoped, is another indication of a movement away from Italian culture since, unlike his other contemporaneous protégé of the period, Alain Delon, she does not play an Italian character in either of her two films for him and in *Il lavoro* she stands out precisely because she is not Italian. As discussed in a previous chapter, the "otherness" of the Swiss Austrian Maria Schell in *White Nights* assumes a related function. And the setting for *The Witch Burned Alive* is not the Italian Alps but Kitzbühel in Austria. In *Ludwig*, Schneider revisits the role that made her a star in Germany in the 1950s, Empress Elisabeth of Austria in the three *Sissi* films shot between 1955 and 1957. In the novel *The Leopard*, Tomasi di Lampedusa refers to the Prince's German heritage, evident in his fair coloring but also in "an authoritarian temperament, a certain rigidity of morals, and a propensity for abstract ideas."[6] Visconti does not use this (Lancaster's fair complexion is a fait accompli) and, if anything, the Prince is situated by the film as deeply Sicilian, his "propensity for abstract ideas" part of a melancholic self-awareness. Such an avoidance of German possibilities was unusual for Visconti by the 1960s, and even though he would continue to stage Italian works, there was an increasingly self-conscious Germanness to some of his theater productions. But it was not postwar Germany that fundamentally interested him.

Both Pasolini and Visconti now looked to the past as a form of rejecting the increasingly chaotic and materialistic world of post-1968 culture, particularly in Italy. For Pasolini, it was the ancient and medieval world of myth and storytelling that became the site of lost utopias. "His cinematic reality," writes Barth David Schwartz of Pasolini, "could not [*sic*] longer reproduce a social reality which Italian prosperity had destroyed."[7] *The Decameron*, freely adapting tales from Boccaccio, thus became "a dirge for a world lost."[8] For Visconti, on the other hand, it was a more recent history that became the site of not so much lost utopias as failed ones, that is to say a Germany and an Austria deeply tied to the Romanticism and Post-Romanticism of the nineteenth and early twentieth century. Visconti was, in effect, asking himself about the origins of a significant aspect of the aesthetic practices and movements informing his own work. The Fascism Visconti and other Italian filmmakers of his generation first embraced and then rejected, with neorealism as its major form of resistance, may also be seen as a rejection of a certain strain of Romanticism appropriated by Fascism (an issue integrated into the seductive style of *The Conformist*). More than any other Italian filmmaker linked with neorealism, the attractions of that Romanticism never deserted Visconti.

The history in these three Visconti films is in reverse order from which the films were made. *Ludwig* opens in 1865, *Death in Venice* reproduces the general period in which Mann's novella was published, 1912, and *The Damned* opens in 1933, ending approximately a year later. Looking at the films in reverse order in terms of production, they chart a trajectory taking us from the height of German Romanticism to its "perversion" in Nazism. By the time *The Damned* was in production, a historical interpretation of Romanticism had formed something close to a tradition and *The Damned* was hardly provocative in that regard. Its provocations were tied to other matters, in particular its status as a spectacle in which Nazism and "deviant" sexualities were conjoined. The X-rated *The Damned* would become Visconti's greatest financial success for reasons strongly related to its violent and sexual content.

Finally, *The Damned, Death in Venice*, and *Ludwig* stand out within Visconti's cinema for the degree to which all of them explicitly address male homosexuality. Homosexuality's presence in later Visconti coincides with the loosening of censorship restrictions and the increased visibility and politicization of gay culture. But even within Italian filmmaking at the time, Visconti was not unique. Pasolini is far bolder in what he is willing to literally show in *Teorema* (1968) or *The Decameron*. In *Teorema*, the suspended erotics of dressing and undressing central to Visconti give way to a world of total stripping down. Near the end of the film, Paolo, the patriarch of a bourgeois family, played by Girotti, stands in the middle of the Milan train station and removes all of his clothes, a literal act of undressing that is also a metaphor for his divesting himself of all material possessions. The father's self-revelation is the culmination of the unexpected visit to his home of a stranger, the Guest (Terence Stamp), who sexually seduces the entire household. For Pasolini, this guest is nothing less than a figure out of the Old Testament, a possible combination of God and the Devil, who speaks to the family through their sexualized bodies otherwise repressed by bourgeois culture. What results is a frenzy of undressing, piles of clothing and underwear scattered everywhere, in which the crotch of this stranger, his bulge visible through his polyester pants, becomes the route either to the sacred or to a revolutionary sense of the profane. In *The Decameron*, the medieval setting of the Boccaccio source material provides a pretext for not simply the film's explicit nudity but also its frequent ties between flesh and fabric. An erect penis juts out of a long shirt, its lower buttons opened, the image having the bluntness of pornography and the suspended erotics of the fetish. Such sudden "freedom" presents new challenges for Visconti in that, as Serge Daney and Jean-Pierre Oudart have argued, "he can no longer inscribe sexuality in the form of a metaphor."[9] But, in fact, he would continue to inscribe it in metaphor (as did Pasolini in a different way) even as he tentatively moved toward more direct forms of representation. The interest of the Visconti films in this chapter is in how they situate this issue of sexuality within the context of history, a political history but also a history of art, a poetics if not an aesthetics, of non-normative sexual desire. The metaphors persist but in some new ways.

Flutterings

Let us start with the film in the middle, *Death in Venice*. And we are starting with the end, the final sequence. A dying Aschenbach sits in a canvas chair and looks out at the sea and, more specifically, at the boy who has been object of his obsession almost from the moment of Aschenbach's arrival in Venice, Tadzio. In a long shot, Tadzio is in the water, right of center in the far distance with his back to the camera, his body in silhouette as the sun is setting. In the far right foreground of this wide Panavision frame is a still camera, mounted on a tripod, a long black photographer's fabric draped over this camera but with no photographer present. In the literature on *Death in Venice*, this shot has been the subject of extensive analysis. So much so that, as with the shot of the Prince looking at the Greuze painting in *The Leopard*, it has come to stand in for the entirety of the film's ambitions. (Both images have been so frequently reproduced that I feel no obligation to show them here yet again.) The idea behind the shot comes from Mann, where he writes, "A camera with no photographer to operate it stood on its tripod at the edge of the sea, a black cloth that covered it fluttering with a snapping noise in a wind that now blew colder."[10] As with the corresponding moment in the film, Mann critics and scholars have extensively analyzed the implications of this sentence, with the more recent literature drawing connections between this still camera and the emergence of the motion picture camera, even though there are no references to the cinema in the Mann and only fleetingly in the Visconti.[11] Visconti had originally intended for this to be a motion picture camera but decided the idea was too obvious.[12] In limiting itself to Mann's description of this moment, the film more richly evokes the cinema than the image of an actual motion picture camera, in its explicitness, could have achieved. But it is not so much the camera that is of interest to the concerns of this book but the cloth on the camera. In the film, the cloth is not fluttering in the wind and making a snapping noise but instead moves almost imperceptibly in relation to a gentle breeze from the sea. The color of the black cloth contrasts with the white of the suit and hat Aschenbach is wearing. But his outfit is soiled and, when seen in tandem with the blackness of the camera cloth, becomes an image of death. In a sequence from *The Man with the Movie Camera*, Vertov's camera, also on a tripod but minus the black cloth, begins to dance due to the magic of stop motion photography. That camera is ecstatic because it imagines it can do justice to the entire social world it is filming. The still camera in *Death in Venice*, on the other hand, is aware that the social world it is capturing is both ending and in a state of transition, with the only slight sense of movement occurring through the fabric.

Aschenbach is an anomaly in Visconti's work, in that he is from the bourgeoisie, his position as a major artist elevating his class status in a way that does not happen with Meursault in *The Stranger*. Typically, if Visconti represents an artist at all he is a secondary (even if essential) figure. Aschenbach is a problem since this is not a cinema interested in directly showing how art is created. We hear feverish arguments between Aschenbach and Alfried about music and the role of the artist but only the tiniest amount of Aschenbach's music is heard diegetically. And he has arrived in Venice in the aftermath of personal and professional crises: a weak heart condition, the death of his daughter, and the disastrous reception of his latest composition. Mann does not give Aschenbach such inciting melodrama for his protagonist's journey. Instead, Mann's Aschenbach sees a man emerging from a Munich mortuary chapel. The man's straw hat makes him appear to Aschenbach as "a traveler from afar," even though what the man is wearing is a "familiar native rucksack strapped to his shoulders and a yellowish Norfolk suit apparently of loden cloth. He had a great mackintosh over his left forearm, which he held supported against his side."[13] The contrasts in the man's appearance, his posture and his demeanor set against the everyday quality of the fabric, create in Aschenbach a desire to get away as this man has, initiating a pattern of Aschenbach seeing negative doubles of himself in various disheveled or grotesque aging male figures. But Aschenbach is not at this moment suffering from any doubts as an artist (it is the irony in Mann's prose that creates a sense of Aschenbach's limitations of which he himself has been unaware) and his desire to travel is more existential than traumatic.

Our first view of Aschenbach in the film is when he sits in a tattered wicker chair on the boat carrying him into Venice. As I have already described in the introduction, he is bundled up in a heavy coat, gloves, and scarf, a blanket on his lap, in muted colors. He is reading a book but looking distracted as a worker behind him adjusts a sail on the boat before walking out of frame. The camera begins to zoom toward him as he closes his eyes, as though trying to sleep; he nods his head, then opens his eyes and tries to resume reading before distraction again takes over. He looks out to the sea and looks back at the book but shakes his head, still unable to concentrate. Following a cut to a long shot of workers wading through the shallow waters of the sea, there is a cut to the top of the boat's white linen canopy, the wind causing the canopy to bubble, as though the boat were a ghost ship pulling the protagonist toward his destiny. We then return to Aschenbach as the camera zooms toward him into a close-up, his scarf now pulled up above his neck, as he opens and closes his eyes, looking pained. This only loosely corresponds to the description of his arrival in the novella, where he is "wrapped in his cloak, a book on his lap." But there he is otherwise expectant, even able to sleep.[14]

At the end of the film, Aschenbach spots Tadzio performing a gesture while standing in the sea, a gesture possibly directed for Aschenbach's benefit, "as if, lifting his hand from his hip, he were pointing outward, hovering before him in an immensity full of promise. And, as so often before, he rose to follow him."[15] This is a culminating moment of a series of references to Tadzio evoking classical Greek sculpture, references the film does not draw upon but only distantly evokes. It is not entirely clear from Mann's description whether Aschenbach literally raises himself up from the chair or whether this act is entirely in Aschenbach's mind. But the film makes this moment literal as a quivering Aschenbach reaches his hand out to Tadzio before he collapses from the exertion and dies. Bogarde does not hold back here and it is a performance that could have been equally effective in silent cinema, even in a diva film made during the period in which the film is set. But the act of looking that brings about Aschenbach's death is a response to his distraction in the opening. Unlike the protagonist in Mann, this Aschenbach immediately and urgently needs something to arrest and transform his gaze and his perception of himself and his art. He must throw off the heavy clothing and blankets in favor of a white summer suit that will nevertheless be the clothing he dies in.

Tadzio, as has been analyzed time and again in relation to both the Mann and the Visconti, upsets Aschenbach's sense of classical order, a schematic obviously drawing upon the Apollonian and Dionysian in Friedrich Nietzsche's *The Birth of Tragedy* (1872). In the Mann, Aschenbach continually places the boy's beauty within classical and Apollonian traditions, as though desperately attempting to contain what the boy's presence unleashes within him. What is unleashed, though, is a force not simply aesthetic but sexual as Tadzio embodies desires exceeding, if not scandalizing, the dominant social order: same-sex desire but also a desire for someone pubescent. This will have negative consequences for Aschenbach, turning him into a failed lover for Tadzio. When he visits a barber in order to make himself look young, the result turns him into a caricature of a dandy, with the white makeup on his face, the black dye in his hair and moustache, and the red lipstick. Daney and Oudart liken Aschenbach here to a transvestite, "but sweating, dirty, his makeup running."[16] But he also resembles a corpse being painted for his showing at a funeral, another version of the walking dead, like Gloria at the end of *The Witch Burned Alive*; or a decayed version of the portrait of Roulin in *Rocco and His Brothers*. Soon after this, as he walks through the streets, Tadzio and his family having just passed by, he begins to pull at the tight collar of his white suit. The gesture of pulling on his collar is an echo of Rocco and Gino pulling at their own collars at critical moments. These are clothes that, however much they connote one's social and economic importance, finally suffocate.

In *Ossessione*, Spagnolo attempts to lure Gino away by pointing to the sea and promising him a world beyond the conventions of heterosexual existence. In *Death in Venice*, the sea offers an even more impossibly transcendent longing, tied to death. Far more interesting than this, however, is the desire to reach out to the boy not as one male desiring another but as an artist attempting to shape something exceeding his gifts and, in the process, destroying him. In the first argument in the film between Aschenbach and Alfried, Aschenbach declares that the artist, due to his exemplary status in the world, "must be a model of balance and strength." Here on the beach, Aschenbach has literally and metaphorically lost both balance and strength. The controversy surrounding the film's prominent use of the adagietto from Mahler's *Symphony No. 5* (1902) is largely tied to the apparent disconnect between this lush post-Romantic score and the aesthetic timidity and classicism of which Alfried accuses Aschenbach. But since we hear so little of Aschenbach's music diegetically, the nondiegetic use of Mahler arguably points to what is not so much absent as latent or repressed in Aschenbach's composing. Alfried makes this clear to Aschenbach as Alfried plays a "demonic" piece of music for him at the piano and then announces it is Aschenbach's own piece. This Dionysian potential emerges through the fully orchestrated and conducted version of the adagietto on the soundtrack, even as this movement from the symphony is ultimately tied to the composer's death. Aschenbach is "outed," unmasked or unveiled.

However, Visconti's filming of this moment is one in which Aschenbach does not just romantically die *for* his art but *outside* of it, becoming an anguished spectator, itself another kind of romantic position. In a film in which metaphor repeatedly announces itself, the alternation of shots of Tadzio in the water and of Aschenbach in his chair becomes one of a spectator enthralled by the "screen" in front of him and by the human subject placed within that screen. Even more than Maddalena watching *Red River*, Aschenbach attempts to abolish the gap between the fantasy created by the screen and the reality surrounding it. Daney and Oudart refer to Aschenbach's "psychosis" being one that has "the effect of marking the breakdown of real/fictive element in the narration and the freeing (which derives from it) of a *supplement of the fabric of the film, of images*" (italics in original).[17] But Aschenbach is unable to fully relinquish his status as a creator and is killed by his own need to give aesthetic order to something at once innocent and diabolical, in which Tadzio becomes both the agent of Aschenbach's death and a figure of aesthetic redemption who causes Aschenbach to finally understand his own deeply turbulent impulses.

In his essay on Antonioni, Roland Barthes writes that what all great filmmakers do is "to gaze at things radically, to the point of exhausting them." Such a look is a threat to the very notion of power, since power "never gazes; if it were to gaze a minute more (a minute too long), it would lose its essence as power."[18] For Barthes, Antonioni is a profoundly modern artist, always open to the possibilities of change in the world. Visconti, particularly in his later work, does not cling to these kinds of cautiously utopian ideas. We are reaching the end of something with Visconti, not the present day (although that is implied) but what has given rise to the present day and to the modern, which is to say, for Visconti, both the Romanticism of the nineteenth century and the cinema as a form and technology perpetuating, extending, and questioning various definitions of the modern and romantic. The camera on the beach at the end of *Death in Venice* with its mournful black cloth hanging over it stands in for a look that can look no more. The camera is not pointed at Tadzio or Aschenbach but is clearly pointed left so that we have a type of profile shot of the camera. Nevertheless, Visconti's ties to neorealism (a movement that has both historically and mythically stood in for the beginning of postwar modern cinema) suggest another method of understanding this shot: an image cannot possibly contain all it needs to express about the ineffable reality of the world. That black fabric, in its small movements, hints at a persistence in looking that is beyond the frame, beyond individual agency, and finally beyond the film itself.

Large Patterns

Visconti considerably expands the implications of the camera in Mann as the film repeatedly makes visible both the camera and its photographer. The most important of these is the first beach sequence. Since *Rocco and His Brothers*, Visconti had been shooting his films using two or three cameras running simultaneously. Such multiple camera practices are not necessarily apparent in the earlier films. But by the late 1960s, with the increasingly central function of the zoom, we have an increased sense that the unfolding action is being caught by multiple cameras. In such sequences the camera is, if not everywhere, certainly attempting to fully encompass what it is filming. Throughout neorealism, as we have seen so far in relation to several sequences in Visconti, the act of looking is one in which that look is given an intensity and, with an equal intensity, problematized. The look of the protagonists and the look of the camera continually shift, overlap, become absorbed into larger patterns. Such intensities are, if anything, stronger in a multicamera film like *Death in Venice*. The first beach sequence is a major example of this and, moreover, one in which the placement of fabric within the shots is crucial to the shifting possibilities of looking.

In the opening shot, Aschenbach enters a low-angle frame wearing a straw hat and a white suit, a newspaper and other items under his arm. He pauses and then moves forward as the camera executes a combination of a reverse track and a reverse zoom while panning to the left as it follows Aschenbach's movements over a brown wooden walkway and under the gray-and-white-striped canvas awning that unfolds toward the beach. As the shot opens wide and frames the action close to ground level, Aschenbach quickly passes two women dressed in formal, light-colored summer attire carrying parasols and wearing hats with enormous veils completely covering their faces. As he nears the end of the walkway he is approached by a young man in a dark bathing suit who, in a gesture of respect, takes off his hat and speaks to Aschenbach although what he is saying to him is not clear. Aschenbach follows the man as a dark-uniformed busboy from the hotel quickly enters the frame, carrying a newspaper. In this shot, which moves from a close view to a wide view, from low angle to low level, there are several ideas central to the film. The sense of order created through the brown walkway and the awning leads to a modified vanishing point at the end of this mobile shot. Aschenbach moves from the center of the shot to being one element of many. This method of positioning him seemingly at the center of the spaces while then just as clearly marginalizing him is one the film will never tire of exploring.

The fabric of the awning is not tightly drawn across the walkway but is relatively elastic and repeatedly dips down in a series of curves as it also moves in relation to the wind from the sea. This provides a tension between the rigid walkway and the flexible canvas awning, a tension between order and expressive (possibly untamable) movement. The film will later return to this walkway but shoot it in a very different manner from what we have here, and a very different staging of Aschenbach's desires will occur there. On this first visit, Aschenbach is largely indifferent to the two women he passes, slightly adjusting his body in order to give them a bit more room to pass him. But the veiled woman so central to *Senso* will be equally central to *Death in Venice*, although for different reasons. When the film then moves directly to the beach, we

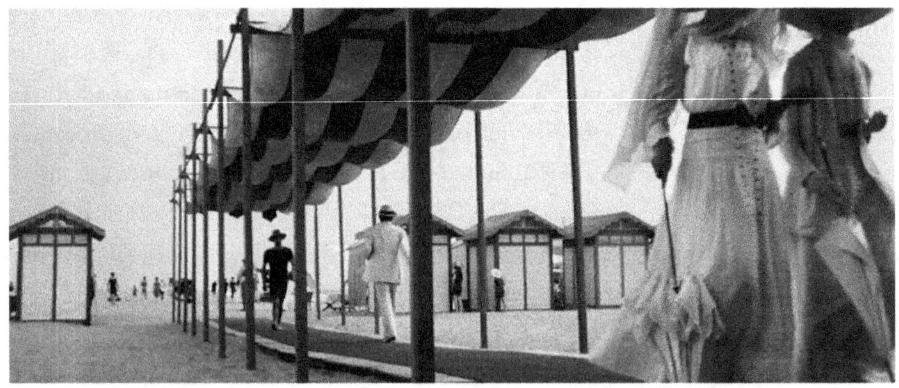

Death in Venice. The entrance to the beach, marked by multiple fabrics.

now clearly see the young man who has just approached Aschenbach. Mann writes of a "barefoot old man in linen pants, sailor shirt, and straw hat" showing Aschenbach to the cabana.[19] But Visconti gives us a young and attractive man in a bathing suit who is soon joined by a similarly attractive man who assists in rolling out the awning and setting up the table and chair for Aschenbach. In *Ludwig*, these kinds of uniformed, working-class male figures will move to the foreground and assume active narrative and sexual functions where their uniforms may come off. On this beach, though, they are like the male servants in *Il lavoro* or *The Damned* with their bright blue uniforms causing them to visually pop in the frame as they move about even as they remain part of the background. In *Death in Venice*, the beach workers are integrated into this mass of carefully directed extras and provide a sense of a frame both realistically detailed and also carefully staged. Neither of these men catches Aschenbach's eye, though, and indeed at no point in the film does Aschenbach show any interest in looking at others, with the exception of Tadzio and, as we shall see, his mother. However, the film at such moments implicitly presents these men for the benefit of a viewer inclined to notice such details.

Throughout this sequence, draping dominates: tents, rugs, blankets, loose-fitting clothing, the veils on the hats of women. All of the fabric creates a sense of abundance for this private beach and also of a sensual femininity, of softness and malleability, but also mobility. Blom has drawn attention to a number of nineteenth- and early-twentieth-century paintings the film (including its beach sequences) drew upon for its visual references.[20] But it draws upon painting in order to demonstrate that the cinema, by virtue of being able to capture movement, completes the project begun in these paintings. The presence of the still photographer here is central not only because, as Blom notes, he marks a passage from the painterly to the photographic. It is also because his presence, in tandem with the ways Visconti's own camera so forcibly makes its presence felt, stands in for the cinema beginning to emerge during the period in which the film is set. It is not just any cinema, though. It is a cinema in which the act of looking, tied to aesthetics and erotics, becomes a structuring element. In this sequence, the still photographer places his camera on its tripod, his head under the black covering, as he takes photos; or he walks about with camera and tripod, as though looking for something else to photograph. Visconti's own camera, though, is moving across and within these spaces in a markedly different manner from that of the photographer. Visconti's camera is panning, zooming, filming the mobility of the human figure, of clothing and décor in a way that a painting can only evoke and a still camera can only freeze in motion. The technical facility of Visconti's camera is also significantly in advance of what a motion picture camera could have accomplished during the period in which the film is set. But if *Death in Venice* is about the expressive power of looking, it is also about a camera's limitations and the limitations of vision in general.

The first appearance of Tadzio on the beach occurs after Aschenbach has settled in to the table in front of his cabana. In a shot taken with a very long lens, Tadzio, first seen at some distance, walks alone, looking about, as the camera pans and slowly zooms closer to him until the boy stops and continues to look around. The convention of this kind of long lens shot implies a character's point of view, and we wait for the reverse angle of Aschenbach looking at the boy. There is, in fact, a cut to Aschenbach immediately following this but he is not looking at the boy. He gives money to the young man who helped him to set up the cabana, as Aschenbach then takes out a cigarette and looks off in what appears to be Tadzio's direction. We cut back to Tadzio in the same camera set-up as the previous shot, the boy now walking over to a group of Russians who are under an enormous tent with the diverse women of the group wearing layers of clothing, a man in a loose beach robe, and a woman in a babushka, as rugs and other drapings surround and are piled up everywhere. Among this group, as we will clearly see later, is a woman who paints (Renata Franceschi). In order to paint she must lift her veil so that her vision is unimpeded. But we never see the painting she is working on. Still photography and the cinema are historically not replacing this gaze but reducing its centrality as a representational art. Tadzio, as though dissatisfied by the spectacle, walks away and toward the camera. As the zoom tightens on him we can begin to make out, at the top of the frame and on its left edge, the awnings that hang in front of the cabanas. Is this the awning to Aschenbach's cabana or simply another one of the many cabanas we have already seen? A cut back to Aschenbach shows him fanning himself with a letter as he looks to his left, probably in the boy's direction. The gesture is almost comic, as though he is fanning himself due to sexual excitement. But the gesture, like so much of what we have seen so far, is ambiguous, as it is not entirely clear if he is seeing Tadzio. He tilts his head to the left and we cut back to the same shot of Tadzio walking forward. But any desire we might have for a confirmation of this being Aschenbach's point of view is further frustrated by the interruption of the sound of offscreen voices calling out Tadzio's name as the boy runs off in the direction of these voices.

As Tadzio and a somewhat older male friend, Jaschu (Sergio Garfagnoli), walk away from the shore, we first see them at the end of a long panning movement. At the end of the pan, a slow reverse zoom shows Tadzio and Jaschu step into the frame, both wearing vertical striped bathing suits, as the frame itself opens out to a wider view of the beach. As Tadzio and Jaschu walk deeper into the space, and if one is vigilant in trying to spot him, Aschenbach is just barely visible in the left center of the frame, writing. A sudden cut to a closer single of him shows him doing a double take as he spots the two boys walking toward him. Fabric is not the only thing that drapes in this film. At the shore, we have already seen Jaschu drape his arm around his friend and, as they walk together toward Aschenbach, Jaschu's arm is around Tadzio as he speaks to him in Polish, leaning in to him in a confidential manner. As they approach the area where Aschenbach is sitting, Jaschu, still with his arm around Tadzio, gives him a kiss. The cut back to Aschenbach shows his reaction: a slight twitch of the mouth, a tightening of his fists as he drops his pen and then nervously places his left hand (wedding ring clearly visible) against his mouth, as though imagining he has been the recipient of a male-to-male kiss. The gesture quickly changes course when he looks around, as if afraid of being noticed. He moves his hand along his cheek and then returns his hand to his lips and chin. But as though in a gesture of contemplation he looks off and the camera slowly zooms into his face, a face attempting to connote its neutrality even as its expression unwittingly reveals his emotional response to what he has just witnessed. Hanging behind him is a green-and-white-striped fabric, marking the entrance to the cabana. This fabric is moving in relation to the wind, a movement realistically situated given the proximity of the cabana to the sea. At the same time, given the immediate dramatic context, the movements acquire an expressive function in relation to Aschenbach's emotional state in seeing the kiss. The fabric behind him does not simply move but, more accurately, flutters.

Looking in this film, then, is the source of an agonizing, an uncertainty. It is tied to something that is, within the historical and cultural context in which the film is set, forbidden, even as the film itself is made during a period of transition in relation to what can or cannot be shown in a film produced and distributed under these conditions. The film enacts and represents both this need to look and the equal need (socially imposed) to look away or to feign indifference, for fear of being caught, of being something looked at. The photographer moving through the beach has no such problems because everything he photographs is socially sanctioned. At the same time, the film situates the photographer in such a way that his look is, in a different way from Aschenbach's, caught up in another set of contingencies.

Our closest view of the photographer directly follows Aschenbach noticing the kiss. The photographer appears at the end of a panning and zooming movement across the Russians, the photographer almost directly facing Visconti's camera as he pulls his head out of the black fabric and begins to take a photo. The camera is not pointed at the Russians, though, but at the sea, and in the next shot Aschenbach is standing near the water but is almost lost in the crowd, placed at the far left of the very wide, distant framing. It is his white suit that causes him to stand out, as does his placement to the far left of the frame, isolating him from the crowd. Through a cut, Visconti's camera moves closer to what the photographer could not capture with his camera on its tripod: the melancholic expression on Aschenbach's face and the look of aimless searching we have seen since the opening sequence. Tadzio is still, at this point in the film, not quite enough, his presence incomplete in relation to Aschenbach's needs. What breaks Aschenbach's melancholia here is the offscreen sound of a woman's voice calling Tadzio's name. That voice, as we are about to see in the next shot, is Tadzio's mother (Silvana Mangano). And Visconti's *Death in Venice* is as much about the desires put into play by Tadzio's mother, in particular by the clothing she wears, as it is about those put into play by Tadzio himself.

Maternal Visions

The first time Tadzio's mother appears is not on the beach but in the lobby of the hotel, on the first night of Aschenbach's stay. Mann writes of the general effect of the attire of the hotel occupants in this lobby: "Evening dress, the universal uniform of cultured society, provided a decorous external unity to the variety of humanity assembled here."[21] In the film, the mother stands apart from the "universal uniform." The film gives her what can only be termed, in theatrical parlance, an entrance as she walks across the lobby and greets her children and their governess (Nora Ricci). Mann describes a woman "dressed in gray and white and richly bejeweled with pearls" where "the cut of her clothes displayed the taste for simplicity favored by those who regard piety as an essential component of good breeding."[22] In the film, the mother is adorned in jewelry but given a pink (possibly silk) gown. The change in color may have reflected little more than choosing a color that would look flattering on Mangano and stand out in this mobile shot. But several other aspects of her entrance are worth noting.

It is in this lobby where Aschenbach first spots Tadzio. From Mann's description it is the collective sound of Polish being spoken that draws Aschenbach's attention to what will turn out to be Tadzio sitting in the lobby with his sisters and governess. Aschenbach sees the outfits on the sisters being "disfiguringly chaste and austere," the specific outline of their figures "suppressed and obscured by their uniformly habit-like half-length dresses, sober and slate-gray in color, tailored as if deliberately unflattering, relieved by no decoration save white, turned-down collars." Tadzio, by contrast, is dominated by a soft, almost feminine appearance, with his flowing hair and a sailor suit that "made his slim figure seem somehow opulent and pampered with all its decoration, its bow, braidwork, and embroidery."[23] The film essentially cuts and distributes Aschenbach's act of looking and listening into three separate moments. The final look, ostensibly tied to Aschenbach, zooms back from a close-up on Tadzio to showing the entirety of what he is wearing: a white sailor's suit with blue trimming, in contrast to the dark blue drabness of his sisters and governess. His sisters, largely confirming Mann's prose, are austerely dressed so that Tadzio is the most eroticized figure in the group, with his eroticizing tied to his androgyny. But the zoom continues beyond this reveal to include Aschenbach in the foreground, a spectator of the very spectacle he himself has partly initiated.

And it is here where the mother makes her entrance, at first not even noticed by Aschenbach. In a film so otherwise dominated by the zoom, the camera dollies in response to the mother, the camera moving across the lobby toward her as a slight push on the zoom eventually permits a closer view. Moreover, once Aschenbach notices her he turns his head and follows her movements as she walks over to her children and the governess, all of them standing as she formally greets them. Given the spectacular nature of the mother's entrance, it is as though Aschenbach's look at the boy is not complete until the mother arrives. This idea is repeated when she makes her entrance on the beach, where her voice causes Aschenbach to notice her. The next shot, however, as she arrives waving at Tadzio and calling out his name, is not his point of view. The governess walks alongside her, a white towel open and waiting for Tadzio. Like the women Aschenbach passes on the walkway to the beach, the mother is dressed from head to toe in oatmeal-colored linen attire, with gloves, holding a parasol and wearing a hat and heavy veil. She and the governess are walking forward in the shot but the governess soon walks ahead of her and disappears as the camera slowly zooms into the mother, isolating her from the surrounding environment. Aschenbach looks over at her but then quickly looks away, as though imagining he might be caught staring. But his look away could just as easily be directed toward what is in the next shot, Tadzio running out of the water, although, again, the camera setup does not logically follow Aschenbach's point of view. Tadzio runs into the waiting towel being held by the governess as she dries him off and he turns his head to his right, as though looking for someone: Aschenbach? Cut back to Aschenbach, the slight movements of his head indicating an intent look at something. The next shot is of Tadzio being reunited with his mother, her parasol now closed, as he begs her for strawberries being sold by a man who is now in the frame. The mother refuses and an unintimidated Tadzio grabs a strawberry out of the basket, prompting the governess to playfully chase him as the mother laughs at the escapade. As this action comes to a close, out of nowhere the photographer slowly walks in the foreground of the frame, moving from right to left, the camera, tripod, and black fabric on his shoulder, before walking out of the shot, shaking his head. The mother, not taking any notice of the photographer, adjusts her veil and tells her daughter it is best for all of them to return to the hotel. But the photographer does not point his camera in the direction of this family. It is as though the film reserves its right to have unmediated access to them.

The film's investment in the glamorous appearance of the mother exceeds the descriptions of the mother in Mann. The mothers addressed so far in this book are essentially figures in black, highly individualized forces of nature whose energies are directed beyond the domestic sphere, staging dramas of their own making. The mentally unstable mother in *Vaghe stelle dell'Orsa* is initially shown in a white chiffon gown but, in the final sequence, she, too, must be in the color of mourning. The Princess in *The Leopard*, on the other hand, is (like the mother in *La terra trema*) an almost recessive figure, her body covered in layers of fabric, even when shown in bed with her husband. The mother in *Death in Venice* is something of an anomaly and contrasts as well with the mothers in *The Damned* and *Ludwig*. Sophie in *The Damned* and Marie of Prussia (Izabella Teleżyńska) in *Ludwig* are, in their relationships with their respective sons, antitheses. Sophie is dressed in chic early 1930s outfits, the cut of them (typical of the period) close to her body, accentuating lines and exposing cleavage. Sophie also receives her moment in black, during the funeral procession for Joachim, in which she wears an ornate outfit with a full-length veil, an absurd performance of mourning over a man whom she has conspired to murder. Marie, on the other hand, engenders revulsion on the part of her sons, both of whom explicitly reject her embrace, and the film's most indelible image of her shows her alone in an enormous bed propped up on large white pillows as she greets Ludwig and congratulates him on the news of his impending marriage to his cousin Sophie (Sonia Petrovna), a marriage that would continue the royal lineage but would also continue the pattern of incestuous relations. These two extreme visions of the mother are counterbalanced by the mother in *Death in Venice* but the three women are closer to one another than they might initially appear.

Some of the intensity with which the mother in *Death in Venice* is presented is traceable to Mangano's star presence, to associations she brought with her, in particular the degree to which she had historically been cast in roles at once mythic and maternal. (The same year in which she played Tadzio's mother she appeared as the Madonna in *The Decameron*.) In *Ulysses* (Mario Camerini, 1954), a film version of Homer's *The Odyssey*, she enacts a dual role of the witch Circe and the faithful wife Penelope, and the two women are dialectically linked with one another not only through physical resemblance but also through their respective acts of weaving. As the mother of Tadzio, Mangano plays another heavily veiled character and one that again imparts to her a mythic and maternal power. *Death in Venice* is a film not only about death but also about the potential for rebirth, and Aschenbach projects himself onto Tadzio, becoming the idealized son for an idealized mother. The voice of the mother forms a type of audio umbilical cord effectively shared by Tadzio and Aschenbach, and the connection achieves its maximum force when it is heard by Aschenbach at the sea. In relation to the voice of the mother in *Sansho the Bailiff* (Kenji Mizoguchi, 1954), Michel Chion writes of how that film's mother, brutally separated from her two children, is miraculously heard by them through a voice that "becomes autonomous, lives a life of its own."[24] Such suspended female voices evoke the mythical figure of the siren, a voice tied to the border between land and sea.[25] In *Death in Venice*, the mother is also poised on that border, as is her son. The film gives her Polish dialogue, barely audible, in which virtually everything she says expresses concern for the health of her children.[26]

In the second beach sequence, there is a remarkable shot of her in a wicker chair, under a canvas awning, reading a book. In a wide shot, Aschenbach passes her but only slightly looks in her direction before there is a cut to a closer view, not from his perspective. She is elaborately dressed, wearing a large summer hat with flowers on top of her head and a veil that comes down over her hair and flows all the way behind her. She sits at a cloth-covered table as various towels and other items are draped on chairs or hang on poles around her. She looks up from her book and off at something, presumably her children in the water, before resuming her reading. The shot isolates her, with no children or governess surrounding her, although everywhere in the shot, through the fabrics, there are indexical signs of their presence. This contrasts with the shot of Aschenbach at the beginning of the film. He also has a book on his lap but is unable to concentrate as he sits bundled up in heavy clothing whereas the mother here calmly alternates between keeping a watchful eye on her children and concentrating on her book.

In neither Mann nor Visconti is there a reference to Tadzio's father, leaving the mother available for Aschenbach's projections. In the first hotel lobby sequence,

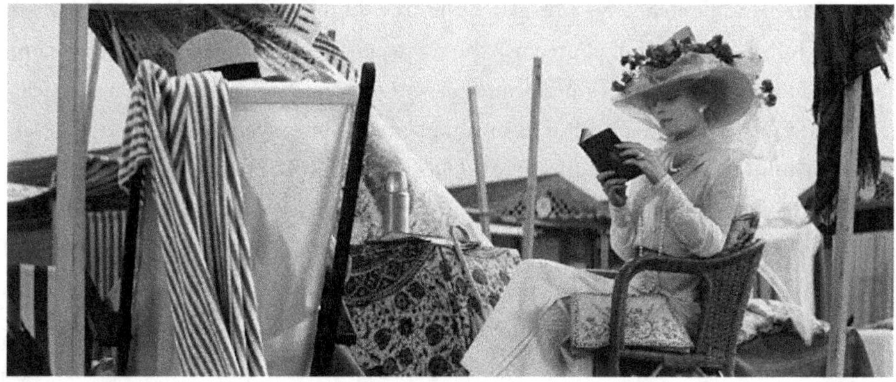

Death in Venice. The idealized mother, surrounded by fabric.

among the musical pieces the orchestra plays are themes from Franz Lehár's operetta *The Merry Widow* (1905), a text not referred to in the Mann and which creates at least the possibility that the mother is without a husband. The mother in this shot on the beach becomes not simply an idealized image but an implicitly oedipal one in which the father has been eliminated and the "son" (Tadzio, Aschenbach, the camera) has the mother all to himself and in which the flowing fabrics surrounding her become central to this idealization, fetishes for the maternal body. In *Edipo Re* Mangano, as in *Ulysses*, enacts a dual role, playing the mother in the prologue and then Jocasta in the central portion of the film, the latter unaware that the man she has married is, of course, her own son, her eventual knowledge of this causing her to hang herself with a red scarf. In *Doctor Faustus*, there is only one woman who is able to seriously tempt Adrian Levurkühn into the possibility of marriage, the designer Marie Godeau, who has an "expertise in costume history" and who is meticulously described in terms of the relationship between what she wears, the black of her expressive eyes, and the "warm, winning timbre" of her voice evoking the voice of Leverkühn's mother.[27] An absolute vision of the mother becomes one in which she is draped in fabric, the maternal manifested in both voice and wardrobe.

Child Labor

Düttmann has argued that children in Visconti most often function as "pure witnesses with no ulterior motive and no real function in the plot."[28] The witnessing child recurs in neorealism, as does a related function of the child as victim of the very events and social conditions it witnesses. The boys who commit suicide in *Germany, Year Zero* and Rossellini's *Europa '51* (1951) are major examples of this, as is Maria in *Bellissima*, although her fate is ultimately played out in a comic and lyrical vein. But childhood is also an ideal (hence impossible) state in Visconti, and the potentialities of this are present in his adult characters who evoke children. In the opening sequence of *Ludwig*, Father Hoffman (Gert Fröbe) prepares the eighteen-year-old Ludwig for his forthcoming coronation, and Berger's performance, with disheveled, curled hair and quickly batting eyelids combined with framings that make him seem small, suggests a child inadequate to the task before him. Hoffman's admonition of humility in leadership is reinterpreted by Ludwig as a justification for opening his kingdom to the artists for whom he hopes to build monuments. The final shot of the sequence is a wide one of the room, Ludwig and Hoffman jammed into a corner as the camera pans to Ludwig's bed, the pillows and bedding scattered, until the camera eventually tilts up into the darkness. This is the first of film's many beds, and in this sequence the bed becomes an image of childlike disorder while also foreshadowing the various other disorders (historical, political, sexual, psychological) to come and, often in response to these disorders, the frequent need of the characters to retreat to their beds.

Contrast this with the opening of Eisenstein's *Ivan the Terrible* (1944/1958). Ivan (Nikolay Cherkasov, an actor at one point considered for the role of the Prince in *The Leopard*), although in reality seventeen years old at the time of his own coronation, is not, in Eisenstein's film, given the appearance of a child. Instead we see a cunning, alert individual fully in a position to confront the challenges facing him from the Boyars. All of this is sharply laid out through the mise en scène, framing, and montage and focused on what Yuri Tsivian has referred to as a coronation's two principal rituals, robing and gilding.[29] The coronation in *Ludwig* is the film's second sequence, and all of the women of the court wear matching red coronation robes. Unlike the opening of *Ivan the Terrible*, the formal construction of the sequence is handled in a slow, almost de-dramatized manner, closer to Rossellini's *The Taking of Power by Louis XIV* (1966) than to *Senso* or *The Leopard*. As the personages involved in the ceremony arrive and greet one another, Visconti's use of long lenses, with much of the action framed from the waist or neck up, creates both distance and intimacy. In one shot the camera is at low level as it films the backs of the women. This framing draws attention to how their red coronation robes hang down and drape over the red carpeting. When the women are filmed in this way, their faces hidden or obscured, they merge into a grandiose ceremonial female image, almost immobile, as the eyes of the spectator are fixated on the robes. This is immediately followed by a close shot of the crown that will be placed on Ludwig's head, the crown sitting on a red cushion that matches the robes of the women, as the camera pans from the crown to an enormous red hem that initially looks as though it could be the hem of another red ceremonial robe. As the camera tilts, though, we see that this robe is being held by two young male attendants, in blue-and-white uniforms, as Ludwig and his entourage, behind the two attendants, step into the room. The robe is placed on Ludwig's back as other final touches are applied to his regalia. In the reverse-angle cutting that then briefly ensues, Ludwig is positioned from the front, where white and blue (the colors of the Bavarian flag) dominate the frame; when cutting to him from behind, red and white dominate. Ludwig is now king but, in terms of color and fabric, he is aligned with the women more than the men, as the cross-cutting in color values implies Ludwig's own ambivalence over what he is about to undertake. Ludwig is not interested in masculine values of aggression and conquest but another kind of conquest, a more feminine one of colonizing and cultivating artists, with Wagner to assume a central position.

One of the curiosities of the film is that it does not explore homoerotic implications in the relationship between Wagner and Ludwig. Helmut Käutner's *Ludwig II: Glanz und Ende eines Königs* (1956), while produced and exhibited under far more restrictive circumstances, goes further than Visconti in this regard. Wagner in the Visconti is more of a father figure, replacing Hoffman as a male authority in Ludwig's life. The great consummated love story of *Ludwig* is the one between Wagner and Cosima von Bülow, where Mangano, as Cosima, again functions as a mother. In the first sequence of the film, in which both Wagner and Cosima appear, the latter still married to Hans von Bülow (Mark Burns), she has no dialogue but is an observer of the exchanges between her lover and her husband. Cosima is either in close-up or filmed in a strikingly composed image sitting on a couch. Her brown-and-white-striped gown is spread out over this couch, with paintings on the wall behind her, and on each side of the Panavision frame there is a drawing of a set design for Wagner's operas, turning Cosima into an objet d'art. At the end of the sequence, in a long, panning shot, Cosima and Wagner ascend a flight of stairs as the train of her gown drags along the steps. As the panning unfolds it reveals that the stairs have gold draping along the bannister, all the way to the top and across the railing on the second floor. The couple is ascending to a magic kingdom worthy of Wagner's own operas. As they step into another space after they reach the second floor landing, Cosima utters her first words: "A child will soon be here." It is as though the mother from *Death in Venice* has migrated to this film and has now become Cosima, even as our own historical awareness of the biographies of Cosima and Richard Wagner provides a counterweight to the romanticism of the moment.

Tsivian has written on bisexuality in relation to *Ivan the Terrible*, where it functions less as an attempt to directly dramatize the ruler's real-life bisexual nature (an impossibility given the historical and cultural context) than as a matter of aesthetic form, in particular its effect on dialectical structure and montage. Eisenstein's fascination with doubling is also tied to this interest in bisexuality, and in *Ivan the Terrible* the individuals surrounding Ivan are partial doubles of Ivan, "facets of his contradictory self."[30] While Visconti is not attracted to the problems faced by the dialectics of ecstatic conflict, the possibilities of an unstable identity and image (sexual and otherwise), central to his cinema from the very beginning, increasingly preoccupy him. Moreover, if in *Ivan the Terrible* Eisenstein's characters are conceived of as doubles of Ivan's contradictory self, in Visconti's later work the characters are less doubles of one another than they are constantly shifting signifiers in terms of sexuality, gender, and power where the links between children and adults are central.

The first sequence in *Ludwig* between Elisabeth and Ludwig clearly lays out his attraction for her as one in which she functions as a female version of himself. In one early shot, as they sit and face one another and Ludwig removes his fur coat, they are wearing almost identical outfits (hers for the purposes of horseback riding) with matching black hats, her veil being the feature most strongly differentiating what each is wearing. But the attraction he has for her is also tied to their childhoods together, with the opening movements of Robert Schumann's *Scenes from Childhood* (1838) accompanying this sequence pointing toward Ludwig's impossible desire to return to these "scenes," prior to the onset of adult sexuality. During their second sequence, Ludwig nudges Elisabeth into remembering a signal he would send to her, in which he would fly the Bavarian flag high on the Isle of Roses. The flag in *Ludwig* has none of the nationalist implications of the Italian flags in *Senso* or *The Leopard*, or the Nazi flags and banners in *The Damned*, but is instead tied almost entirely to the personal and the sexual. The flag is later shown ascending and then fluttering in the wind as Elisabeth arrives at Ludwig's home on the island but it is also in this sequence that Elisabeth most forcefully attempts to break the spell Wagner has over Ludwig, a spell that is, in turn, tied to Ludwig's own romantic delusions, including a delusion about enjoying any heterosexual relation with his married cousin. The first major task Ludwig will later give to an attractive servant, Richard Hornig (Marc Porel), who serves as Volk's replacement, is for Hornig to hoist the flag. Ludwig assists him, jerking at the flag as it briefly fills the frame before ascending.

Elisabeth's sister Sophie becomes the unfortunate victim in the impossible love story. The sequence in which Sophie speaks of Ludwig's inability to express anything resembling love for her is a tour de force of blocking and framing. The women appear to be doubled in one shot, both briefly filmed from behind, Sophie on her bed, Elisabeth at the dressing table, with their extremely long hair hanging down and matching one another. Their hair is so long and voluminous it becomes de facto fabric. But the possibility of Elisabeth and Sophie being doubled through their hair is interrupted by Elisabeth. Elisabeth wants to break away from a possible link with her passive sister (the stiffness of the green-and-white drapings over Sophie's bed serves as a corollary of her sexual inexperience) as Elisabeth begins to pace about the room in her elaborate white nightgown, its train dragging along the floor. She walks over to a heavily curtained window and faces it as Sophie tearfully describes her situation, culminating with her accusation that Ludwig and Elisabeth are in love with one another. She receives a slap in the face for this and Elisabeth's prompt contrition. But as her dialogue in the first sequence in the film between Elisabeth and Ludwig has made clear and as she reiterates here, she sees herself in Ludwig, even as she also regards him as still a child. As she attempts to reassure Sophie, there is a cut to the train of her gown with her hair hanging down over much of it as the camera slowly tilts up and finds the two women facing one another. The shot is an echo of the one of the train of Ludwig's coronation robe but with the elaborate hair of the female monarch becoming of a piece with the fabric of her nightgown. Here we move from the public costume of the coronation robe to the private wardrobe of the bedroom, to female attire, and to things that flow. At the first meeting between Ludwig and Horning, as Hornig lights the fire, Ludwig watches while partially covering his face with his black leather gloves as he instructs Hornig to take off his own gloves. Hornig does so but also removes the cap of his uniform, revealing the long hair hiding underneath it, as he seductively tosses his head back and displays this hair for Ludwig. Like Aschenbach on the beach, Ludwig watches the male object of desire while partly masking or veiling that look upon the forbidden. At the same time, this gesture evokes the black-gloved gesture of Sandra's mother at the funeral in *Vaghe stelle dell'orsa* when she, too, has to look at something that is too much to bear, the gesture of a mother from one film migrating to the gesture of a "child" from another.

In *The Damned*, both Martin von Essenbeck (Berger) and his uncle Konstantin von Essenbeck (Reinhard Kolldehoff) partly function as children, with Konstantin equally functioning as an unsympathetic father to cello-playing son Günther (Renaud Verley), whose sensitivity, according to Konstantin, is entirely traceable to the young man's now-deceased mother. If the mother in *Death in Venice* functions as a symbolic merry widow, Konstantin is a literal merry widower, away from the oppressive nature of his wife's feminine sensitivity, his newly found freedom now manifested through his role as a SA officer. The SA creates for Konstantin a framework within which his same-sex desires are enacted. But in the opening sequence of the film he remains the son of Joachim, as the elderly patriarch continues to sit at the head of the dinner table and make the final decisions in relation to the steelworks, until the end of the sequence, when Joachim ultimately decides to promote Konstantin.

The ambivalence that dominates Visconti reaches one of its apotheoses in the Night of the Long Knives sequence, in which Konstantin is killed. The relationship of the sequence to historical reality is, at best, tenuous, but it is after something other than precise recreation. The sequence has interesting parallels with (and deviations from) the Dance of the Oprichniki from *Ivan the Terrible*, both centered on all-male bacchanals arising in the midst of moments of political frenzy. In Eisenstein's film, only one person is killed, the infantile Vladimir of Staritsa (Pavel Kadochnikov), who is also Ivan's primary challenger to the throne. Vladimir's desire for this throne is nonexistent and he is entirely being masterminded by his ruthless mother, Efrosinia (Serafima Berma). This relationship is loosely paralleled in *The Damned* between the initially apolitical Martin and his ambitious mother, Sophie. Joan Neuberger has written on how the *oprichniki* in *Ivan* emerge out of the tradition of the *radenie*, which was "intended to produce a state of spiritual and sexual ecstasy in believers." Historically it had been an "all-male gathering of subversive, religious heretics whose swirling dances were assumed to end in all-male orgies." Reportedly central to Joseph Stalin's anger in looking at the second part of Eisenstein's film was this dance, an anger "triggered by [its] subversive, homosexual innuendo."[31] In *The Damned*, Nazi flags dominate the bacchanal and the Nazi anthem where the "Horst Wessel Song" is performed, with its opening lyrics instructing Nazis to raise the flag high. The gathering of SA officers begins largely as an all-male romp, including many of the younger officers running nude into the lake. Eisenstein has no such luxury as male nudity available to him in order to evoke "homosexual innuendo." Instead, he creates feverish images of his male environment through a montage of swirling fabric. He describes how "the black of the cassocks first engulfed the gold of the robes of the *oprichniki*; then *oprichniki* in their black robes covered the gold of Vladimir's mantle; and finally the whole mass of black *oprichniki* swamped the inside of the cathedral."[32] No women are present in the sequence until the end, when Efrosinia, shrouded in black as usual, enters and discovers her son's dead body. In the bacchanal from *The Damned*, some women are present but they appear to be bar maids. While they participate in the drunken revels, their most important function is related to their clothing, which gradually migrates from being worn by the women to being worn by the men. In the *oprichniki* from *Ivan the Terrible*, it is Fyodor Basmanov (Mikhail Kuztnezov) who assumes the female role in the dance, wearing a *sarafan* and periodically holding up a female mask as he sings. The mask is intended to evoke Ivan's first wife, the murdered Anastasia. (Fyodor is the son of one of Ivan's most trusted lieutenants and he was reportedly one of the czar's lovers although the film goes no further than dramatizing an extreme case of hero worship.)

What is particularly striking about this sequence from *The Damned*, so famed for its decadence, is the childlike behavior of the men, gay sons dressing up in Mommy's outfits, a world of homosexual anarchy. During the 1930s, Visconti reportedly admired *Triumph of the Will* (Leni Riefenstahl, 1934),[33] a film that went into production not long after the actual Night of the Long Knives. Riefenstahl devotes one sequence to a Hitler youth camp, canvas tents lined up everywhere, in which shirtless men help one another to bathe, shave, comb hair; they cook and eat together and playfully box and roughhouse. If for *The Man with the Movie Camera* the Soviet Union is largely built on the collective energies of weaving women, *Triumph of the Will* creates another kind of energy, entirely male, homosocial, and homoerotic. As with the *oprichniki* from *Ivan the Terrible*, Riefenstahl's sequence has striking parallels with the bacchanal in *The Damned*, and culturally and historically it is, of course, much closer to it than what is found in *Ivan*. But Visconti not only makes overt the repressed homosexual aspects to what Riefenstahl films, he introduces women's garments into this all-male paradise. In *Ivan the Terrible*, the culminating act of Vladimir's murder emerges from within the bacchanal, a cunningly staged maneuver on the part of Ivan to eliminate his rival. Ultimately, there is nothing utopic about the sequence. In *The Damned*, the violence unleashed is external to the SA paradise, with the arrival of the SS also involving "adults" triumphing over "children." That the children are also Nazis compounds the ambivalent attractions of this world.

The first SA soldier to hear the arrival of the SS, as he stands on the hotel terrace in the early morning hours, is shirtless, wearing a woman's black panties with black hose and garters. The outfit evokes what Martin wears the first time he is shown in the film, on a stage in the Essenbeck mansion. There he is performing a song of Marlene Dietrich's from *The Blue Angel* (Josef von Sternberg, 1930), "Kinder, heut' abend, da such' ich mir was aus" ("A Man, Just a Regular Man") and is wearing an outfit loosely approximating Dietrich's signature look. In *Ivan the Terrible*, Vladimir wears a woman's outfit. But his mannerisms are not markedly effeminate and his body is completely covered, whereas Martin's female attire exposes androgynous male flesh emerging through the gaps. His gestures and mannerisms and his somewhat lisping, thin voice, combined with our first view of him in drag performing a song by a queer icon like Dietrich, all give the appearance of homosexuality. But Martin's gayness will be refused by the film, as though it is *only* an appearance, and it will be the aggressively masculine Konstantin who engages in sex with men.

Martin's link to childhood is further inscribed by his molestation, dramatized twice in the film, of little girls: Thilde (Karin Mittendorf), the daughter of Martin's cousin Herbert Thallman (Umberto Orsini), and Lisa Keller (Irina Wanka), who lives in an apartment next to the one occupied by Martin's girlfriend, Olga (Florinda Bolkan). In both instances, the molestation also becomes political metaphor, fabric integrated into the nature of what is shown and not shown. In the case of Thilde, a thick cloth hangs over the table under which the molestation occurs. The act itself is not directly represented but implied through a confused set of ellipses and reactions (the sound of a screaming governess, the grandfather in bed looking disturbed by this sound, then a zoom into a close-up of Martin, presumably still under the table). What is ultimately important with Thilde is that Martin has molested the daughter of a vociferous opponent of National Socialism, a member of the family who has also been employed by the steelworks, even though Martin at this point has no political interests. The handling of the Keller molestation is more detailed and prolonged.

It has often been noted that Keller's molestation is based on a suppressed chapter from Dostoevsky's *Demons* in which the wealthy Nikolai Stavrogin admits to having seduced a working-class girl of somewhat indeterminate age, Matryosha.[34] Lisa is a tiny, wide-eyed witness to and participant in her own demise, her status as witness intensified through the absence of dialogue given to her. The only sounds she makes are screams. In *Demons*, as in *The Damned*, the girl's response to the actions of her assailant is suicide. In *Demons*, the suicide is tied to a Christian sense of guilt. The agonies connected to Lisa's death are not of the same order since Lisa is Jewish. Visconti retains an idea from Dostoevsky of the girl's mother being a seamstress. A model's dummy with measuring tape is in the middle rear of the apartment and a sewing machine is by the window, fabric draped over it. But the mother is, as in Dostoevsky, abusive so that this domestic space in which female labor is tied to fabric is also the site of oppression for the child. On Martin's first visit to the apartment, as soon as he hears the mother's voice offscreen, he runs back to the safety of Olga's apartment, this voice the antithesis of the voice of Tadzio's mother. (In fact, we never see Lisa's mother.) After he flees to Olga's apartment, the voice of Lisa's mother is heard through the walls, yelling at her daughter, causing Martin to panic and, as with Rocco, Gino, and Aschenbach, anxiety causes him to pull at his collar. When Martin first visits Lisa she is doing needlepoint on a piece of red cloth, and a little boy, presumably her brother, sits on a bed observing what threatens to unfold but this encounter is abruptly terminated by Lisa's refusal (she moves away from him and stands in a corner with her back to him) and by the subsequent arrival of her mother. It is when Lisa is later in Olga's apartment, sweeping the floor, that the molestation occurs. The act itself is not directly represented, but her happy reciprocity in the face of his performance of tenderness and generosity (he gives her a pearl necklace) is groundwork for her subsequent guilt-induced illness.

When Martin visits Lisa in her sickbed, she is in an opposite state to Maria, peacefully sleeping in the final shot of *Bellissima*. The sheer size of Lisa's bedding causes her to look very small, almost like an Edward Gorey figure, her head sunk into two large pillows, a white sheet pulled up to her chin. The red fabric she had been working on earlier now migrates to her bright red blanket and the red scarf hanging over the lamp on the wall. He touches her through the blanket and sheet and while the gesture is, at this moment, most likely tied to his concern for her health, she rises from the bed and in a repeat of their initial encounter she walks across the room and faces the wall while also turning around to him and nodding her head. A strange cut follows, one that initially appears to be a reverse angle of him sitting on her bed but which, we quickly ascertain, is the bed in Olga's apartment. Behind him, through the open door, is Lisa, gray knitted scarf around her neck, walking up a flight of stairs. This is interrupted by a brief sequence of Günther escorting Elisabeth Thallman (Charlotte Rampling), her daughters, and their governess to a train station, all of them under the delusion the Thallmans are to be reunited with Herbert when, in fact, they are, we will soon discover, being taken to Dachau. When we cut back to Lisa, all that is visible are her bare legs and feet and her gray scarf dangling: she has hanged herself with the knitted scarf. The girl's response to the molestation by becoming ill and then committing suicide are all in *Demons*. But changing her identity to a German Jewish child in 1933 considerably shifts the implications. The silent Lisa's guilt is also a question of her own status as a Jew involved in a "perverse" situation with a German. Visconti takes the basic idea from Dostoevsky of the mother's profession as seamstress and builds upon this larger ideas about fabric that are, in turn, tied to guilt, molestation, and complicity. And whereas Matryosha hanging herself is not described at length, in *The Damned* we not only see the bottom half of Lisa's dead body hanging but she has, like Jocasta, hanged herself with her own scarf, with the hanging occurring in a space of hiding and refuge, the attic. Fabric and sewing, traditionally linked to the maternal and the feminine, to female labor, even to the possible creation of new worlds, are now linked with murder and suicide. Things can no longer be stitched together.

Bringing Down the Curtain

No less than *Death in Venice* or *Ludwig*, *The Damned* is about a battle over culture, in particular cultural forms of their German Romantic and post-Romantic incarnations. This has often been noted in the literature on *The Damned*, and indeed the film's awareness of the history of these forms is persistent. In the same sequence in which Martin performs the Dietrich song, Günther performs a Bach cello sonata as his father looks bored by the display of somber high German culture, one undoubtedly linked in his mind, as virtually everything is in terms of his son, with the feminine. It is Wagner, *the* central great artist to be embraced and partially co-opted by the Nazis, that Konstantin is later heard singing in the film. He sings the "Liebstod" from *Tristan und Isolde* (1859) at the SA bacchanal, the film attempting not simply ironic contrast but also a foregrounding of the sexual ambiguities at work in much of Wagner. Martin's emergence on the same stage in drag directly following Günther's recital was clearly designed by Martin to be a provocation to the traditional values of the Essenebecks. But the reference to *The Blue Angel* does not involve a simple contrast between the high art of the Bach cello piece and the popular music of the Dietrich film.

The Blue Angel is a major product of the late Weimar period and as such would be antithetical to the cultural values of National Socialism. Blom has offered a detailed analysis of the use of mirrors in *The Blue Angel* and of their possible influence on Visconti in general.[35] Without going so far as to point to any direct influence, Sternberg's use of fabric in the film offers additional insight. For example, there is the manner with which Professor Rath (Emil Jannings) employs his handkerchief. Rath is meticulous with his students but surrounds himself with filth and disorder. He carefully uses his handkerchief in the classroom, pulling it out of his jacket pocket in order to blow his nose while also using it to clean his glasses, the same fabric tied to covering up germs and to spreading them around. In *Death in Venice*, as Aschenbach is in his hotel room putting the final touches to his formal dinner attire he flourishes a white handkerchief and then puts it in his lapel before going downstairs, where he will see Tadzio for the first time. In *The Damned*, just as Herbert and Elizabeth are about to leave their rooms in the mansion for the dinner downstairs, a servant hands Herbert a folded white handkerchief. Herbert performs a flourishing gesture as he puts it in his pocket, slightly delaying his exit from the room and causing Elizabeth to turn around and tell him to hurry. It is at this dinner where Joachim will make the decision to remove Herbert from the steelworks. When Ludwig's teeth begin to rot, he takes to his bed due to the pain, two thirds of his face covered in a white bandage, leaving only one eye visible, as he also holds a large white handkerchief against his face. When he gets out of bed, in anger he pulls the white bandage off as he paces about and shouts, now using a more decorative red scarf to cover the side of his face swollen from pain. *The Blue Angel*, *The Damned*, *Death in Venice*, and *Ludwig* are narratives of degradation and death for their male protagonists, their use of white handkerchiefs the final, desperate flourish of their ties to a world slipping away from them. When Rath steps into the Blue Angel nightclub where the singer Lola (Dietrich) performs, he gets entangled in the nets hanging near the entrance that are part of the seafaring decor of the club. The film will use fabric as part of a pattern of Rath's degradation in the midst of the temporary satisfactions of his affair and subsequent marriage to Lola, and her ruffled panties (an item of exchange backstage during his first visit to Lola's dressing room) will become central in magnetically drawing Rath to her. Lola has a total command of fabric, later confidently wrapping her nude body around a curtain in her dressing room as she gives orders to a degraded Rath.

Behind Martin on the Essenbeck stage hangs a white sheet with multicolored lights projected onto it. A white sheet will soon be used prominently again, after Joachim is shot in his bed later that evening, as the sheet is used in order to wrap his corpse. But before it is wrapped around Joachim, the sheet is briefly stretched out and held up by the police, linking this sheet with the one on the stage where Martin's performance was a source of such disgust for the grandfather. We also may be reminded here of the white tablecloth at the picnic in *The Leopard* where the whiteness and scale of that tablecloth was the sign of potentialities. The sheet is the site of potentialities in *The*

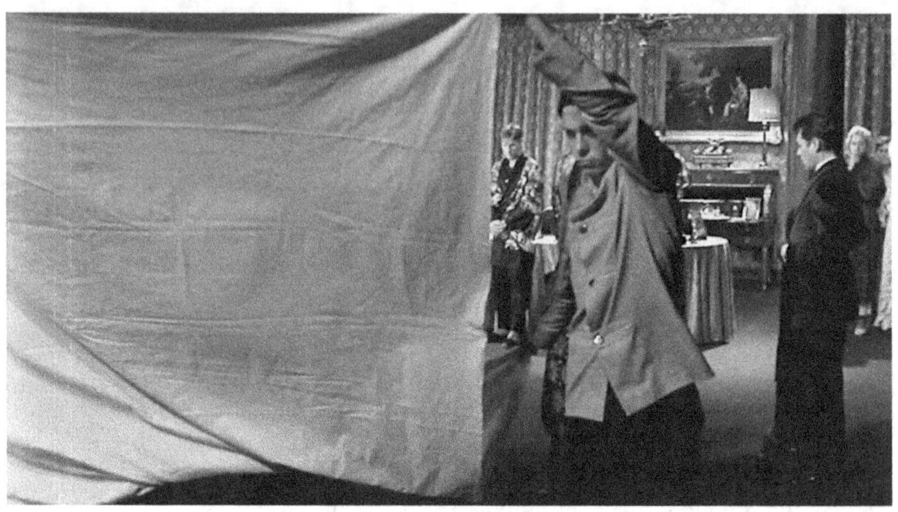

The Damned (1969). The white sheet as site of fascist negation.

Damned as well, but those are now aligned with death, whiteness as negation, the beginning of Nazism.

The conversation among the family members that soon follows the discovery of Joachim's body takes place in front of the stage where the white sheet still hangs, the sheet now bathed in a red light. It is here we have the first extended sequence devoted to Martin's legal power as heir in relation to the steelworks, making him a desirable figure for his mother, Friedrich, Konstantin, and Aschenbach, all of whom wish to court his favor. As Martin fumblingly begins to realize the extent of his power, he is standing in front of the white sheet and the brown stage curtain as though this stage represents the next step in the unfolding drama. Daney and Oudart have referred to the film's SS officer Aschenbach (Helmut Griem) as "the mythical Nazi, a lever who is omnipresent and ideally castrated, with no erotic interests."[36] If Nazism is to be understood as a form of political theater, an elaborate mise-en-scène (with *Triumph of the Will* as the ultimate cinematic record of this), Aschenbach's power is tied to his status as the actual *metteur en scène* of the unfolding spectacle in *The Damned*. He has no desires because, like Mephistopheles, he establishes himself as a figure beyond such desires, all the better to manipulate those of others. But his triumph does not manifest itself before he is challenged by other figures who likewise wish to engage in this political aestheticism, principally Sophie and Friedrich, the Macbeth and Lady Macbeth of the film.

"As an image of a man," Eisenstein writes, "Macbeth is almost inseparable from Lady Macbeth, because both are mutually dependent on a complex of circumstances."[37] Eisenstein's reading of *Macbeth* is of a piece with his interest in bisexuality. Macbeth and Lady Macbeth do not embody fixed states of masculine and feminine but exchange such states in relation to what is otherwise clearly a patriarchal, militaristic order. Friedrich remains, throughout *The Damned*, the weaker of the two figures but Sophie, as a woman, cannot assume such power alone and must continually prod her lover into carrying out specific actions, such as murdering Joachim or collaborating with Aschenbach in the elimination of Konstantin. Unlike Friedrich, Sophie has a vision and it must come to life at the expense of male figures whose weaknesses she can control. "Every symbol in *Macbeth* turns out to be something real," Eisenstein writes.[38] The same argument cannot be made for *The Damned*, in which the symbols and the metaphors are rendered with such an intensity that the real and the historical become subsumed into them. What finally eludes Sophie's control is an oedipal scenario, engendered by Aschenbach and played out with Friedrich as the substitute for Martin's biological father. (Sophie is another merry widow but her relationship with Friedrich compromises her status within the symbolic logic of the film.) Martin's rape of his mother is a "perversion" of this scenario where the son does not desire the mother so much as the mother desires the son, a realization on Martin's part brought about by Aschenbach. But the rape occurs because Aschenbach turns Martin's love for his mother into hate. Visconti's world of dressing and undressing reaches its limit point and ultimate state of inversion when Martin completely undresses in front of his mother and then flings his clothes at her as she sits on the bed.

Neuberger has written of the influence of Caroline Spurgeon's *Shakespeare's Imagery* (1935) on Eisenstein in *Ivan the Terrible*, in particular Spurgeon's emphasis on clothing in *Macbeth* in which the title character is often wearing clothes too large for him, signaling a gap between his ruthless ambition and his fundamental discomfort in the role he has assumed. In *Ivan*, there is a trope of the removal of Ivan's ornate, official wardrobe, signaling "a vulnerable shedding of royal power and a removal of the burdens of rule."[39] For the sequence culminating in her rape, Sophie arrives as though prepared for it, in an elaborate, ruffled blue chiffon gown, frillier and more feminine than anything else she wears in the film. A nude Martin walks over to her and rips off the top layer of her dress as she screams. But she does not actively resist or attempt to run away. It is as though the scream is simply a matter of form, what she feels she is expected to do under the circumstances, and in the sequence that immediately follows of the two of them in bed together, her face registers only postcoital bliss.

The incest, while it invigorates Martin no less than his molestation of Lisa Keller, destroys Sophie. She regresses into some state of infantile motherhood tied to the period of Martin's own infancy, as she sits alone and fondles his baby shoe, his sailor's hat, and a ribbon with a lock of his hair (which she compares with her own), all of them blue.

The color of the gown she has chosen to wear for her rape is also the color of Martin's childhood. At the point of Sophie's total withdrawal, she writhes on her ornate bed of many pillows in an off-white nightgown. In *The Damned*, the "veils" of a mother are torn off as idealization gives way to sexual violence and eventually murder in the guise of Sophie and Friedrich's double suicide, engineered by Martin, who exchanges Dietrich drag for a Nazi uniform. Their suicide by cyanide capsules given to them by Martin is immediately preceded by their wedding ceremony, where Martin is the *metteur en scène*, carefully arranging and then lowering the veil on his mother's violet wedding hat. But what are we to make of Sophie's breakdown and willingness to commit suicide? It would seem to contradict what we have seen of her ruthlessness throughout the film. Is incest for her the ultimate taboo? If it strengthens her "creation," Martin, who now channels his energies into Nazism, why would it not do the same for her? Unlike Lady Macbeth, she does not have any guilt over the murders to which she has been connected or that she has masterminded. I would argue that it is less guilt over incest that precipitates her downfall than her awareness of her loss of control of the situation within her family, in particular her awareness that it has been engineered by her son (via Aschenbach), whose control over Martin she believes to be absolute. She is like a machine that has begun to malfunction.

The mechanics of the great creators in these films (Wagner in *Ludwig*, Aschenbach in *The Damned*) are only partly visible, if visible at all. In Wagner's first sequence in the film, he tells von Bülow that he must be surrounded by the right sort of luxurious decor in order to create, as though creation itself is predicated on an extravagant mise-en-scène. In the aftermath of Wagner's break with Ludwig, Ludwig stages the most elaborate mise-en-scènes imaginable. But all of these are tied to an intertwining of romance and sexual desire that leaves him more "exposed" than Wagner or Aschenbach. When Elisabeth pays a visit to three of Ludwig's castles near the end of the film she is dressed entirely in black and wearing a hat with a veil. As she is guided through the castle by a servant she notices a black veil over an entire piano, the veil almost transparent, and she is told that Ludwig had it placed there after Wagner's death. The monumental mise-en-scènes that Ludwig constructed finally cause Elisabeth to burst out laughing over their absurdity. As she rides away in her carriage, her head remains covered in her veil. She is shot in left profile from the neck up, mostly surrounded in darkness, with the brightest point of light on her face. Her face registers a nervousness, her head slightly twitching, as though she can hear Ludwig's voice calling her.

This is immediately followed by a cut to a close shot of Ludwig with a red blindfold around his eyes, mouth open so that his decaying teeth are visible, and it is he who now laughs. A reverse zoom shows him surrounded by a group of his male servants,

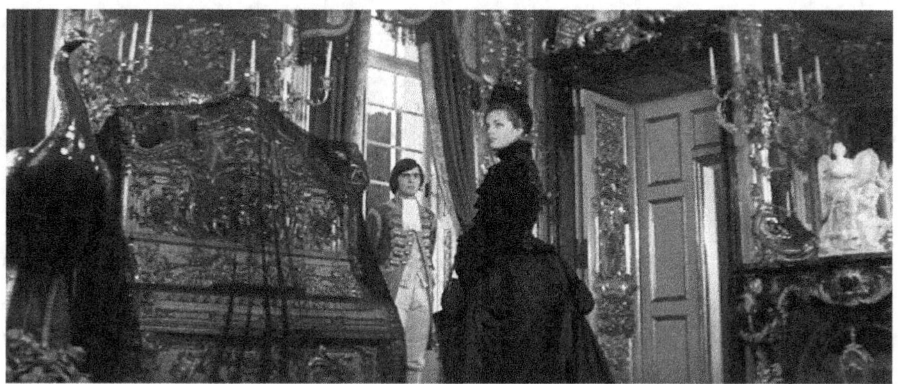

Ludwig (1973). Richard Wagner's veiled piano, in mourning.

an enormous green draping on the wall behind him, as the men begin to exchange the blindfold. What follows, with its inebriated, partially dressed and nude men dancing and singing but mainly languorously lying about, has clear parallels with the bacchanal that precedes the Night of the Long Knives. But this bacchanal does not terminate in violence, and Ludwig merely walks away from his own mise-en-scène. Like the blindfolded Gloria in *The Witch Burned Alive*, Ludwig is the star attraction of this setting, but unlike Gloria he is also its creator. Neither of them, though, have the capacity to transform their environments in such a way that their individual needs are met: in Gloria's case her status as a product precludes this and in Ludwig's case the preclusion arises through his status as a ruler who is also a homosexual aesthete disinterested in politics. But the side-by-side placement of the veil-covered Elisabeth in the carriage with the blindfolded Ludwig suggests still another impossibility facing Ludwig: the desire for his female cousin. Both the homosexual environment with which Ludwig now surrounds himself and the desire for an alternative to it through Elisabeth are the sites of blindness and veiled visions. Henceforth, the spaces of the film become increasingly tight.

For Ludwig's downfall and eventual arrest, which dominate the last fifty minutes of the film, the curtains become thicker and it is always raining, as though his world is closing in and his view is more attenuated. This becomes particularly acute once he is confined to the rooms of Berg Castle, these rooms heavy in fabric, from curtains to lace tablecloths, while the bed he has been given is small, enough for one person only, and draped in silk. It is a world of bourgeois comforts evoking childhood, with a music box and portraits of children on the walls. Just before his death, as he is walking in the rain with Doctor Müller (Karl-Heinz Windhorst), he refers to the myth of the moon being maternal in contrast to the sun's paternal nature. But for Ludwig, the night is neither of these and night is appealing because it is a space of the kingdom of heroes and of reason. Ludwig has finally been granted a tragic self-awareness, a world beyond male and female, masculine and feminine, in favor of a world of the infinite, the sublime (itself a romantic idea), ironically contrasted with the finite space and minor delicacies of lace tablecloths and green curtains.

Ludwig will soon disappear, only to have his dead body discovered in the lake. His disappearance is first indicated through a panning movement from his hat to his coat to his jacket, all abandoned in the rain. The final shot of the film is a freeze frame of his corpse laid out along the shore of the lake, rain pouring down. Within the context of the cinema of fabric, the film's original ending would have been more evocative, in that it was intended to show a servant noticing a bullet hole in Ludwig's coat, indicating Ludwig had been shot.[40] But perhaps the ending as it now stands is more inevitable in relation to how the film has chosen to represent Ludwig. At the end of his life, the material world is taken away from him and he substitutes for this a romantic embracing of the infinite, even as the brutal image of the dead body of the king in the final shot of the film returns us to the real, the material.

In conclusion, let us return to the beach of *Death in Venice*. Not the ending this time but a sequence occurring after Aschenbach has decided to return to Venice, in spite of warnings an epidemic is spreading. He continues to take pleasure in observing Tadzio and his mother. When Tadzio comes running out of the water, his mother tells him how dirty he is because of the wet sand clinging to him. It is the governess, though, who primarily uses the towel to wipe him off as the mother mainly touches his face, pulls back his wet hair, and then finally uses a bit of the towel to wipe his face, a superfluous gesture in terms of its actual effect in making him clean, but in its touch it imparts a strong sense of the maternal. The mother is abundantly clean, veiled, covered up from any possible contamination. The governess helps Tadzio remove his top and she covers his body with the towel before instructing his sister to get out of the chair she is sitting in so her brother can assume that position, as though Tadzio were a crown prince. All of this is presumably seen by Aschenbach, whose face will sometimes register amusement, but the ambiguous point-of-view structure of the earlier beach scenes remains in place. As Tadzio sits, Aschenbach rises from his beach chair as though to get away from him and goes over to his tiny desk in front of a cabana as Mahler begins to be nondiegetically heard. It is no longer the adagietto we hear but the fourth movement from *Symphony No. 3*, "Midnight Song," the text taken from Nietzsche's *Thus Spake Zarathustra* (1883–91). As Aschenbach sits down to furiously write, as though attempting to push the boy out of his consciousness for a moment, in a medium long shot are the striped awnings of the cabanas shaking in the wind, perhaps responding to something larger than simply the natural environment. Suddenly Tadzio, towel wrapped around his body, crosses in the extreme foreground of the shot, slightly out of focus, only his body from the shoulders to just below his knees visible. Aschenbach does not see him. The next image is a wide shot in which Aschenbach is in the right mid-foreground of the frame, Tadzio on the left middle background. The framing now shows that the towel Tadzio has wrapped around himself comes all the way to the ground so that only his head and left shoulder are visible. In *Ludwig*, Wagner describes Ludwig as being like a young god descended from Olympus. Here Tadzio evokes such emotions while looking both male and female, a god but also a source of temptation, the left shoulder and returned gaze beckoning to Aschenbach, Tadzio as androgynous siren. As this image presents itself to Aschenbach, the soprano voice on the soundtrack reinforces the siren-like atmosphere as she sings of the importance of taking heed. This becomes, within the context of the moment, at once a warning and an invitation. Tadzio turns to look at Aschenbach and Aschenbach, sensing his presence, looks over at him at the same time. The boy turns away and proceeds walking toward the sea as Aschenbach resumes his writing, as though temptation has been temporarily put at bay.

But the "Midnight Song" continues to be heard over the succeeding sequences, of Aschenbach awakening in his hotel room and opening the shutters to look out at the sea and then at the beach again, as he returns to it. Upon returning, again wearing a white suit, he passes over the walkway through which he made his first visit there, its grandiose entrance now visible in an establishing shot that was absent earlier, as veiled women in summer attire again pass him. This time, though, Visconti shoots the walk differently. Instead of one brief, extended take of Aschenbach quickly walking, the sequence is broken into several different shots. He stops as he reaches the entrance and spots Tadzio standing there in a red-and-white-striped bathing suit and straw hat and talking to Jaschu and another boy who quickly break away from Tadzio and run off. A cut to a closer view of Aschenbach, from his left side, shows him hesitating in moving forward now that Tadzio is standing there alone. He slowly moves forward, as does Tadzio, who does not, at first, look around. This movement is shot with a long lens, the flattening of distance between them accentuated by the placement of the poles as Tadzio swings around one pole and then another. With each swing he briefly makes eye contact with Aschenbach as the camera slowly zooms forward. Aschenbach raises his right hand, as though wanting to touch the boy, and then withdraws it as the boy continues moving forward and again swings around a pole before running off to the beach, and a shaken Aschenbach must hold on to that pole for support. A cut to a wide shot of him shows him standing not, as we might have imagined from the previous shot, close to the edge of the walkway but all the way at the back of it as three veiled women pass him and he changes direction and walks over to the cabanas to his left. As the camera slowly zooms toward him, a cabin boy walks past, a stack of towels on his shoulder, the boy not noticed by Aschenbach. Throughout all of this the soprano continues to sing Nietzsche's references to a world far deeper than one had imagined, of a pain that is deep but a joy that is deeper still, a joy seeks deep eternity. But as Mahler's music and Nietzsche's text imply a world of transcendent expression and desire, we see a suffering, middle-aged man in a white suit, veiled women passing by, their bodies fully covered, as the forbidden object of desire, in a tight-fitting red bathing suit, has once again offered himself and then disappeared. In the final shot of the sequence, the reality of the social world around Aschenbach continues to circulate even as the other human figure here, the cabin boy, is himself not fully outside the film's structure of desire.

FADING

6

Beginnings and Endings

We are reaching the end. So let us start at the beginning. First film: The sound of an explosion followed by the credits, white letters on a black background, which read *Conversation Piece* or, if one is watching an Italian print, *Gruppo di famiglia in un interno*. As the credits continue, they fade in to the tape of an electrocardiogram slowly moving downward as Franco Monnino's mournful musical theme is nondiegetically heard. The camera then slowly rises (the tape, we now can see, is on a carpeted floor) and it becomes possible to discern the gold hem of a maroon or brown tablecloth. But before the movement reaches its destination there is a dissolve to a magnifying glass moving over an eighteenth-century painting as a man holding the glass searches for salient details in this portrait of a family.[1] A slow reverse zoom reveals the man from the back, evidently aging, wearing a dark jacket and a white shirt. A cut to a closer view of him, taken from his left side, shows that the actor in this role, about to be referred to as the Professor, is Burt Lancaster. Head down, still looking at the painting, he utters a single word: "Exquisite." Second film: A camera quickly zooms into a book, Gabriele d'Annunzio's *L'innocente*, a fourth edition of it, as a superimposed credit reads "Un film di Luchino Visconti." The book is placed on a table covered in red satin or velvet. As the credits continue, the camera quickly zooms back as a man's hands enter the frame from the right and slowly turn the pages of the book, pausing long enough for us to see a two-page, black-and-white illustration by Guido Sartorio, just before the title page, of a crucifixion. The hand continues to turn the pages as the camera zooms back to its original position and the credits, accompanied by another mournful Monnino theme, finish.

Conversation Piece and *The Innocent* are Visconti's final films, made following a stroke he had during the editing of *Ludwig*. In different ways, they are films about the end, not just in terms of physical decline but also as films with an evident awareness that the forms they assume are fading in importance. In 1974, De Sica died; Pasolini would be murdered the following year; Rossellini would die in 1977, a year after Visconti's own death. (Visconti died during postproduction on *The Innocent*.) Not quite enough to announce a definite end to an era (Antonioni, Fellini, Bolognini, Rosi, and others would continue) but enough to create a feeling of the inevitable. All of these directors who died were working up through the end. Of these final works it is Pasolini's *Salò, or the 120 Days of Sodom* (1975) that is the most useful as point of contrast and comparison with Visconti's final two films. As its subtitle indicates, *Salò* adapts the Marquis de Sade's *The 120 Days of Sodom* (1785/1904) but the Sade text coexists with a number of other texts. Officially a repudiation of the celebration of eros in the *Trilogy of Life*, Pasolini's choice of Sade pushes the issue of literary adaptation onto an entirely different level from anything in Visconti. With Sade, Pasolini is filming the impossible, the unrepresentable due to the fundamentally literary nature of the sexually explicit and scatological language of Sade.[2] In *The Innocent*, on the other hand, Visconti is doing yet another literary adaptation, with a text posing none of the challenges of the Sade. But the process involved in this use of d'Annunzio has its own complex historical and political awareness.

It is now confirmed, but was widely guessed at the time, that the hands in the credits for *The Innocent* are Visconti's own. They are clearly the hands of an old man, the arm covered in a dark blue jacket, the sleeve of a blue shirt with white diamond patterns emerging from the jacket's sleeve. Aging and decay are everywhere in the shot, in Visconti's hands but also in the small brown stains on the pages of the book, as though the book itself has liver spots. The book is, like Visconti's own body, fragile and must be treated delicately lest it crack. Cracks are also evident in the "exquisite" painting the Professor is looking at through his magnifying glass. While the literature on Visconti often compares the Professor to the Prince in *The Leopard* (a comparison encouraged by Lancaster playing both roles), he does not look at this painting in the same way the Prince looks at the Greuze. The Professor shows no evidence of seeing his own death in the painting (and unlike the Greuze, the painting is not one of death anyway) but rather his appraisal of it is that of the connoisseur. But his control of his own situation is about to change.

In contrast to all of Visconti's prior features, *Conversation Piece* is small in scale, shot in a studio in Rome and set entirely in interiors, those of the Professor's home. The staging and shooting style is, for the most part, quite simple in a film heavy in dialogue, with a reliance on alternating singles as the characters address one another while standing or seated, these patterns often broken by cutting to wider shots. The film was made in an atmosphere of reduced expectations in the aftermath of Visconti's stroke and an awareness that his long-cherished project of adapting *In Search of Lost Time* was clearly not going to happen. Enrico Medioli (who would eventually collaborate on the script with Suso Cecchi d'Amico and Visconti, as he also would on

The Innocent) suggested the basic idea for *Conversation Piece* because of its restricted setting. *Conversation Piece* is another "original" screenplay but unlike Visconti's prior ones it does not give itself such rich literary evocations and intertextuality, although Thomas Mann's novella *Disorder and Early Sorrow* (1925) is distantly evoked. The source of the explosion we hear at the beginning of the film is shown near the end, and the shock of it sends the Professor to his bed, hooked up to the electrocardiogram. The Professor was partly based on the literary and art critic Mario Praz, whose study of the eighteenth-century English genre painting of the group portrait *Conversation Pieces* (1971) served as a source for not only the film's English-language title but also the book's emphasis on a genre for which the Professor has a particular fondness. (These paintings dominate the walls of his home.) Such group portraits are typically those of families, and *Conversation Piece* is, among other things, another Visconti film about the family, albeit a family of a very unusual nature.

That *The Innocent* is adapted from d'Annunzio's novel is made overt in the credit sequence. But that the volume is decaying is one indication of the film's intent in positing its literary source as something of a ruin. Conversely, Pasolini uses Sade in an immediate manner, marshaling its implications for a film set not in France in the eighteenth century but in the Republic of Salò during the final nineteen months of Italian Fascism. But Pasolini's methods address larger historical and philosophical questions about the origins and ongoing nature of fascism. While the villa used for the exteriors of the dominant location was built in the early nineteenth century, the interiors are filled with futurist art and art deco, consistent with the film's attempt to link aesthetics with fascism. Moreover, the film is equally an allegory about the Italian present day of consumer capitalism, for Pasolini another manifestation of the fascist impulse. Visconti is not interested in this kind of marshaling of vast swaths of history and culture in order to force an analogy with the present day. For Visconti, the interest of the d'Annunzio work is that it is a once-fashionable object, the book's placement on red fabric for the credits also an indication of the film's ambitions. This fabric looks luxurious but also a bit garish and, like the book resting on it, and indeed like the style of the credit sequence itself, something of an anachronism.

In terms of its integration of costuming and decor into larger formal effects, *The Innocent* is one of Visconti's richest films. Much of this is due not only to the opportunities offered by the period setting but also to its use of the fabric references in d'Annunzio's prose. D'Annunzio does not simply describe clothing and decor; his prose luxuriates in their details. Visconti's first choice in adapting d'Annunzio was *Il Piacere* (1889) but the rights were unavailable. *The Innocent*, though, borrows as much in its general atmosphere from *Il Piacere* as it does from its official source.[3] The first-person narration of Tullio Hermil in the d'Annunzio novel is forsaken for a more "objective" approach. Hermil imagines he is an example of the Nietzschean superman and, as a result of this, beyond conventional moral categories. Duplicating this for the film would threaten to lock the viewer into sharing, however critically or dialogically, this quasi-fascistic subjectivity. The film instead opens up this perspective. And while Tullio (Giancarlo Giannini) is in the majority of sequences, the film's visual and rhetorical strategies create a much stronger sense of a social world surrounding Tullio than in the novel. In the film his perspective on this world becomes secondary.

There has been a tendency to read some of Visconti's later period films as Proustian in a displaced manner. I briefly alluded to this in an earlier chapter in relation to *The Leopard* and it has also been addressed by others in relation to *Death in Venice*, *Ludwig*, and, especially, *The Innocent*. Ivo Blom cites statements from Piero Tosi and Visconti's frequent production designer, Mario Garbuglia (who also designed the sets for *Conversation Piece*), that there was a conscious attempt to evoke Proust in *The Innocent*.[4] The beautifully appointed upper-class rituals of *The Innocent* are central to this Proustian ambition. Crucial to the dovetailing of Proust and d'Annuzio is the sense of a world in which all conduct is theatricalized, a world of role-playing in which the reality of a situation is typically a question of interpretation. Pasolini will take such a strategy and push it to extremes in *Salò*, in which the young men and women of the film, arrested by the Fascists, are stripped naked, raped, assaulted, forced to eat excrement, and murdered, and done so through an overt theatricalizing of the environment in which they are imprisoned. There is no suspended eroticism, no veiling in the film through the dressing and undressing of these attractive young people. Instead, the act of undressing is bluntly handled, an enforced exposure of genitalia for the arousal of the four libertines whose desires determine the staged sexual activities. "In Sade," writes Roland Barthes, "no striptease. The body is uncovered at once (save for a few young men who are allowed to 'let their pants fall agreeably down over their thighs')."[5] Supplementing this perspective of the four libertines is the presence of the "storytellers," three middle-aged women elaborately costumed who narrate sexual and scatological anecdotes designed to arouse the libertines. As the young people are forced to listen, a fourth woman accompanies these stories by playing piano works by that fundamental composer of the Romantic era, Frédéric Chopin, who is also heard during the soirées of *The Innocent*.

If the desire to turn one's own life into an elaborate mise-en-scène is central to a number of Visconti films (these desires doubling those of the *auteur*), such a desire is already evident in d'Annunzio. Of the protagonist of *Il Piacere*, d'Annunzio writes that "his house was the most perfect theater; and he was an extremely skillful designer. But he almost always invested all of himself in this artifice; he lavishly spent in it the richness of his spirit; he would sink so far into oblivion within it, that not infrequently he would be deceived by his own insidiousness, wounded by his own weapons, like an enchanter trapped within the circle of his own spell."[6] Such a description, in which sensuous aestheticism is tied to self-destruction, is typical of d'Annunzio's relationship with Decadentism as well as with symbolism and aestheticism, movements Praz would notably address in *The Romantic Agony* (1933), a book that ends with an extended analysis of d'Annunzio as the "most monumental figure of the Decadent movement."[7] One of Pasolini's ambitions with *Salò* is to imply a connection between Romantic and Decadent thought, with its roots in the Enlightenment, and fascism. At the end of the opening sequence of *Salò*, one of the four libertines declares all things are good when taken to excess, a paraphrase of Oscar Wilde's "nothing succeeds like excess." In the film that follows, such "excess" becomes the height of fascistic brutality, as though the film wishes to both reproduce and repudiate the (largely homosexual) tradition of decadence and camp. Visconti's ambivalence causes him to be less dogmatic about these forms and traditions, the nuanced irony he displays in *The Innocent* foreign to the Pasolini of *Salò*. But if examined closely, the visual and dramatic rhetoric of Visconti's final films has its own sense of imminent destruction, of enchanters trapped within the circles of their own spells. In *The Innocent*, decor and costuming have an all-consuming power.

At the time of the film's production Visconti stated of d'Annunzio in relation to contemporary Italian culture that "we're all his children. We've all come via him. . . . Despicable things have been written about him, especially by Moravia, Pasolini and those people. If only they could write the things D'Annunzio wrote."[8] The "despicable things" about d'Annunzio (his reactionary and nationalist politics, his ostentatious theatricalizing, his decadence) offer to Visconti something similar to what melodrama and grand opera assumed for him in *Senso*. In 1975, d'Annunzio was no longer fashionable, unlike Sade, who had by then achieved canonical status, a status made explicit in the credits to *Salò*, which have the audacity to give the viewer a Sade bibliography. With *The Innocent*, it is up to Visconti to revive d'Annunzio but in a very particular manner, not only nostalgically but (as with his treatment of melodrama and grand opera) critically. With d'Annunzio and his cult of the self what historically culminates is fascism. Unlike the Risorgimento in *Senso*, however, political upheaval is not dramatized in *The Innocent*, given that the film has chosen to confine itself to the period in which the novel was written, minus any contemporary interpolations. The upper-class characters in *The Innocent* are not affected by eminent political changes, and the adulterous nature of the story does not metaphorically stand in for the changes to come: The hypocritical Tullio, unable to accept that his passive wife, Giuliana (Laura

Antonelli), has not only had an affair but become pregnant by her lover, eventually murders the baby rather than accept it in his own household. As Visconti was very much aware, the example of d'Annunzio's literature cannot be *reduced* to nothing more than a foreshadowing of the era of Mussolini. Decadence is not a simple dead end but in its attraction to "abnormal" sexual desires also clarifies the repressiveness of the dominant social orders. D'Annunzio is both embraced and critiqued, revived by the film and used by it as a historical ruin, a past retrievable only under the most nuanced of conditions.

The political backdrop to *Conversation Piece* is more immediate, the story picking up on the tensions between extreme right- and left-wing forces in Italy in the early 1970s that have given rise to terrorism and neofascism. The character of Konrad (Helmut Berger) has ties to the political Left but his roots (he claims) are in the culture of 1968, although he has quickly become something of an anachronism. He now spends his time as the "kept boy" of a wealthy woman, the Marquise Bianca Brumonti (Silvana Mangano), whose husband (never shown in the film) is a right-wing industrialist, with possible fascist sympathies. Bianca arranges for the rental of the apartment above the Professor so that Konrad can move in, along with Bianca's daughter, Lietta (Claudia Marsani), and her boyfriend, Stefano (Stefano Patrizi). Their move into this space becomes a literal and metaphoric awakening for the Professor, in terms of the former due to the noise they bring with them and in terms of the latter for what happens to the Professor once they all begin to share this space. Of these four "intruders," Konrad will become the pivotal figure for the Professor. It is Konrad who is the victim of the blast that begins and ends the film, the blast from an oven in the kitchen of the upstairs apartment. But the explosions in the film also carry larger connotations tied to the politics of both the moment in which the film was made and the Second World War. *Conversation Piece* and *The Innocent* address the issue of Italian Fascism not head-on, as was becoming increasingly typical during this period. Instead, they address the topic from two different historical directions and in a more specific manner than Pasolini: fascism's latency during the period in which *The Innocent* is set and its potential for persistence in the present day in *Conversation Piece*, where the Professor's home becomes an attempted refuge from the contemporary world. In this regard, the two films complete some of the implications of the films in the trilogy that immediately preceded them. But this is not all that these two films accomplish.

Lifting the Veil

For one last time, veils. In *Conversation Piece* they are used most prominently in two brief sequences occurring over an hour into the film, both sequences set in the past.

In the first of these we see the Professor's mother (Dominique Sanda) and in the other the Professor's wife (Claudia Cardinale). Our first view of the mother is instigated by the Professor hearing offscreen sounds intruding into his library, including the sounds of a ringing telephone and Bianca talking to her chauffeur and to the Professor's maid, Erminia (Elvira Cortese). Also heard here is a parrot given to the Professor by the "children" who will only be quiet once a piece of fabric is draped over his cage. Hearing all of this produces in the Professor a mood of reflection, indicated through Lancaster's far-away facial expression and in which he looks almost directly into the camera. The image of his face dissolves into a lavish room dominated by pink, in the silk wallpaper, in the silk lining of the couch, in the chairs, in the tablecloths, and in the roses, as the audio of the telephone in the present day gives way to the ringing of a doorbell from the past. As the dissolve begins, the camera pans over one wall, showing the paintings hanging there (barely discernible portraits and not the "conversation pieces" to come), before the camera pulls back as a maid dashes from offscreen left, responding to the offscreen right voices, into the outside hallway, excitedly calling out to another servant. Rather than cut to the source of the voices, the film continues with its slow reverse tracking movement as a woman's voice states she is happy to be back. It is here where the woman who has just been speaking enters as the nondiegetic music romantically swells. The woman is wearing a formal suit intended for travel and a hat with an enormous veil hanging from the top of the hat down to her shoulders and falling down her back. The veil is so heavy that the features of her face are not fully discernible. Standing in profile and looking out the window, the woman lifts her veil and then turns around and walks through the room, in a close mobile shot, before sitting on the couch as the maid says, "So, that's our little American boy?" The woman turns and looks into the camera and then looks away as the maid tells her the boy resembles this woman: the Professor's mother. This is followed by a cut to a wide shot of the room as two men, another maid, and a woman have just entered the space. In the wide shot, the mother and the maid address the boy by looking to their left, to some undefined area just out-of-frame. But in the return to the close-up of the mother, who again looks into the camera as though the camera is in the same position as the boy, she and the maid discuss the possibility of giving him candy, and the maid remarks upon the boy's shyness. At the maid's reference to his shyness, a cut returns us to the present day, where we now clearly see that the room the mother entered was the same library where the Professor is now sitting. In the present, though, the pink decor is replaced by brown and green, the room becoming darker, more somber. The Professor is in a chair at the far right of the frame, the same spot where his mother and her maid were addressing him when he was a child.

The links between the Professor and Aschenbach in *Death in Venice* have been frequently noted, both men emotionally reserved, aging aesthetes whose lives are thrown into turmoil by the unexpected arrival of figures much younger than themselves. This sequence of the mother in *Conversation Piece*, in its emphasis on the mother's voice in relation to the perceiving male child, in its idiosyncratic handling of the act of gazing upon the mother through impossible point-of-view editing, and in the mother's body covered from head to toe, culminating in a veil that is then raised in order for her face to be revealed, has ties to the presentation of the mother in *Death in Venice*. The decision to shoot an intimate film like *Conversation Piece* in Todd-AO 35, a short-lived anamorphic widescreen process, would appear to be counterintuitive. But the wide screen in the film produces a number of advantages, and one of them is evident in this close-up of the mother's face, the veil pulled over her hat, in which she literally fills the enormous frame as she looks into the camera. By contrast, the mother in *Death in Venice* is barely aware of Aschenbach. She has her own children to focus on, whereas the mother here has the child's full attention. The loving gaze of the mother not returned to Aschenbach is returned here to a child who beholds a mother whose beauty is so overpowering he is unable to speak and is therefore reduced to being virtually a spectator. This is not just a generalized maternal image but one that, as with the mother in *Death in Venice*, connotes great economic and social privilege and one in which the voice of the maid engages in a type of duet with the voice of the mother, supplementing her function as a mother, as with the nanny in *Death in Venice*. When we see the Professor in the present day it is as though he has not developed beyond this position as the "little American boy." As in *Death in Venice*, *Conversation Piece* shows us a world without fathers. As the Professor runs his magnifying glass over the family portrait in the first sequence, he examines the mother and two children but ignores the father.

The footage involving the Professor's wife emerges slightly after the view of the mother, when he is in bed with a book in his lap, listening to the andante from Mozart's *Sinfonia Concertante K 364* (1779). Like Aschenbach in the opening of *Death in Venice*, he is distracted, and the music generates a memory of his wife. The footage crosscuts from first showing her in a wide shot of what is presumably their bedroom, the wife wearing a pink nightgown as she weeps while sitting in a green chair at the foot of the bed. From this we quickly cut to a close shot of her even further in the past, lifting the veil of her wedding gown, the gesture filmed in slow motion, with pale red or deep pink curtains and silk wallpaper behind her. As she continues to raise the veil and then remove the crown to which the veil is attached we gradually notice that she is looking at herself in a mirror as she places the crown and veil down on something below the frame. A cut quickly takes us back to the bedroom, to a close-up of the wife crying as she tells the Professor she wants to confess everything. As in the footage involving his mother, the Professor is not visible, and when we cut to him in the present day, still in bed, he telegraphically raises his arms in despair as if to indicate he failed his wife. Maynard Solomon has written of the "suppressed undercurrent of feeling, compounded of anxiety and longing" sections of this Mozart andante produce and of the andante's "long yearning phrases."[9] The aptness of this music for the Professor's melancholic reverie is then interrupted by contemporary Italian pop music invading his space and coming from the library, breaking him out of the past and forcing him into the present day.

Both mother and wife are linked through the gesture of lifting their veils, as well as by the color pink dominating the library's decor in the mother's sequence, then migrating to the curtains behind the wife in front of the mirror, and then to her nightgown in the bedroom. The Professor witnesses the lifting of the mother's veil but it is not clear if he is in the room when his wife lifts hers. The subjective aspect of nostalgia in the raisings of these veils also places these images slightly outside of "reality," whereas the footage of the wife as she is crying is handled in a more straightforward manner. Why is she crying? What does she need to be forgiven for? Presumably some sort of infidelity brought about by the Professor's sexual indifference to her and one he was unable to resolve. The implication is that the idealization connected to his heavily veiled mother prevents him from satisfactory sexual relations with his wife, as though to commit such an act would be a violation of the incest taboo. The beautiful veiled mother is a figure of worship but also of anxiety, inducing his shyness. In this regard, she has ties to the Romantic and Decadent image of the Fatal Woman in which, as Praz writes, "the man dies under the eyes of a frigid woman, devoted to the cult of the Moon, herself an idol, and his death is her involuntary act." Praz quotes from Swinburne's *Atalanta in Calydon* (1865), in which Meleager implores the virgin, "hide my body with thy veil/and with thy raiment cover foot and head."[10] In the chapter from *The Leopard* not used in the film, Tomasi di Lampedusa writes of the Prince's vision of his own death as he himself lies dying. As with the father in the Greuze painting, the Prince is surrounded by family members when a mysterious young woman appears, "in brown travelling dress and wide bustle, with a straw hat trimmed with a speckled veil which could not hide the sly charm of her face. . . . When she was face to face with him she raised her veil, and there, chaste but ready for possession, she looked lovelier than she had had when glimpsed in stellar space."[11] The costuming of the mother in *Conversation Piece* is remarkably close to this description, an ambivalent image of both beauty and death.

The most striking use of the veil in *The Innocent* occurs not in relation to a Fatal Woman but in relation to Giuliana getting ready to go to an auction, where she is observed by Tullio. What draws Tullio to his wife's room is the sound of her singing an aria from Gluck's *Orpheus and Eurydice* (1762), "J'ai perdu mon Eurydice." Like a Siren, her voice acts as a lure as her husband follows its sound to her room, although in this instance there is nothing premediated about the singing. These details of Tullio hearing his wife sing, and even the aria itself, are taken from d'Annunzio, although in the film the song is initially heard earlier in the narrative, when a professional singer performs it as part of a recital at a soiree attended by Tullio and Giuliana. When Tullio enters Giuliana's room, this is how d'Annunzio describes it: "She was standing near a table trimmed with lace, and on which scintillated the scattered innumerable little articles that serve nowadays to beautify women. She wore a dress of vigonia, of a dark color, and held in her hand a light-colored shell comb mounted in silver. The dress, very simple in cut, set off her slim, graceful figure."[12] The film supplements and substitutes this already evocative prose. She is not wearing a dress of vigonia but instead one of gray fabric with a silver-buttoned front. The set is dominated by heavy, pale pink curtains in the main area of the bedroom, white and pale blue lace tablecloths on small tables and stands, salmon-colored wallpaper, and white curtains in her dressing room. When she steps into this dressing room in order to apply the final touches, including spraying herself with perfume, there is a cut to a closer shot of her pulling down a pink veil adorned with pink and violet flowers on top. Behind her, to the left of the shot, is a small white garment of some kind and a mirror on the opposite wall shows a reflection of her as she looks at herself in the mirror in front of her. Unable to successfully pin the veil, she walks into the other room. She asks Tullio to help her as she steps over to a mirror on the wall on the far right of the room and we see their reflection as he helps her with the pinning. He notices she is wearing a new scent, Crab Apple (an English perfume, she tells him, a detail from the novel), as he walks away and the principle musical theme of the film begins to be ominously heard, nondiegetically.

The veil Giuliana needs assistance in pinning is not given a great amount of descriptive detail by d'Annunzio. The film, by contrast, creates an uncanny image of a veiled woman, possibly taking its cue from another passage in *L'innocente* when Tullio writes of narrating a "fabulous tale" of a young prince rejoining with a woman he loves. "But a veil seemed to render this smiling lady intangible, a veil of unknown substance, so subtle that it was confounded with the air; and, nevertheless, this veil was a barrier that prohibited the young man from clasping the woman he loved to his heart."[13] This notion of a woman's veil serving as a barrier to the desiring male's access is, in this sequence, a fabric so thick and, once pinned, so tight on her face that it presses down on her features and slightly disfigures them. It is as though a symbolist image of woman is about to give way to a surrealist one. The central question here is why the film goes to such extremes in rendering Giuliana in this manner. At least two possibilities present themselves. One is that the veil becomes a metaphor for the sense of entrapment she experiences within the marriage, as though she is in a gilded cage. Giuliana does not have the political commitment and emotional fervor of Livia in *Senso* and must internalize her situation, a quiet suffering in contrast to Livia's veiled exhibitionism. Another possibility (only clearer when the narrative is seen in retrospect) is that she has already begun her affair with the writer Filippo d'Arborio (Marc Porel), a friend of Tullio's brother Federico (Didier Haudepin). After helping Giuliana to pin her veil, Tullio leafs through a copy of d'Arborio's *La Fiamma* and notes the inscription to his wife, this inscription becoming an inciting incident for the melodramatic conflicts dominating the second half of the film.

The sequence of her standing in front of her dressing room mirror is a variation on two sequences discussed in earlier chapters: Gino's exploration of Anita's room in *Ossessione* and Natalia in front of the mirror of the boarder in *White Nights*. In both of those sequences, the desire for the body of the potential new lovers is manifested in attention to the decor of their rented rooms and where the scent of cologne or hair gel becomes central. In *The Innocent*, however, Giuliana is in her own private space, the perfume her own. But she is preparing herself for the man who will supply her with the sexual satisfaction that her husband is incapable of providing. She does not attend the auction for which she claims she is getting dressed, and returning home she goes straight to her room and to the mirror where her husband had earlier helped her to pin her veil. She raises the veil and pensively stares at her face in the mirror, one hand placed in front of her mouth, as though nervous about something she has just done—presumably sex with Filippo, the encounter that will lead to her pregnancy. (Reflected in the mirror is a portrait of a child on the opposite wall.) The veil in the sequence with Tullio becomes not simply an indication she is hiding something but a foreshadowing of the disastrous consequences of this secret.

A significant change from novel to film is the function of Teresa Raffo (Jennifer O'Neill). In the novel, Tullio occasionally refers to his mistress but she does not emerge as a fully formed character. In the film, she is central. She dominates the first soiree, wearing a vivid red gown with a high collar, attended by men in tuxedos and dark blue uniforms. Surrounded in this way, her redness stands out much more vividly in a room where red walls and curtains dominate. In another room, where a piano recital is taking place, many of the women are in varying shades of red and pink. It is as though Teresa's brazenness, embodied in red, permeates her environment. Even Giuliana is not exempt from this and wears a gown of maroon. How Teresa sees herself is made explicit during the first extended sequence she has alone with Tullio, in her home, and directly following the soiree. She is waiting for him in a room in which the decor is dominated by red, in the wallpaper, the curtains, the furniture, and the pillows, and in her own gown, which she has not changed since returning home. It is here where she declares herself to be free and liberated, just as he is. Moreover, in making such a declaration, she is implicitly telling him she is assuming a masculine role within their social world. Such freedom of expression becomes something strongly drawing him to Teresa even as it is also the source of anxiety due to his lack of control over her. This function for Teresa is markedly unlike that of the more passive Giuliana, Teresa representing a new conception of the modern woman who engages in reversals of standard social protocols based on gender.

Contrast this with the first bedroom sequence between Tullio and Giuliana, set in Tullio's bedroom. This room is dominated by closely intermingled grays, soft greens, and whites, in the curtains, the wallpaper, and the bedding, as Giuliana enters dressed in a pale blue and white nightgown. To her right is a portrait on the wall of a male subject, his clothing and white wig connoting his relationship to (most likely) the eighteenth century, an Enlightenment figure. But as she crosses the room and sits down, in a corner of the room above Tullio's desk is a sculpture of a nude male, his crotch covered by gold draping, similar to the draping in the crucifixion in the Sartorio illustration in the credits. In these two works of art, there is a contrast between the rationalism of the world of the portrait (and such portraits recur in the film) and the eroticism of the world of the sculpture, both of them facets of how Tullio imagines himself. She sits on a bench in front of the bed but on a bench with a bright red pillow on it, as though the presence of Teresa lingers as Tullio speaks frankly to his wife about his obsession with his mistress. As Giuliana is forced to listen to this cruel exhibitionism masquerading as honesty, she is framed by white drapings on each of the four bedposts, two on the immediate sides of her and two behind her. Two sets of white pillows are stacked at the rear of the bed, all of this a strong image of sexual neglect.

At the auction Giuliana claims to be attending, Tullio searches the room for his wife but, in the process, unexpectedly spots Teresa. They make eye contact and walk toward each other as the auction continues. Teresa steps up very close to the camera to the point where only her eyes are visible, a black semitransparent veil covering what we see of her face as she looks at Tullio. *The Innocent* is another late Visconti film shot in an anamorphic process (in this instance, Technovision), and Teresa's veiled eyes create an overwhelming impression as they fill the frame, a gaze that is acute and in which Teresa's power resides in her capacity to return this look to Tullio or to anyone in the world around her. At the first soiree, she boldly walks over to the Princess and apologizes for her early departure, even though Giuliana is sitting next to the Princess during this exchange. At the second soiree given by the Princess where the Gluck aria is performed, red is largely gone from the environment and is only visible through lingering details such as the wallpaper and vases of roses. Giuliana is now in black and the other women in the room are mainly in dark colors, the pattern occasionally broken by the appearance of a gown of pale pink. Teresa is not there. This black fabric is partly taking its cue from the content of the aria, as though the entire room has been plunged into mourning over Orpheus's loss. But the dominance of black also announces one of several major developments in the narrative. Once Teresa, in the early sections of the film, is no longer in a space, she seems to take the red with her. From the extreme close-up of her veiled eyes at the auction there is a cut to Giuliana returning home with her heavy pink veil covering her face. Two very different women, both linked with Tullio, are contrasted through their veils, Giuliana's a veil of intense, agonizing secrecy and Teresa's a veil virtually transparent and tied to a look fully able to equal the powerful gaze of the male figure.

By the time of *Conversation Piece*, the veil is mainly connected to the past. But there is one sequence in which Bianca, in a dark gray dress ensemble, wears a hat with a veil, and this occurs when she yells at the Professor, somewhat illogically defending herself in relation to his anger over the destruction Konrad, Stefano, and Lietta have caused to the apartment upstairs. Throughout the film, Bianca's appearance is not fully of the period in which the film is set. Her pencil-thin eyebrows, for example, evoke those of Martin for his Dietrich impersonation in *The Damned*. The outfit she is wearing in this sequence with the Professor could have easily been worn in the late 1930s. That her husband is not only right-wing but, near the end of the film, accused by Stefano and Konrad of being a fascist would supply a pretext for visually linking her to that earlier history of Italian politics as well an indication of the persistence of fascism in present-day Italy. Strictly in relation to her character's psychology, though, it is in this sequence when she confesses to the Professor that Konrad is her "kept boy" where the veil becomes an extension of her own desire to keep this truth at a slight remove. Livia's veils in *Senso* are an earlier incarnation of this idea of the older wealthy woman having a secret, younger male lover who is also a "kept boy," a role more traditionally assumed by men, heterosexual or homosexual. But Livia's secret lover is precisely a secret and, as already discussed, her veils perform a dual function in indicating both the shame and the excitement she experiences through this scandalous relationship. This is not quite the case with Bianca, whose affair with Konrad is an open secret, her veil smaller because she has less to hide, and in which her lover's politics, antithetical to her own social world, are connected to his past rather than his present.

Lavishly dressed and often wearing fur, Bianca is the last in a group of overpowering Visconti mothers. As with Sophie in *The Damned*, the specter of incest hovers around her family relations. Bianca has no male child although the Professor initially mistakes Stefano for her son, which she contemptuously laughs off. But this early moment in the film establishes an atmosphere of uncertainty surrounding what we might call, in fashionable terms, "boundaries" within her family. Not only is Lietta blissfully undisturbed by her mother's relationship with Konrad but Lietta herself is most likely also having sex with Konrad. The Professor walks in on Lietta, Stefano, and Konrad, all of them nude and swaying together to pop music in the Professor's library (a sexual invasion of this space otherwise devoted to strictly platonic aesthetic contemplation). Any possible feelings of guilt from them in relation to this are not addressed. In fact, there is an implication that this is one of the reasons Bianca has set the three of them up in the apartment, Bianca functioning as a devious *metteur en scène*. "A slightly incestuous family," is how Stefano later describes them all but his irony only serves to veil the truth. As a mother, Bianca is not a figure in black, simultaneously overpowering and repressive, like Rosaria in *Rocco and His Brothers*. Overpowering she is but she is also abundantly sexual although the film's ambivalence prevents her from embodying any strongly positive force, even as she directly expresses her own ambivalent attraction to Konrad when she states, "I may be infatuated with Konrad but that doesn't mean I don't know what sort of person I'm dealing with." In a phone conversation between Konrad and Bianca witnessed by the Professor, Konrad repeatedly calls her "bitch" and "cunt" and says she is someone who will "break your balls." That it is Mangano playing the role and in such an emphatic style makes her the antithesis of her mother in *Death in Venice*. But such emotionalism and grand gestures also link her with the sacred monster tradition of the diva. Her ostensible monstrosity is reinforced through the furs, or coats trimmed in fur, that she wears, creating a stronger impression of her character than any of the fabrics she wears, the diva mother as beautiful animal. Konrad contemptuously gives her the Sadean nickname of "Madame la Marquise de merde." She could almost walk directly from the set of *Conversation Piece* onto the set of *Salò* and play one of the storytellers without having to change her wardrobe or makeup.

In *Salò*, one of the storytellers, Signora Maggi (Elsa Di Giorgi), describes a client who was only attracted to women who had been condemned to death and who paid enormous sums for these women to show him their rear ends and defecate in front of him. Maggi is wearing a black veil that falls down from the top of her head to just below her shoulders, the collar of her black gown trimmed in black fur, and she is wearing expensive-looking jewelry. The power of the image arises not through a simple contrast between the scatological content of what she is saying and her pristine, aging glamour but in how the film ultimately links her black-veiled appearance with desire, power, and death central to the film's project, the storytellers themselves transposed from Sade. This in itself, though, suggests a fundamental gap between Pasolini in this particular film and Visconti in his own. Praz writes, "Sade empties his world of all psychological content except the pleasures of destruction and transgression, in which his characters are degraded to the status of instruments for provoking the so-called divine ecstasy of destruction."[14] Bianca is likewise linked with fascistic destruction but in a more equivocal manner, bound up with the complicating factors of Mangano's star presence, the cult of the diva her Bianca evokes, and the fact that she remains a fully realized fictional character in a way the storytellers in *Salò* are not.

In d'Annunzio, the body of the woman in relation to fur and fabric is one of the pinnacles of a fetishistic response to her. In *Il piacere*, he writes of Andrea Sperelli putting on the fur coat of his lover, Elena, as they exit a soiree where he catches sight of her arm emerging from the coat's sleeve. "The sight of that living flesh, emerging from the fur like a mass of white roses from snow, once again inflamed longing in the young man's senses, even stronger than before, due to that strange provocative allure attained by the feminine nude when she is partly hidden by a thick, heavy garment."[15] Near the end of *The Innocent*, Giuliana is about to leave for church services when Tullio gives her a present of a fur coat and muff. She initially resists the extravagance of the gift but he insists, telling her that peasants enjoy seeing their masters wear luxurious items. For Tullio, Giuliana must perform the role of the upper-class wife and enter into his fetishistic circuit of desire, a world of openly displayed, upper-class male sexual power, class distinctions kept sharply in place.

Camouflage

The Professor's memories of his ex-wife and his mother do not emerge simply from the unwelcome sounds intruding into his world. They are equally engendered by what has occurred prior to these recollections, specifically Konrad being assaulted by men linked with political (and potentially terrorist) activities. The Professor tends to Konrad's wounds and wipes off the blood. Laurence Schifano has argued that "Lancaster's way of approaching and treating the young man who seeks refuge with him is maternal rather than paternal."[16] Like Spartaco in *Bellissima*, the Professor becomes a mother in the absence of conventional mother figures. That the film is fully aware of what it is up to in this regard is made explicit later in the film when Lietta jokes the Professor should adopt Konrad; and Konrad will sign his farewell note to the Professor as "Your son, Konrad." Almost anyone who has written extensively on *Conversation Piece* has taken note of the *pietà*-like positioning of the bodies of the Professor and Konrad as the Professor pulls Konrad's dead body away from the blast in the kitchen, the Professor here not only a maternal figure but the ultimate iconic maternal figure of Catholicism, the Madonna. However, the same maternal relationship has been central for those who see the Professor as a repressed homosexual, his sexuality awakened by Konrad. In a film in which so much in relation to the Professor's way of seeing is preceded by sound, it is Konrad's voice he hears immediately before seeing him, Konrad the last of the "family" to make his entrance into the home. As we hear Konrad tell Bianca that the police are about to tow away her car, the Professor looks over, searching for the source of this voice, as there is a rapid zoom into the Professor's face. A cut to a close-up of Konrad, wearing a brown cap, a blue shirt with a white tie, and a trench coat, follows as there is then a cut to a reverse angle of Bianca in the center of the frame and the Professor, behind her and to the right, slightly out of focus, still looking intently at Konrad. Unlike the numerous slow zooms into and away from Tadzio as Aschenbach stares, it is less clear what it is the Professor at first sees (or hears) in Konrad. In *The Innocent*, the initial appeal of Filippo for Giuliana is strongly tied to his voice, one Filippo self-deprecatingly acknowledges is capable of putting people to sleep but one Giuliana clearly finds soothing, if not seductive. She will soon be tied as well to his hypnotic gaze at the second soiree, but it is his voice that precedes this, during their first meeting at Federico's suite of rooms in the family house in Rome. The centrality of the voice as an audio umbilical cord was discussed in the previous chapter in relation to the mother in *Death in Venice*. But in *The Innocent*, such voices are capable of cutting across genders. Late in the film, a nanny explains that hearing any adult voice is soothing to a baby even as the film has already dramatized that such voices serve a similar nurturing function for adults. But Konrad's thin, Austrian-accented voice does not convey this kind of intensity, and the content of what he is saying is too banal to galvanize anyone. Something is meant to be happening to the Professor as he looks and listens. But the film is not yet making it clear why this should be so.

It is not until their first extended sequence together, in his study and directly following his vitriolic phone conversation with Bianca, that the film begins to assemble the necessary details. There is a sequence from *The Leopard*, discussed in a previous chapter, in which a Tuscan general admires the frescoes of draped mythical figures on the ceiling of the Prince's home. This sequence from *Conversation Piece* picks up on some of the possibilities raised in that sequence and, with Burt Lancaster once again present, reimagines them. In both sequences, there is the element of surprise in which such aesthetic inclinations are exhibited by men who would not otherwise seem to be capable of them. In *The Leopard*, however, the Prince's heterosexual nature does not allow for the general to function as a potential object of desire for him, and the film must engage in a complex choreography of looks in order to express other potentials. In *Conversation Piece*, though, the Professor and Konrad have an extended conversation over aesthetics, initiated by Konrad when he takes note of an eighteenth-century English painting hanging on the wall and recognizes the artist as Arthur Devis. Together they listen to a recording of Mozart's aria "Vorrei spiegarivi, oh Dio!" (1783). Konrad gives the impression of being less a scholar than a somewhat relaxed dandy but their exchanges create a general atmosphere of two people drawn to each other through shared aesthetic tastes. Konrad is also, for the Professor, if not raw material at least a figure he can transform, becoming a teacher to him but perhaps also a lover. When the two men examine the Devis painting, Konrad places his hand on the Professor's shoulder. The film keeps the two men at a "respectful" distance from the camera in a wide shot but Konrad's gesture is enough to add just the slightest element of the erotic to this moment. The Professor does not pull away but neither does he show a sense of being overwhelmed by the moment. Nevertheless, his response to being touched contrasts with a moment earlier in the film when Lietta touches his shoulder and he slightly recoils at her boldness.

The Mozart aria the Professor plays for Konrad is about loving someone but being unable to directly express it except through a language of veiling. This is central to how the film handles the relationship between the two men and where a word other than veil becomes important: camouflage. Late in the film, in the midst of a political argument with the entire "family" over the persistence of fascism in the current political climate, the Professor argues, against a skeptical Stefano, "It [fascism] does exist, even more dangerously today than ever. Because it's camouflaged." But to be camouflaged in *Conversation Piece* exists on two overlapping levels, one of them political and the other sexual. In an early sequence, when Stefano accidentally presses against a bookcase in the Professor's study, the bookcase gives way to an apartment hidden behind it. The Professor explains that his Italian mother had constructed this apartment during the Second World War as a way of hiding and protecting Jews and partisans. (The Professor, part American, had fought in the Fifth Army.) The mother is linked with hiding and protecting but she died before the war ended. When the new tenants first move into the Professor's home and begin the process of blasting from the inside for the purposes of remodeling, Erminia specifically compares this drilling to the war. And indeed the interiors of the second floor resemble wartime devastation, made explicit in the dialogue when the outraged Professor declares, "My house is filled with rubble." The wreckage seeps down into other parts of the house, necessitating that much of the decor be covered in white sheets. The family takes this whiteness to an extreme level through the redecorating initiated by Bianca, who will transform the second floor into a trendy modern environment, with avant-garde art hanging on blindingly white walls, contrasting with the muted colors and dim lighting of the Professor's space. This new space has no history, no traces of anything, its refurbishing paid for with right-wing money from Bianca's husband. It is in the mother's wartime apartment where the Professor will hide Konrad after he has been attacked, undressing him and helping him into bed, Konrad's white T-shirt and white underpants spotted with blood, as his head rests against two large white pillows. Konrad begs the Professor to let him spend the night in this apartment, to at least temporarily be hidden. It is up to the Professor to continue his mother's project, the film pointing to the persistence of the issues at stake during the war. When Konrad expresses his fear over being shut in the apartment overnight, with the bookcase door closed and locked, the Professor keeps the door open and sleeps on the couch in the library, like a mother helping a frightened child to get through the night.

When Emilia discovers the Professor asleep on the couch the next morning, the shot is framed so that a sculpture of a sleeping figure on the coffee table is aligned with him. It is *Sleeping Hermaphroditus*, whose figure is largely nude as she sleeps facedown but, in Bernini's 1620 revision used here, she is placed on a mattress with sheets flowing down from under her head, trailing along the outside of her body until they finally wrap around her left ankle and right foot. Blom has argued that the preponderance of nude and seminude sculptures (most of them of men) in the Professor's home implies the Professor's repressed homosexual desires.[17] Within such a context, the female figure of the draped Hermaphroditus is not so much an object of desire as a female double of the Professor, or at least a figuration of his repressed feminine self. And it is soon after he has been awakened by Emilia that his first memory of his mother occurs. With his veiled mother in the study, the pink decor implies her feminine sensibility has dominated that space. The Professor represses this possibility and, in the aftermath of her death, has taken her space and made it progressively more masculine. It is Konrad who has the potential to break through this but in a film in which virtually everything occurs too late for any decisive transformations.

In both *Conversation Piece* and *The Innocent*, a male figure around whom sexual fascinations and anxieties revolve is seen nude, showering. In *Conversation Piece*, this occurs the morning after Konrad has been attacked and he stands in a bathtub and showers the dirt and blood off. The Professor is in the library and engaged in another kind of cleaning: with a cotton ball in his hand he is carefully wiping the dirt off of one of his paintings. Wiping his hands with a rag, and bundled up in an Aschenbach-like pale brown sweater, he follows the sound of showering to the bathroom where he finds Konrad. But Visconti does not stage and edit the sequence in a way that immediately suggests the Professor sexually desires Konrad. There are no telegraphic facial expression of pained closeted desire as in *Death in Venice*, nor does Konrad express any embarrassment in being seen in this way. As Konrad steps out of the shower, he wraps an enormous white towel around himself and steps over to the mirror, looking at his wounds. White towel still around him, he walks into the main space of the hidden apartment. There he attempts to continue his conversation with the Professor from the night before. He does not, unlike Tadzio, use this towel seductively in the presence of the Professor but keeps it tight around his body. Konrad wishes to confess things, to no longer hide or camouflage his fundamental nature. The towel is one indication of this desire to come clean, its whiteness linked with the slight movements of the white curtains on the opposite side of the room. But the Professor's defensiveness over this potential causes him to abruptly leave the room rather than give Konrad the full dignity of the moment. This is immediately followed by the Professor's memory of his wife, the wife also wishing to confess to an offscreen Professor who, as has become increasingly clear, is resistant to such transparency. Konrad awakens not simply the Professor's past but his relation to his mother and his wife, Konrad becoming the wife and the Professor becoming his mother.

The towel in *The Innocent* assumes a different function, as does the man who uses it. The man is Filippo and the man observing him is Tullio. The sequence follows the one in which Teresa tells Tullio she did not see Giuliana at the auction. She taunts Tullio with the prospect that his wife now has a lover, increasing his suspicion of Filippo. In the sequence in which Tullio observes Filippo, he is first introduced to Filippo at the fencing club. Filippo removes his black fencing mask and Tullio is able to see his face, the mask serving here as a raised veil. The most immediate purpose of this raising of the mask is to show Tullio that Filippo is handsome, the first step in Tullio's anxiety. The two men engage in a straightforward match and the shower immediately follows. Tullio

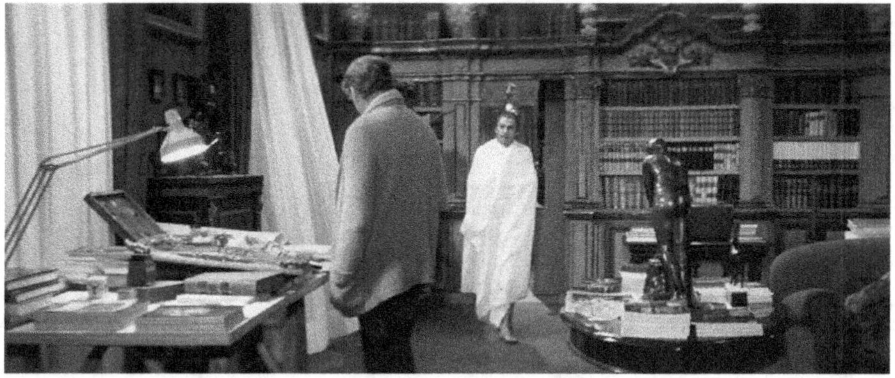

Conversation Piece (1974). The white towel tied to a need to confess.

sits and smokes as he blatantly stares at Filippo in the shower, the camera tilting up Filippo's body as an extension of Tullio's point of view, although the camera is closer to Filippo's body than is Tullio. The stare is so intense that Filippo himself looks over at Tullio before resuming his activity. In a wide shot showing Tullio still on a bench, Filippo enters the frame from the left, nude. Hanging on racks on the wall above and to the right of Tullio are various white robes and towels and Filippo takes one of the towels and wraps it around his body before walking out of the shot, center right. Such an encounter is present in d'Annunzio, who writes of this environment having "an acrid, sickening smell of men. All those in it, naked save for their large white dressing gowns, were smoking and slowly rubbing their chests, arms, shoulders, and chaffing one another loudly." In the midst of this he spots Filippo, "the frail form of Arborio, whom my eyes sought involuntarily. And, once again, the odious image was formed."[18] In the film Filippo is not frail and he will die unexpectedly from a disease caught in the "dark continent" so central to the Italian imagination of the period, later culminating in fascist conquest, Africa. In this sequence he is a potent image of male sexuality, not only in terms of face and body but also in terms of the substantial size of his penis. It is this, more than anything else, engendering Tullio's sexual jealousy. Filippo's penis is not visible to us until he steps out of the shower and moves over to where Tullio sits. Here he turns away from Tullio as he wraps the towel around himself and faces the camera, where the full force of what is upsetting Tullio is made clear. The shot where Filippo faces the camera is more for the spectator's benefit than it is for Tullio, who has already seen Filippo's genitalia. The intensity of Tullio's gaze indicates no expression of sexual desire for Filippo, whereas the comparative blankness of the Professor's look at Konrad creates a puzzling absence, almost a desire on the part of the spectator for the Professor to directly show us *something* when looking at Konrad. As we saw in the first chapter in relation to the shower sequence from *Rocco and His Brothers*, Simone is stared at by the trench-coated Morini in such a prolonged manner it exceeds his professionalism and speaks to a need of another sort. The male-to-male act of looking in the shower sequences of these two final films of Visconti's is more explicit due to the nudity. However, the framing of the showering men is only partly contained within the subjectivity of the men who are looking. This in itself is nothing new in Visconti, who, as we have often seen, will routinely use and then move beyond the desiring looks of the protagonists. But the men who look in these sequences from *Conversation Piece* and *The Innocent* remain outside of a direct expression of same-sex desire, in the case of Tullio because such desires are not part of his repertoire and in the case of the Professor because he remains camouflaged, unwilling to make (as is the film itself) his desires clear.

The White Angel

There is a sequence in *The Innocent* that is one of the film's fabric high points while announcing the shifting concerns of the film's second half. The setting is the Villa Lilla that belongs to Tullio and Giuliana. Giuliana is staying with Tullio's mother (Rina Morelli) at the family estate in Badiola while Tullio remains in Rome but he has arrived at his mother's as part of a concerted attempt to woo Giuliana. If the red of Teresa's clothing and decor dominates the color schemes of the first forty-five minutes of the film, the sequence at Villa Lilla moves other colors to the foreground. In the sequence immediately preceding Tullio's departure to the country, he is in Teresa's red-dominated room seen earlier in the film where, in this later sequence, an enormous fur covers the couch. All of this red and thickness is about to give way to another world, more strongly (but not exclusively) tied to Giuliana. Tullio's hopes for reconquering his wife are central at Villa Lilla but the fabrics and the colors associated with the sequence, beginning here and then throughout the remainder of the film, point toward his failure.

He is initially confident when he arrives in the country, and the shot of him at the family estate, lying in a white hammock in an oatmeal-colored suit and hat, tasseled pillows around him and cigar in hand as he talks to his mother and Giuliana, conveys a man who imagines himself to be in full possession of his masculine powers. When Tullio and Giuliana arrive at Villa Lilla and step into the house, the furniture and chandelier in the entrance are covered in white sheets, Tullio is in a suit matching and complementing these colors, and Giuliana is wearing a black jacket and hat with what initially appears to be a white dress underneath, signs of her hesitation in stepping over into Tullio's world. Tullio is attempting to move backward in time and rewrite his history with Giuliana, first by returning to this space from the first days after their marriage, where Giuliana lost her virginity. At the entrance to the house, he steps toward Giuliana, unpins and then lifts her veil, the importance of this gesture underlined through the forward zoom as he does so. The white sheets covering the Professor's furniture in *Conversation Piece* are almost entirely related to the evocation of a wartime environment while simultaneously pointing toward present-day destruction. In *The Innocent*, the white coverings and white muslin curtains carry other connotations. Most immediately they connote the overwhelming sense of a lost world, a history no longer to be recovered. Nevertheless, the pristine whiteness and beauty sufficiently move Giuliana to reluctantly accompany her husband on this journey, as her black hat and jacket come off, revealing a white dress with thin black stripes, and they stroll through the house and the gardens before his seduction.

In the bedroom, the camera pans and tilts over her discarded outer and under garments as Tullio says he wants them to now behave like two people who are meeting for the first time. The camera continues to move until it reaches the couple in bed, both of them nude. When we finally see them, the image itself looks veiled, with some kind of gauze placed over the lens, as though the film cannot bring itself to look directly at this somewhat false arrangement. Suddenly a flash of light enters the right of the frame and almost fills it up before there is a cut to a reverse angle of white curtains billowing in the window, these curtains presumably the diegetic source of what slightly obscured the end of the previous shot. In a few seconds of screen time, the film offers a condensed lexicon of the cinema of fabric, moving from the raw material of discarded clothing items, to relations between the lens of the camera and fabric obscuring what is being filmed, to a bright light approaching a state of abstraction, before the film returns us to fabric, that bright light (we retroactively see) itself a piece of fabric.

When the camera returns to them in bed it is has moved to the other side, the sense of romantic distance created through veiling gone as we look at two sweating naked bodies, the film participating in the naturalist desires of *Ossessione* (and Massimo Girotti will return in this film, playing a count infatuated with Teresa) but here enacted through the upper classes. There are two sex scenes in the film between Tullio and Giuliana, this one and later, when she is in her bedroom at the family estate. In both of these sequences, Antonelli's nude body is the primary focus and not Giannini's, whose nudity is camouflaged. Prior to working with Visconti, Antonelli's stardom was built upon several erotic films in which her nude body was a focal point of interest. *The Innocent* would not disappoint those who came for such a spectacle. In the first sex scene, Tullio promises he will now teach her the pleasures of sex, a task he had previously neglected. But Giuliana's writhing, nude body implies an experience in these matters of which her husband is unaware. Her reluctant body language at Villa Lilla would initially indicate that her hesitancy is due to his infidelities. But in reality it is due to her pregnancy by Filippo, something Tullio will soon discover. The white fabrics dominating Villa Lilla, as though initially announcing the possibility of making a clean break with the past, begin to migrate across later sequences, as though persistently mocking Tullio's presumptions.

For the second sex scene, he steps into Giuliana's bedroom, where she is wearing a white nightgown and doing needlepoint, a crucifix and a portrait of a Madonna in a gold frame to her left on the wall above her. There are two red chairs in this room, to the right of her bed, breaking the dominance of the cooler colors but also serving as a reminder of what is being increasingly marginalized in this world. His task is again to persuade her to come over to his way of thinking but the task before him is more complicated than the one he thought he was facing at the villa: he now wants Giuliana to abort her baby. Framed just behind him as he begins to talk to her is a portrait of what appears to be a little girl in a red dress. (In a later sequence we will see the entire portrait, which is of a mother and child.) He keeps up a steady stream of talk while also lying her on the bed, lifting up her nightgown, ravaging her, and then literally tearing the gown off of her, ripping it. He remains fully dressed. This casts a slight spell over her but, even as she lies nude across the bed, she does not fully succumb. Like Spagnolo with Gino in *Ossessione*, but reversing the politics involved, he is attempting to get her to reject the values of her world for the values of his. It is here where he most explicitly articulates his theories of himself as a Nietzschean superman for whom God has no meaning. The room's decor, with the Madonna and crucifix, makes clear the ethical and philosophical divide between husband and wife, and this will become stronger in succeeding sequences. In a sequence from the first half of the film, Teresa, after having spent the night in bed with Tullio, is surrounded by white sheets, blankets, and pillowcases, and she is wearing a white nightgown. In this bed, mocking Tullio, she shows a mastery of these sheets, pulling them toward and away from her as a way of demonstrating her ability to control him. When Tullio leaves Giuliana's bedroom, she pulls the sheet up to her face, only the top of her head from the eyes up visible, the moment more immediately connoting her sense of shame over what has just happened but, when situated within the context of the entire film, hinting at the games of subterfuge she herself has begun to play with him. She has begun to master this world of appearances but on her own terms.

When Giuliana first steps out of the carriage after the arrival at Villa Lillia, she opens a black silk parasol and walks about the grounds. The blackness of the fabric of this parasol, with the high sun shining on it, creates a beautiful image. But it also hints at the resilience of the seemingly weak woman carrying it. The parasol and umbrella recur in Visconti's cinema. The first shot of the street fair in *Ossessione* is of an umbrella suspended in the air and then falling into the hands of a barker selling the item to naive potential buyers on the basis of its leak-proof resilience. This umbrella becomes another of the film's many rhetorical flourishes in relation to questions of persuasion, seduction, and movement. A parasol, on the other hand, connotes feminine gentility. In terms of the former, *Death in Venice* shows how central the mother carrying a parasol is in conveying a sense of upper-class maternal. But it is more than this, not only in Visconti but elsewhere. In the Odessa Steps sequence from *Battleship Potemkin*, one of the motifs Eisenstein establishes just before the slaughter is of parasols carried by the bourgeois women on the steps, waiting for and waving at the approaching ship. When the gathered crowd is suddenly fired on, the first image that follows the overlapping close-ups of a woman reacting to the gunfire is of another woman, in black, rushing toward the camera, her white parasol open and eventually filling the frame. In this shot, we pass from the gentility of the parasol to the parasol now becoming a weapon of resistance. The needlepoint Giuliana engages in is an indicator not simply of her feminine, domestic nature but of a diligence, like Penelope's weaving in *The Odyssey*, in attempting to control a situation. As will be shown near the end of the film, her indifference is a performance given by her for Tullio's benefit in order to protect the child from Tullio's potentially murderous inclinations.

The white dominating the film's second half increasingly begins to turn on Tullio as Teresa herself loses virtually all of her connection to red. When Tullio makes an unexpected return to his house in Rome, he discovers that the furniture is tightly covered in white sheets because the house is being cleaned, the red and gold curtains (matching the wallpaper) still hanging in the windows. It is as though Tullio is being excluded, if not erased, from his own environment as fabric increasingly becomes the dominant image of this erasure. In the sequence directly following this one he is reunited with Teresa, who is now wearing green, red relegated to the very dark curtains behind them in the restaurant where they are seated. When he later returns to his home, this time with Federico, the furniture still has its white coverings. Lying in one of these covered chairs, he suddenly awakens from a restless sleep and finds Federico there. The sequence is entirely built around a discussion of Filippo, whom Federico refers to in a surprising way. Federico refers to him as not only a great artist but an angel, someone who almost makes Federico feel ashamed of himself. If Rocco is a type of saint, then, Filippo becomes a type of angel. As with Rocco, being an angel does not preclude a man from being sexually desirable, if not sexually active, and Filippo is both of these. He is an angel who has become not only a celebrity figure but an object of desire to

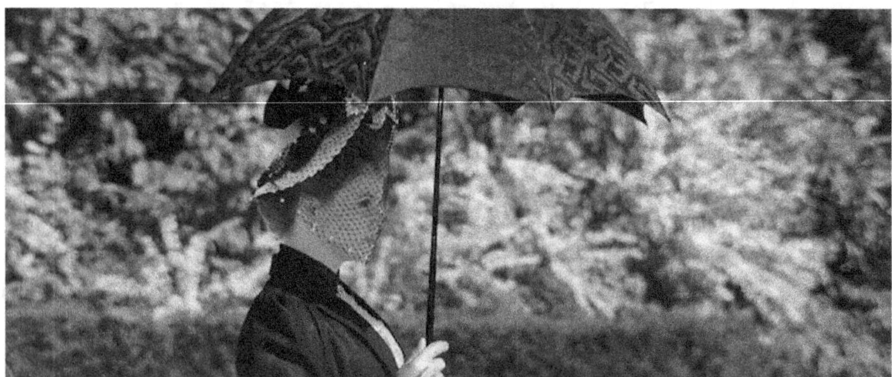

The Innocent (1976). The black parasol and the resilience of the woman carrying it.

many women in Rome, in this regard bringing him close to the Guest in *Teorema*, but his powers are entirely heterosexual and he remains, in fundamental ways, a specific fictional character rather than a symbolic figure. His angelic status, at least to Federico, is because his class origins are unlike his and Tullio's. Federico dismissively refers to the well-traveled and well-educated upbringing he and his brother were given, as though this has created something monstrous and unlike what Filippo represents. In the sequence in which Filippo is introduced, he explains his impoverished background and that, while he went to the same boarding school as Federico, he had to pay for it himself, through lessons he would give to other students, including Federico. Presumably, Filippo's status as angel is also a matter of him being a self-made man, not so much an artist of his own life as an artist. It is not entirely clear, however, what we are to make of him as a writer. The title of his novel we are given in the film, *La Fiamma*, is close to the title of a later d'Annunzio novel, *Il fuoco* (1900), which would suggest that if he is not based on d'Annunzio (the somewhat recessive personality would suggest otherwise, as would Filippo's very different class origins) he is at least a d'Annunzian writer and, like d'Annunzio, a powerful seducer of women. But if he is an angel, this suggests he is a potentially redemptive figure. This potential is not directly dramatized. (The character is too undeveloped for this.) Instead, his presence and, more specifically, his death bring about changes in the behavior of the characters as well as in the look of the film, in how colors and fabric begin to be increasingly used.

After Giuliana gives birth, Tullio steps into her bedroom, where the birth has taken place, and discovers a decor dominated by white in the bedding and other fabrics hanging or draping. This contrasts all the more strongly with the fabrics in the other rooms, dominated by browns and golds. Filippo is now dead but the white fabric throughout the room suggests at once the persistence of his angelic status and the innocence of his newborn son. The bassinet in which the male child (named Raimondo) is placed is covered in white lace, with white blankets and pillows in the bassinet itself, all of this delicate and refined, and when Tullio's mother holds Raimondo up he is tightly wrapped up in white. Just above his bassinet is a portrait of what appears to be Jesus Christ. In *Salò*, Christianity has been reduced to iconography that has ceased to have any metaphysical significance, an extension of the Decadent aesthetic of draining religious meaning from Catholic iconography so that it, along with its surrounding rituals, takes on purely decorative and fetishistic functions. If, as we have already seen in relation to other Visconti films, Catholicism is present it is because of its social rather than directly religious influence. But Catholicism is not negated or reduced to the merely decorative even as Filippo's status as an angel is ambiguous. If Christ, via the portrait, is in this room with Raimondo, are we to read Filippo as a Christ-like figure, dying for the sins of those around him? For the world of this film, in particular its women, Filippo's quiet sexual power, his working-class origins, his aestheticism focused on his work as a writer rather than on turning his life into a work of art, in themselves are an alternative to the narcissistic bravado of men like Tullio. But is Filippo enough for the challenges an "angel" might face in this particular world?

Tullio's murder of Raimondo, taking the baby outside in the cold and leaving him there on a slab of marble, would suggest Filippo has arrived too late, that this child represents too insignificant a form of resistance. The murder itself is dominated by white fabric (including diapers) in the baby's room. The murder is ironically cross-cut with Giuliana and other members of the household attending a Christmas mass as another form of white—snow—is quietly falling. Just before he takes the baby out into the cold, sheer white curtains blow inward from the windows but this movement is markedly different from the same kind of movement of white curtains from the opening of *The Leopard*, where it marked the beauty and fragility of that particular environment. "The curtains separated me from an abyss," Tullio writes in the novel.[19] And here, the fabric in this room quickly transitions from connoting the innocence of the child and its father to a foreshadowing of the child's death. Before taking the baby out of the bassinet, Tullio does not simply remove the baby's blanket but violently jerks it down, an echo of the gesture of his ripping the top of Giuliana's white gown during his first concerted attempt to convince her to abort. Giuliana's revulsion over what Tullio has done to the baby engenders a full confession from her as she stands outside of her room, the door open and crucifix visible on the wall. She states that, contrary to her actions and words prior to this, she has always loved the child and will always love the child's father. This has already begun to be evident, even to Tullio, prior to the murder, but the explicitness of the confession makes it clear she is now firmly engaged in a full-scale rejection of Tullio, one sending him back to Teresa. In *L'innocente*, Giuliana and Tullio already have two children before she becomes pregnant by Filippo. Eliminating this not only intensifies the singularity of her pregnancy, it also rids the marriage of any connotations of family, leaving both spouses isolated at the end of the film, each taking their own particular journey in relation to guilt and penance.

Deceitful Disguises

Both *The Innocent* and *Conversation Piece* resolve themselves in ways requiring leaps of faith from the viewer. When Giuliana makes her confession to Tullio, both are dressed primarily in black. A bit of white emerges through the blouse underneath the top of her gown, the white crawling up the gown's middle front and reaching to a high collar, the collar's top border trimmed in black. This black on Giuliana begins to migrate as she herself disappears from the final moments of the film and white is no longer central. From Giuliana's confession, a sudden cut takes us from a close-up of Tullio's face to the inside of a carriage in which Tullio and Teresa are passengers. Again Visconti takes advantage of the wide anamorphic frame, Tullio and Teresa kept in singles throughout the sequence, with no master shot or two-shots. One effect this wide frame creates is that both figures are engulfed in blackness through the lining of the inside of the carriage and their clothing, a white scarf peeking out from the top of Tullio's coat. The couple will soon head to his house in Rome, where the final sequence will unfold. Teresa has already terminated her relationship with Tullio and told him she no longer loves him. And here in the carriage, as he narrates his story of placing Raimondo out in the cold, her eyes are filled with tears. It is not made explicit what is causing these feelings of pathos and they are, at this precise moment, uncharacteristic. Possibly she is crying over Tullio's narration of the death of the child even as she also attempts to convince him of the inherent resilience of babies. She implies a more poetic, fatalistic reason for its death: the baby did not wish to live. Tullio does not accept this and, uncharacteristically, assumes moral responsibility for what he has done. At the same time, he clings to his traditional ways of seeing, regarding his wife's affair as a second-rate romance fiction, as short-lived and meaningless as Federico's other affairs. And possibly his obtuseness is what is producing tears from Teresa, crying over the ongoing blindness of the man she once loved. But no dialogue makes this explicit.

Suicide is crucial to the endings of both films. Departing from d'Annunzio, Tullio shoots himself. Konrad's death can be more properly thought of as a murder/suicide, in that Konrad's gesture will soon lead to the collapse of the Professor from shock and grief. He is visited by Bianca and Lietta, Bianca in pale yellow and Lietta in white, both apparently atoning. Bianca resentfully regards the suicide as Konrad's way of "having the last word," as though Konrad was attempting to wrest control of the narrative away from "Madame la marquise de merde" and to be the ultimate *metteur en scène* of the situation. Lietta, on the other hand, insists to the Professor (after Bianca has left the room) that Konrad did not kill himself. "They murdered him," she states. Who are "they"? Possibly she is referring to Bianca and the absent Stefano, the latter having denounced him in a sequence prior to this one, although the precise terms of the denunciation are not clear. But Stefano's denunciation is particularly virulent in being expressed along class lines. When Stefano dismisses Konrad's emergence into the world as occurring through the servants' entrance, Konrad responds, "Right, with a frayed shirt and a corduroy jacket which I couldn't button because I'd outgrown it." Unlike Don Ciccio in *The Leopard*, Konrad is unable to boast of the ragged nature of his clothing because he has no peasant or working-class culture from which he could proudly smack the decaying seat of his pants. What Lietta is referring to, then, is not simply her mother and her boyfriend but the sociopolitical world around Konrad. Like the Prince, Konrad has outlived his era. His parasitic ties to the upper classes that served as a refuge from his period of political commitment are now also eluding his grasp. But following Lietta, should his final act of the film necessarily be taken as a suicide?

When the Professor pulls Konrad's body away from the oven and drags it into the living room of the modern apartment, Konrad still has in his hands a black-and-white-striped woolen scarf. The "children" of the film are initially shown wearing scarves that look expensive, chic indicators of their social status. In *Salò*, scarves are linked with the bourgeois and proletarian youth arrested by the fascists, or with children who observe the arrests. As one boy is taken away, soon to become a guard at the villa, his mother chases after him because he has forgotten his scarf. But the son repudiates this attempt at maternal care as he almost willingly marches off with two officers wearing trench coats and black hats. The scarf has become a superfluous item in relation to what is to follow. The scarf Konrad is holding at the end of the film, however, belongs to Stefano and, unlike Konrad and Lietta, Stefano continues to wear this scarf so that it becomes a signature look. But the Professor, preoccupied with Konrad's bloodied body, does not take particular note of the scarf. There are no closer shots of it and it is never referred to in the dialogue. The scarf suggests a link between Stefano and the death of Konrad (the bomb, perhaps, simply another camouflage to give the appearance of suicide, the scarf inadvertently left behind in a mad dash to escape) although how all of this precisely transpired, or what Stefano's motivations might have been, are never clarified. The scarf simply becomes a metaphor for "they."

When Konrad flees the gathering after Stefano's accusations and the failure of the Professor and Bianca to defend him, the Professor has a monologue and, in a surprising move, professes his love for the people before him in the room, as well as, implicitly, Konrad. "I love this wretched family," he tells them. This self-evidently ambivalent expression of love, and the monologue that follows, is delivered as he first stands in front of a window with its sheer white curtains closed. The Professor refers to a writer whose books he keeps on a table near his bed and reads from time to time. The words uttered are an evocation of Proust, who writes of a tenant moving stealthily above him who suddenly vanishes but then eventually returns, becoming a constant presence: "He is Death." The end of his life has been announced to him all along in one of Death's many "deceitful disguises." In yet another surprising shift, the Professor says the presence of Bianca and the others has had the opposite effect on him. "You've awakened me from a sleep as profound, as insensitive and as deaf as

Death itself." Throughout this monologue, there is only one brief reaction shot of the family, although all of them appear to be moved by what the Professor is saying. But halfway through, as the Professor looks up, there is a cut to a tracking and panning movement around all of the paintings hanging high on the walls of the study. He continues with the monologue through this movement, culminating with his expression of gratitude to this family for disrupting the insular nature of his prior existence. But as the circular movement finds its way back to the Professor, he is not facing the family but facing the window he had been standing in front of. The curtains are open and it is now daytime, the family gone as Erminia enters with Konrad's farewell letter, the upstairs blast soon to follow. The movement across the paintings makes a clear connection and contrast between the eighteenth-century families in these conversation pieces and the flesh-and-blood reality of the present-day (and very noisy) family above him. It is precisely this noise that has awakened him, as the camera moves across history and brings itself up to a present day the Professor is finally willing to embrace, to open the curtains and look out at the world. But it will turn out to be too late and the final noise from upstairs will put an end to this possibility, an explosion evoking both war and terrorism.

In an early sequence from *Salò*, one of the fascist libertines quotes Proust but in a way that becomes both a perversion of Proust's intent and also, for Pasolini, an inevitable culmination of its sensibility into fascist decadence. In his monologue, the Professor does not wish to negate the sensibility of a Proust or any of the other art objects with which he surrounds himself but to see them in new ways. The camera movement in the study still includes these paintings in its movement, containing the Professor within its circularity while also acknowledging the possibility of this aestheticism opening out to what is beyond the window. Instead, the death of Konrad sends the Professor back to that central item of decor in Visconti, the bed.

In *The Innocent*, Tullio and Teresa are in Tullio's living room. The *coup de théâtre* of Tullio taking a gun out of a drawer and shooting himself at the end of this lengthy sequence is the most mysterious death in all of Visconti because so little has prepared us for this sudden reversal in psychology. His statement to Teresa that he would kill himself if he no longer had a taste for life still seems, strictly in psychological terms, inadequate for his final gesture. The portrait of Christ in Raimondo's room could also be seen as an ironic commentary on Tullio regarding himself as dying for the sins of the values of his own world, referring back to the illustration of a crucifixion from the novel, shown in the credits. But the point of the suicide is clearest if we move it away from psychological coherence and instead situate it in historical and political terms. The white sheets covering the furniture in the living room are gone and the large leather maroon chairs and black leather sofa seen early in the film are again visible. As Teresa looks around, she tells Tullio these interiors are strange because they so strongly resemble him, a statement with clear ties to the Romantic and Decadent notion of domestic environments being dominated by the taste and sensibility of their owner. Yet she also alludes to an ugliness there, but one she will only tell him about later. Moreover, Teresa herself is uttering statements outside of the character we have previously witnessed. If earlier in the film she proudly assumes a masculine role in her society, seeing herself as free as Tullio, she now speaks of a certain equality of the sexes, of her right to walk side by side with a man, something she also acknowledges is an impossibility with Tullio because he is, like all other men, monstrous. The possibilities of play in roles of dominance and submission the couple previously engaged in are gone, as Teresa sounds close to a feminist of the 1970s. The film must eliminate Tullio—and Teresa must forcefully reject him—not simply because he is a negative figure within the period in which the film was made but also because he anticipates fascist ideals of the coming years. But if he is a political metaphor, he is also a metaphor for a *metteur en scène* who has lost control of his vision, and the suicide becomes his final romantic gesture.

It is the concluding images of *Conversation Piece* and *The Innocent* that will bring this book to its own conclusion. In the first film, white fabric dominates; in the second, black. The Professor is propped up in bed by two large pillows, and he is wearing white pajamas and surrounded by white bedding, covered up to his waist by a fur blanket, with a book open on his lap. The table to his left, on top of which sit medicinal items and a few books, has a white tablecloth covering it. Teresa, on the other hand, is outdoors, fleeing Tullio's home. It is dawn and there is mist. Her dashing away is captured in three separate shots, interrupted by a brief cutaway to Tullio's body lying sprawled on the floor. The first is an establishing shot of the house. As Teresa steps out of this house, nervously glancing over her shoulder, she looks diminished in a film where she has otherwise dominated spaces. Her black evening gown, in the morning light, is beginning to look incongruous, almost surreal, as there is a cut to a close view of her, still dashing, but shot with a long lens, magnifying the sense of her agitation. The final shot of the film is the one that most commands attention: A wide shot of Teresa from behind walking down the path to the house as we see the movements of not only her body but also her black gown, its hem dragging in the dirt, as she carries a black wrap and a white handkerchief, before the image freezes and the final credits roll. In *Conversation Piece*, the Professor weeps and folds his hands in a gesture of prayer or pleading as he then hears footsteps overhead. The Professor (and the spectator) would now know what those sounds mean, that they are at this moment no longer a "deceitful disguise" but understood to be death itself, come to take the Professor. At the same time, they could also be nothing more than the sound of someone on the second floor walking about. The Professor closes his eyes as his head falls to his right and the image freezes, bringing the film to an end.

In one shot, a figure largely immobile, confined to his bed, his death imminent if not implicitly made visible. In the other, an agitated figure in motion, moving toward an uncertain future. As a method for conveying the Professor's death, the film has chosen to end itself on an image that does not so much clearly signify death as convey things being halted, suspended, returning the Professor to the long, metaphoric sleep he was in before the arrival of the new family. But that sleep, too, he has already acknowledged, was a type of death. If for Pasolini in *Salò* Romantic and Decadent art has the potential to culminate in fascist oppression, for Visconti in *Conversation Piece* such potentials do not turn outward, in aggression, but inward, destroying the self. But it is the whiteness of things here, articulated through fabric, that gives this image much of its ambiguous power, a white of sickness and death but also of a certain paradoxical beauty, the white fabric surrounding a movie star. Yet this is also an image of an *aging* movie star, playing a character who is, if not dying, fading, the medical apparatus tied to him bringing us back to the reality of the physical.

With the shot of Teresa, Visconti's cinema has come full circle. In her nervous movements out of doors in elegant clothing, she evokes Livia in *Senso*. But even more than this she is the last in a line of Visconti women in black. Teresa's lucidity has given way to agitation, her direction uncertain. Her movements are like Giovanna's in *Ossessione* when she steps out of the insurance office in her black widow's weeds and lifts up her long veil, anxiously looking for Gino in order to talk about the money she will receive.

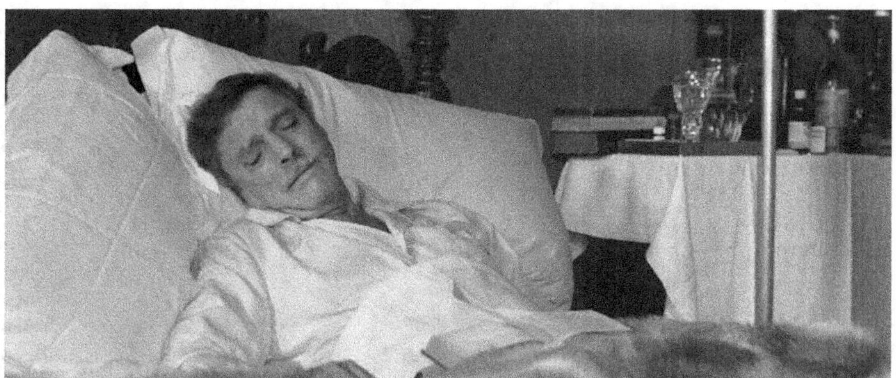

Conversation Piece. The white bedding of sickness and death.

Teresa has no such financial concerns, though, nor is she gripped by an uncontrollable sexual passion, like Livia. She runs because she is scared, as though wishing to completely distance herself from this world within which she is both a central figure and something of an exception. At this moment, neither role is adequate for what has just happened, and within a long tradition of neorealism she has beheld something that has outstripped her normal modes of perception. When the Prince walks slowly into the darkness of the final shot of *The Leopard* he does so with a full awareness of the death of his own culture. As an Italian female subject of the late nineteenth century, though, where is Teresa going? Within the film's rereading of d'Annunzio, what lies ahead is fascism, where the values Teresa espouses will have no place. But beyond this is the history and culture that culminated in putting this film together. When Teresa moves from the lush fabrics of d'Annunzian decadent interiors to the outdoors of the film's final shots, it is as though she has become a nascent neorealist subject, her black gown inadequate for what she is now facing.

But throughout this book I have also situated Visconti's films within another context, not of an official film movement but of a trope, the cinema of fabric. Through this trope, we not only understand anecdotal and decorative details in a film's use of fabric but tie these to fundamental questions about the cinema and the social, historical, and political forces shaping it. Visconti's homosexuality is crucial to this history. Fabric, as we have repeatedly seen, is often a privileged, if not at times overdetermined, method of shaping the form and social and political intent of any given Visconti project and in which tensions and relations between male and female, masculine and feminine, heterosexual and homosexual are enacted *through* fabric. But Visconti's cinema is also, crucially, one of suspended desires, of things left uncertain, ambiguous, unfulfilled. How apt that the final images of his two final films are literally suspended

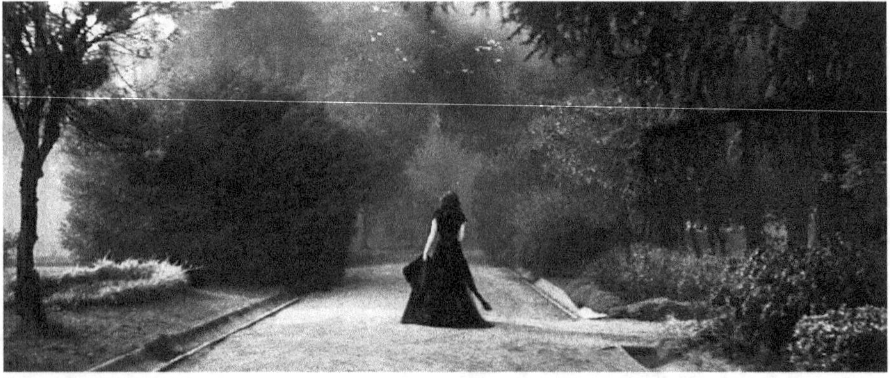

The Innocent. The black gown as incongruous image: the past and the future through fabric.

ones. But they are also images of white fabric in one film and black in the other, a return to basics, the colors of shadow and light. These images evoke not so much literal death as suspended forms of it, this suspension itself the source of ambivalent, if not fetishistic, pleasure for the spectator, and where the cinema of fabric becomes the very fabric of cinema.

NOTES

Introduction

1 D. A. Miller, "Second Time Around: *Rocco and His Brothers*," *Film Quarterly* (Fall 2008): 13.

2 Cited in Mira Liehm, *Passion and Defiance: Film in Italy from 1942 to the Present* (Berkeley: University of California Press, 1984), 126.

3 For a useful description of the relationship between Visconti and the Italian Communist Party, see Laurence Schifano, *Luchino Visconti: The Flames of Passion*, trans. William S. Byron (London: Collins, 1990), 228–30.

4 Serge Daney and Jean-Pierre Oudart, "The Name of the Author (on the 'Place' of *Death in Venice*)," trans. Joseph Karmel, in *Cahiers du Cinéma, 1969–1972: The Politics of Representation*, ed. Nick Browne (Cambridge, MA: Harvard University Press, 1990), 313.

5 Ibid., 314. The first book-length biography of Visconti in English, Monica Stirling's *A Screen of Time*, published in 1979, three years after the director's death, makes no mention of his sexuality.

6 Miller, "Second Time Around," 13.

7 Ibid., 14.

8 Christian Metz, *The Imaginary Signifier*, trans. Celia Britton, Annwyl Williams, Ben Brewster, and Alfred Guzzetti (Bloomington: Indiana University Press, 1982), 77–78.

9 Jean-Luc Godard, *Godard on Godard*, ed. and trans. Tom Milne (New York: Da Capo Press, 1972), 222.

10 Ibid.

11 Alberto Moravia, "Visconti, The Leopard Man," trans. Raymond Rosenthal, *Vogue*, July 1963, 105.

12 Alexander García Düttmann, *Visconti: Insights into Flesh and Blood*, trans. Robert Savage (Stanford, CA: Stanford University Press, 2009), 46.

13 Colette, *Colette at the Movies: Criticism and Screenplays*, trans. Sarah W. R. Smith, ed. Alain and Odette Virmaux (New York: Frederick Ungar, 1980), 31.

14 Colette, *Colette at the Movies*, 19.

15 Cecelia Ager, "Another Dawn," in *American Movie Critics: An Anthology from the Silents Until Now*, ed. Philip Lopate (New York: Library of America, 2006), 84.

16 Maurice Zolotow, *Billy Wilder in Hollywood* (New York: G. P. Putnam's Sons, 1977), 69.

17 Gaia Servadio, *Luchino Visconti: A Biography* (New York: Franklin Watts, 1983), 62.

18 Schifano, *Luchino Visconti*, 75.

19 Marcel Proust, *In Search of Lost Time: The Captive, The Fugitive*, trans. C. K. Scott Moncrieff and Terence Kilmartin, rev. D. J. Enright (New York: Modern Library, 1992), 291.

20 Roland Barthes, *The Language of Fashion*, trans. Andy Stafford (London: Bloomsbury Publishing), 101.

21 "When I was in Paris [in the 1930s], I was kind of an imbecile, not a Fascist, but unconsciously affected by Fascism, 'colored' by it." Rhonda K. Garelick, *Coco Chanel and the Pulse of History* (New York: Random House, 2014), 252.

22 Barthes, *Language of Fashion*, 100.

23 In the 1950s, Schneider appeared in several remakes of seemingly unremakable Weimar classics: Harald Braun's *Der letzte Mann* (1955, a remake of F. W. Murnau's 1924 film), Géza von Radvány's *Mädchen in Uniform* (1955, a remake of Leontine Sagan's 1931 film), and Pierre Gaspard-Huit's *Christine* (1958, costarring Alain Delon, and a remake of Max Ophüls's 1933 film *Liebelei*, starring Magda Schneider).

24 Dziga Vertov, *Kino-Eye: The Writings of Dziga Vertov*, ed. Annette Michelson, trans. Kevin O'Brien (Berkeley: University of California Press, 1984), 5.

25 Ibid., 34.

26 Annette Michelson, introduction to *Kino-Eye: The Writings of Dziga Vertov*, ed. Annette Michelson, trans. Kevin O'Brien (Berkeley: University of California Press, 1984), xxxviii.

27 Ibid., xxxix.

28 Ibid., xxxvii.

29 Yuri Tsivian, *Ivan the Terrible* (London: BFI, 2002), 65.

30 Sergei Eisenstein, "The Structure of the Film," in *Film Form: Essays in Film Theory*, ed. and trans. Jay Leyda (New York: Harcourt Brace Jovanovich, 1949), 166.

31 Ibid., 168–69.

32 Ibid., 167.

33 Ibid., 173.

34 Daney and Oudart, "Name of the Author," 307.

35 Ivo Blom, *Reframing Luchino Visconti: Film and Art* (Leiden: Sandstone Press, 2017), 289.

Chapter 1: Interwoven

1 Sam Rohdie, *Rocco and His Brothers* (London: BFI, 1992), 25.

2 Guido Aristarco, "Luchino Visconti: Critic or Poet of Decadence?" trans. Luciana Bohen, *Film Criticism* (Spring 1988): 59.

3 Fyodor Dostoevsky, *The Brothers Karamazov*, trans. Richard Pevear and Larissa Volokhonsky (New York: Vintage Classics, 1991), 636. Eisenstein refers to this passage in his memoirs where he writes of the importance of the interlacing of details in aesthetic construction, this passage from *Karamazov* "no better example" of how "the entirety and the part" are combined so "harmoniously" that "both are equally noticeable." Sergei Eisenstein, *Beyond the Stars 2: The True Paths of Discovery*, trans. William Powell (New York: Seagull Books, 2018), 29.

4 Émile Zola, *Au Bonheur des Dames*, trans. Robin Buss (New York: Penguin, 2001), 15.

5 Sergei Eisenstein, "Lessons from Literature," in *Film Essays and a Lecture*, ed. and trans. Jay Leyda (Princeton, NJ: Princeton University Press, 1968), 79. Sumiko Higashi has written that a passage in *Au Bonheur des dames* in which Zola describes two simultaneous dramatic high points (women engaged in a buying spree on the main floor of the department store as an entrepreneur attempts to seduce an "innocent" woman) is able to "exemplify" parallel editing. Sumiko Higashi, *Cecil B. DeMille and American Culture: The Silent Era* (Berkeley: University of California Press, 1994), 104.

6 James M. Cain, *The Postman Always Rings Twice* (New York: Vintage, 1992), 51.

7 Ibid., 4.

8 Ibid., 3.

9 See also a discussion of the differences between the presentation of Girotti in *The Iron Crown* and Girotti in *Ossessione* in Mauro Giori, *Poetica e Prassi della Trasgressione in Luchino Visconti 1935–1962*, 2nd ed. (Milano: Libraccio Editore, 2018), 57–58.

10 Geoffrey Nowell-Smith, *Luchino Visconti* (London: BFI, 2003), 21.

11 Eisenstein, "Structure," 169.

12 Zola, *Thérèse Raquin*, trans. Robin Buss (New York: Penguin, 2004), 10–11.

13 Cain, *The Postman Always Rings Twice*, 8.

14 Ibid., 97.

15 In the Carnè film of *Thérèse Raquin* this erotic treatment of the torn T-shirt worn by a male figure occurs through a character who is not in Zola's novel, a blackmailing sailor played by Roland Lesaffre. Richard Dyer has written

that this fetish for the ripped T-shirt on men, boldly displaying a nipple, is an iconic image from 1950s gay pornography. Richard Dyer, *The Culture of Queers* (New York: Routledge, 2002), 128.

16 Zola, *Thérèse Raquin*, 27.

17 Guido Aristarco, "The Earth Still Trembles," *Films and Filming* (January 1961): 12.

18 Henry Bacon, *Visconti: Explorations of Beauty and Decay* (Cambridge: Cambridge University Press, 1998), 105. For a detailed analysis of the influence of Mann, Dostoevsky, and, especially, Testori in relation to the film, see Mauro Giori, *Rocco e i suoi fratelli* (Torino: Lindau, 2011), 109–32.

19 Rohdie, *Rocco*, 25, 28.

20 Luchino Visconti, *Three Screenplays: White Nights, Rocco and His Brothers, The Job*, trans. Judith Green (New York: Orion Press, 1970), 150.

21 Sergei Eisenstein, *Beyond the Stars 1: The Boy from Riga*, trans. William Powell (New York: Seagull Books, 2018), 147. For Eisenstein, the two "superlative" accounts of "the subject of beds" are Groucho Marx's *Beds* (1930) and Maupassant's "Beds" (presumably "Le lit," 1882).

22 See André Bazin, "Cinematic Realism and the Italian School of the Liberation," *What Is Cinema?*, trans. Timothy Barnard (Montreal: Caboose, 2009), 215–49.

23 Bazin, "De Sica: Metteur en Scène," in *What Is Cinema? Volume II*, ed. and trans. Hugh Gray (Berkeley: University of California Press, 1971), 65–66.

24 Ibid., 64.

25 Ibid., 64–65.

26 André Bazin, "*Bicycle Thief*," in *What Is Cinema? Volume II*, ed. and trans. Hugh Gray (Berkeley: University of California Press, 1971), 45.

27 Ibid. Nowell-Smith argues that *La terra trema's* "cinematic models are [Robert] Flaherty and Eisenstein," (*Luchino Visconti*, 33).

28 Amédée Ayfre, "Neo-Realism and Phenomenology," trans. Diana Matias, in *Cahiers du Cinéma*, ed. Jim Hillier (Cambridge, MA: Harvard University Press, 1985), 187.

29 Miller, "Second Time Around," 14.

30 Noa Steimatsky, *Italian Locations: Reinhabiting the Past in Postwar Cinema* (Minneapolis: University of Minnesota Press, 2008), 115.

31 Nowell-Smith, *Luchino Visconti*, 39.

32 Parker Tyler, *Screening the Sexes: Homosexuality in the Movies* (New York: Holt, Rinehart and Winston, 1972), 259.

33 Giovanni Verga, *The House by the Medlar Tree*, trans. Raymond Rosenthal (Berkeley: University of California Press, 1983), 24.

34 Ibid., 12.

35 André Bazin, "*Senso*," *Bazin at Work: Major Essays and Reviews from the Forties and Fifties*, ed. and trans. Bert Cardullo (New York: Routledge, 1997), 161.

36 Ayfre, "Neo-Realism and Phenomenology," 190.

37 Daney and Oudart, "Name of the Author," 322.

38 Schifano, *Luchino Visconti*, 177.

39 Ibid.

40 Giuliana Minghelli, "Haunted Fames: History and Landscape in Luchino Visconti's *Ossessione*," *Italica* 85, nos. 2/3 (2008): 183.

41 Ibid.

42 Ibid., 187.

43 Ibid.

44 Mauro Giori, *Homosexuality and Italian Cinema: From the Fall of Fascism to the Years of Lead* (London: Palgrave Macmillan, 2017), 14.

45 Mighelli, "Haunted Fames," 190.

46 Arthur Miller, *A View from the Bridge*: *The Penguin Arthur Miller* (New York: Penguin, 2015), 469.

47 George Lukács, *Essays on Thomas Mann*, trans. Stanley Mitchell (New York: Grosset and Dunlap, 1965), 55.

48 Thomas Mann, *Joseph and His Brothers*, trans. John E. Woods (New York: Everyman's Library), 238.

49 Sigmund Freud, *Totem and Taboo: Some Points of Agreement between the Mental Lives of Savages and Neurotics*, ed. and trans. James Strachey (New York: Norton, 1950), 194.

50 Visconti, *Three Screenplays*, 96.

51 Rohdie, *Rocco*, 74.

52 Ibid., 69.

53 Mann, *Joseph and His Brothers*, 473.

54 Fyodor Dostoevsky, *Crime and Punishment*, trans. Richard Pevear and Larissa Volokhosnky (New York: Vintage, 1992), 91.

55 Blom, *Reframing Luchino Visconti*, 52.

56 Marcel Proust, *In Search of Lost Time, Volume VI: Time Regained*, trans. Andreas Mayor and Terence Kilmartin, rev. D. J. Enright (New York: Modern Library, 1993), 173.

57 Blom's research has drawn attention to Visconti's fascination with this portrait, in particular for the hat worn by Roulin (*Reframing Luchino Visconti*, 119–20).

58 Meyer Schapiro, *Vincent Van Gogh* (New York: Harry N. Abrams, 1950), 84.

59 Mann, *Joseph and His Brothers*, 515.

Chapter 2: The Diva, Draped

1 Cited in Liehm, *Passion and Defiance*, 148.

2 Jacques Doniol-Valcroze and Jean Domarchi, "Interview with Luchino Visconti," *Sight and Sound* 28, nos. 3/4 (1959): 146. Translation uncredited.

3 Bazin, *What Is Cinema?*, 234.

4 Cited in Liehm, *Passion and Defiance*, 150.

5 Cited in Bacon, *Visconti*, 62.

6 Schifano, *Luchino Visconti*, 280.

7 Ibid., 288.

8 Millicent Marcus, *After Fellini: National Cinema in the Postmodern Age* (Baltimore: Johns Hopkins University Press, 2002), 43

9 Proust, *Time Regained*, 509.

10 Doniol-Valcroze and Domarchi, "Interview with Luchino Visconti," 147.

11 Angela Dalle Vache, *Diva: Defiance and Passion in Early Italian Cinema* (Austin: University of Texas Press, 2008), 6.

12 Drake Stutesman, "Hide in Plain Sight: An Interview with Piero Tosi," *Framework: The Journal of Cinema and Media* 47, no.1 (2006): 108.

13 Ibid., 114.

14 Marcus, *After Fellini*, 52–53.

15 Blom links *Senso* and *Gone with the Wind* in that both evoke "romance during wartime." *Gone with the Wind* was not released in Italy until 1950 and he argues that the film would still have been fresh in the minds of spectators at the time of *Senso*'s release, 51.

16 Blom, 150–51.

17 Blom writes of the connections between Livia's outfits and the designs of Christian Dior, Balenciaga, and Pierre Balmain that were contemporaneous with the film's production (*Reframing Luchino Visconti*, 110).

18 Nowell-Smith, *Luchino Visconti*, 76.

19 Aristarco, "The Earth Still Trembles," 38.

20 Düttmann, *Visconti*, 90.

21 Camillo Boito, *Senso (and Other Stories)*, trans. Christine Donougher (Sawtry: Dedalus Books, 1993), 27.

22 Blom, *Reframing Luchino Visconti*, 109.

23 See ibid., 131–37.

24 Boito, *Senso*, 22.

25 Jean Cocteau, *The Art of Cinema*, trans. Robin Buss (New York: Marion Boyars, 1992), 136.

26 Dalle Vacche, *Diva*, 151.

27 Boito, *Senso*, 52.

28 Angela Dalle Vache, *The Body in the Mirror* (Princeton, NJ: Princeton University Press, 1992), 154.

29 Boito, *Senso*, 54.

30 Dalle Vacche, *Body*, 150.

31 *Ibid.*, 140.

32 Sergei Eisenstein, "Synchronization of Senses," in *The Film Sense*, ed. and trans. Jay Leyda (New York: Harcourt Brace Jovanovich, 1975), 71.

33 For Visconti's version of Blasetti's response to the use of the "Charlatan theme," see Doniol-Valcroze and Domarchi, "Interview with Luchino Visconti," 146–47.

34 Marcus, *After Fellini*, 47.

35 Bazin, *What Is Cinema?*, 217.

36 Ibid., 218.

37 Ibid., 217.

38 Marcus, *After Fellini*, 51.

39 Blom, *Reframing Luchino Visconti*, 47.

40 Bazin, "*Senso*," 160.

41 Ibid., 161.

42 Ibid.

43 Dalle Vacche, *Body*, 145.

44 Margaret Mitchell, *Gone with the Wind* (New York: Scribner, 2011), 418.

Chapter 3: Tight Fits

1 The film is based on a 1949 novel by Vitaliano Brancati and was an attempt to address the impossible ideals of masculinity within Fascist Italy. The film adaptation (cowritten by Pasolini) is set in the present day and examines the ideal's persistence.

2 Fyodor Dostoevsky, "White Nights," in *The Best Short Stories of Dostoevsky*, trans. David Macgarshack (New York: The Modern Library, 1992), 19.

3 Ibid., 26–27.

4 Guido Aristarco, "Three Tendencies: A Postscript to the Venice Film Festival," *Film Culture* 15 (December 1957): 8.

5 Steimatsky, *Italian Locations*, 114.

6 Ibid.

7 Schifano, *Luchino Visconti*, 304.

8 Dostoevsky, "White Nights," 27.

9 Cited in Bacon, *Visconti*, 204.

10 Albert Camus, *The Possessed: A Play in Three Parts*, trans. Justin O'Brien (New York: Knopf, 1960), v.

11 Düttmann, *Visconti*, 24.

12 Ibid., 25.

13 Albert Camus, *The Stranger*, trans. Matthew Ward (New York: Vintage International, 1989), 9.

14 Ibid.

15 Dostoevsky, "White Nights," 1.

16 Ibid., 6.

17 Ibid.

18 Interview with Giuseppe Rotunno, *White Nights* (Criterion DVD, 2005), 11:42–12:40.

19 See Barry Salt, *Film Style and Technology*, 2nd ed. (London: Starword, 1983), 161–62.

20 Dostoevsky, "White Nights," 7.

21 In a review of *Une Vie*, Godard would declare that the "real beauty" of the film is in the "shimming" yellow dress worn by Pascale Petit (*Godard on Godard*, 95). "Astruc is very different here from Visconti [in *White Nights*] with whom it would be silly to compare him" (*Godard on Godard*, 98).

22 Luigi Pirandello, *Naked*, trans. Nina Davinci Nichols (Buffalo: Guernica, 2004), 87.

23 Ibid., 10.

24 Dostoevsky, "White Nights," 27.

25 In the early 1970s, Visconti was interested in directing several films for English and American television, one of them an adaptation of Pirandello's *Tonight We Improvise* (1930). See Monica Stirling, *A Screen of Time: A Study of Luchino Visconti* (New York: Harcourt Brace Jovanovich, 1979), 263. Possibly because of his declining health, none of the television efforts came to pass.

26 Camus, *The Stranger*, 15.

27 Dostoevsky, "White Nights," 41.

28 Camus, *The Stranger*, 21.

29 Nowell-Smith, *Luchino Visconti*, 101.

30 Susan Hayward, "Gender Politics–Cocteau's Belle is Not That Bête: Jean Cocteau's *La Belle et la Bête* (1946)," in *French Film: Texts and Contexts*, ed. Susan Hayward and Ginette Vincendeau (New York: Routledge, 1990), 134.

31 Ibid., 130.

32 Camus, *The Stranger*, 48.

33 Ibid., 55.

34 Schifano, *Luchino Visconti*, 326.

35 Ibid., 360. She also notes a "Cocteau influence" in some parts of *White Nights* (305), but does not specify.

36 Anthony Rizzuto, "Camus and a Society Without Women," *Modern Language Studies* 12, no. 1 (1983): 7.

37 Camus, *The Stranger*, 57–58.

38 Ibid., 59.

39 Ibid., 58.

40 Ibid., 85.

41 Ibid., 123.

42 Roger Shattuck, *Marcel Proust* (Princeton, NJ: Princeton University Press, 1974), 24.

Chapter 4: Classical Forms

1 Edward W. Said, *On Late Style: Music and Literature Against the Grain* (New York: Vintage, 2006), 114.

2 Quoted in Schifano, *Luchino Visconti*, 333.

3 Samuel Beckett, *Proust* (New York: Grove Press, 1931), 17.

4 Jean Collet, "The Absences of Sandra," *Cahiers du Cinéma in English* 2 (1966): 19. Translation uncredited.

5 Thomas Elsaesser, "Luchino Visconti," *Brighton Film Review* 17 (February 1970): 23.

6 Visconti, "Drama of Non-Existence," *Cahiers du Cinéma in English* 2 (1966): 13. Translation uncredited.

7 Aeschylus, *Oresteia: Agamemnon*, trans. Richard Lattimore (Chicago: University of Chicago Press, 1953), 80.

8 Visconti, "Non-Existence," 15.

9 Giacamo Leopardi, *Canti*, trans. Jonathan Galassi (New York: Farrar, Straus & Giroux, 2010), 178.

10 Ibid., 3.

11 Nowell-Smith, *Luchino Visconti*, 107.

12 For a detailed analysis of the use of the Franck in the film, see Suzanne Liandrat-Guiges, *Les Images du Temps: dans Vaghe stelle dell'Orsa de Luchino Visconti* (Paris: Presses de la Sorbonne Nouvelle, 1995), 135–99.

13 On this sequence, also see Blom for a reading that is, in many ways, complementary with my own, although our emphases are sometimes different (*Reframing Luchino Visconti*, 158–59).

14 Giuseppe Tomasi di Lampedusa, *The Leopard*, trans. Archibald Colquhoun (New York: Knopf, 1960), 25.

15 Visconti, "Non-Existence," 15.

16 Ibid., 13.

17 Eisenstein, *Beyond the Stars 2*, 152.

18 Tomasi di Lampedusa, *The Leopard*, 101.

19 Visconti, "Non-Existence," 15.

20 Schifano, *Luchino Visconti*, 348.

21 Tomasi di Lampedusa, *The Leopard*, 29.

22 Schifano, *Luchino Visconti*, 333.

23 Tomasi di Lampedusa, *The Leopard*, 144–45.

24 Ibid., 58.

25 Iris Origo, *A Study in Solitude: The Life of Leopardi: Poet, Romantic and Radical* (London: Pushkin Press, 2017), 139.

26 Blom, *Reframing Luchino Visconti*, 58.

27 Tomasi di Lampedusa, *The Leopard*, 175.

28 Ibid.

29 Rohdie, *The Passion of Pier Paolo Pasolini* (London: BFI, 1995), 45–46.

30 Tomasi di Lampedusa, *The Leopard*, 182.

31 Ibid., 103.

32 Ibid., 73.

33 Ibid., 176.

34 Ibid., 66.

35 Schifano, *Luchino Visconti*, 350.

36 Cited in Schifano, *Luchino Visconti*, 350.

37 Nowell-Smith notes that *Vaghe stelle* reproduces a gesture from the Ford play, in which the brother takes the wedding ring from his sister in order to wear it himself. "But unlike the Leopardi reference, the Ford references are not intended to say anything to the spectator" (*Luchino Visconti*, 110).

38 Euripides, *Electra*, trans. Emily Townsend Vermeule, in *Euripides V*, ed. David Greene and Richard Lattimore (Chicago: University of Chicago Press, 1959), 22.

39 Schifano, *Luchino Visconti*, 307.

40 Tyler, *Screening the Sexes*, 189.

41 Schifano, *Luchino Visconti*, 348.

42 Elsaesser, "Luchino Visconti," 22.

43 For an analysis of the use of the wind in the film, and Leopardi's relationship to this, see Liandrat-Guiges, *Les Images du Temps*, 243–48.

44 Mauro Giori, "Oresti di paglia ed Elettre sepolte. Le suggestioni dell'antico in *Vaghe stelle dell'Orsa . . .* di Luchino Visconti," *LANX* 9 (2011): 87.

45 Blom, *Reframing Luchino Visconti*, 131.

46 Origo refers to a most likely apocryphal story about Leopardi being passionately in love with a woman but, unable to directly state his feelings to her, hiring a boy to dress up in a woman's shawl, thereby allowing Leopardi to directly give voice to his desires (*A Study in Solitude*, 295).

47 Liandrat-Guiges, *Les Images du Temps*, 160.

48 Visconti, "Non-Existence," 15.

49 Elsaesser, "Luchino Visconti," 23.

50 Visconti, "Non-Existence," 15–16.

Chapter 5: Decadent Threads

1 Düttmann, *Visconti*, 98.

2 Aristarco, "Critic or Poet of Decadence?," 62.

3 Bacon, *Visconti*, 150.

4 Nowell-Smith, *Luchino Visconti*, 186–87.

5 Schifano, *Luchino Visconti*, 373.

6 Tomasi di Lampedusa, *The Leopard*, 27.

7 Barth David Schwartz, *Pasolini Requiem* (New York: Pantheon, 1992), 547.

8 Ibid., 573.

9 Daney and Oudart, "Name of the Author," 313.

10 Thomas Mann, *Death in Venice: A Norton Critical Edition*, trans. and ed. Clayton Koelb, Koelb (New York: Norton, 1994), 61.

11 Blom notes the presence of a poster for a Pathé Kok home movie projector in a sequence in which Aschenbach speaks to an employee of Cook's in Piazza San Marco (*Reframing Luchino Visconti*, 91).

12 Ibid.

13 Mann, *Death in Venice*, 4. In an early version of the screenplay, Visconti attempted to adapt this moment for the opening sequence but was defeated by the challenge of transforming it into cinema. "The fact is, the reasons Mann gives in his story cannot be reproduced mechanically" (Stirling, *A Screen of Time*, 209).

14 Mann, *Death in Venice*, 15.

15 Ibid., 63.

16 Daney and Oudart, "Name of the Author," 318.

17 Ibid., 320.

18 Roland Barthes, "Dear Antonioni . . . ," trans. Nora Hoppe, *L'Avventura*, ed. Seymour Chatman and Guido Fink (New Brunswick: Rutgers University Press, 1989), 212.

19 Mann, *Death in Venice*, 25.

20 Blom, *Reframing Luchino Visconti*, 203–5.

21 Mann, *Death in Venice*, 21.

22 Ibid., 23.

23 Ibid., 22.

24 Michel Chion, *The Voice in Cinema*, trans. Claudia Gorbman (New York: Columbia University Press, 1999), 113.

25 Ibid., 114.

26 Nowell-Smith writes: "In *Death in Venice* the ethereal figure of Silvana Mangano in her veil and hat is as much an object of desire as Tadzio. The desire, so to speak, to *be* Tadzio, to be a member of a family group with Silvana Mangano as its head, is as strong as the desire *for* Tadzio, but being less disruptive is less remarked on" (*Luchino Visconti*, 197).

27 Thomas Mann, *Doctor Faustus: The Life of the German Composer Adrian Leverkühn as Told by a Friend*, trans. John Woods (New York: Vintage International, 1997), 440–41.

28 Düttmann, *Visconti*, 21.

29 Tsivian, *Ivan the Terrible*, 21.

30 Ibid., 60.

31 Joan Neuberger, *Eisenstein's Ivan the Terrible in Stalin's Russia* (Ithaca: Cornell University Press, 2019), 327.

32 Eisenstein, *Beyond the Stars 2*, 239.

33 Servadio, *Luchino Visconti*, 47.

34 The most extensive analysis of the ties between *Demons* and this sequence is found in Giori, *Scandalo*, 138–51.

35 Blom, *Reframing Luchino Visconti*, 265–66.

36 Daney and Oudart, "Name of the Author," 312.

37 Sergei Eisenstein, *The Psychology of Composition*, ed. and trans. Alan Upchurch (London: Metheun, 1988), 95.

38 Ibid., 96.

39 Neuberger, *Eisenstein's Ivan the Terrible*, 134.

40 Cecchi D'Amico: "Someone takes a cloth that belonged to Ludwig, and they see that there is a hole. But this scene would have needed something more, I don't know what. I don't think that Luchino would have wanted to put it in the film." Also cut from the film was an image of the dead Elisabeth under a white veil that would have followed the scene of her second visit to him in which she tells Ludwig that one of the privileges of royalty is that they must be assassinated (Bacon, *Visconti*, 173–74).

Chapter 6: Fading

1 Blom identifies the painting as *John, Fourteenth Lord Willoughby de Broke and His Family* (1766) by Johann Zoffany (*Reframing Luchino Visconti*, 71).

2 The most notable example of this position on the film is from Roland Barthes, "Sade-Pasolini," trans. Verena Conley, *Stanford Italian Review* (Fall 1982): 100–102.

3 See Blom, *Reframing Luchino Visconti*, 127.

4 Ibid., 128–29.

5 Roland Barthes, *Sade/Fourier/Loyola*, trans. Richard Miller (New York: Farrar, Straus & Giroux, 1976), 158.

6 Gabriele d'Annunzio, *Pleasure*, trans. Lara Gochin Raffaelli (New York: Penguin, 2013), 17.

7 Mario Praz, *The Romantic Agony*, 2nd ed., trans. Angus Davidson (New York: Oxford University Press, 1970), 399.

8 Schifano, *Luchino Visconti*, 410.

9 Maynard Solomon, *Mozart: A Life* (New York: HarperCollins, 1995), 367.

10 Praz, *Romantic Agony*, 235–36.

11 Tomasi di Lampedusa, *The Leopard*, 193.

12 Gabrielle d'Annunzio, *The Intruder*, trans. Arthur Hornblow (Kansas City: Valancourt, 2009), 32.

13 Ibid., 51.

14 Praz, *Romantic Agony*, 106.

15 D'Annunzio, *Pleasure*, 57–58.

16 Schifano, *Luchino Visconti*, 404.

17 Blom, *Reframing Luchino Visconti*, 72–73.

18 D'Annunzio, *The Intruder*, 40.

19 Ibid., 189.

INDEX

8½ (Fellini), 83–84
1860 (Blasetti), 74, 75, 105
120 Days of Sodom, The (Sade), 174

Adrian, 6
Ager, Cecelia, 6
Alicata, Mario, 34
All'Italia (Leopardi), 108
Amore, L' (Rossellini), 59
Annabelle, 5
Another Dawn (Dieterle), 6
Antonelli, Laura, 178, 194
Antonioni, Michelangelo, 15, 17, 42, 58, 84, 87, 152–53, 174
Aristarco, Guido, 1, 17, 22, 55, 66, 85, 138
Assommoir, L' (Zola), 92
Astruc, Alexandre, 92, 214n21
As You Like It (Shakespeare/Visconti), 86
Atalanta in Calydon (Swinburne), 181
Au Bonheur des Dames (Zola), 18, 209n5
"Au bord du lit" (Maupassant), 7
Avventura, L' (Antonioni), 17, 42
Ayfre, Amédée, 28–29

Bacchanal, The (Titian), 52
Bach, Johann Sebastian, 164
Bacon, Henry, 22, 139
Badalucco, Nicola, 139
Bandito, Il (Lattuada), 59, 60
Barber of Seville, The (Rossini), 97
Barthes, Roland, 8, 146–47, 219n2
Bataille, Sylvia, 7–8
Battle of Algiers, The (Pontecorvo), 87
Battleship Potemkin (Eisenstein), 11–13, 28, 29, 32, 76, 81, 195–96
Bazin, André, 26–28, 33–34, 56, 72, 74, 76
Beauty and the Beast (Cocteau), 68, 98, 99–100
Beckett, Samuel, 112
Before the Revolution (Bertolucci), 88, 126–27
Bell, Marie, 107, 128–29
Bell'antonio, Il (Bolognini), 84, 213n1
Bellissima, 14–15, 49, 55–62, 72, 80–81, 83, 85, 137, 156, 163, 187
Bellocchio, Marco, 88, 126–27
Berger, Helmut, 138, 156, 160, 178
Bertini, Francesca, 56, 128
Bertolucci, Bernardo, 88, 126, 140
Bête Humaine, La (Renoir), 18
Bicycle Thieves (De Sica), 26–28, 52, 60, 61, 62
Birth of Tragedy, The (Nietzsche), 145
Blasetti, Alessandro, 14, 19, 71–72, 74–75, 80
Blom, Ivo, 15, 65, 67, 73, 121, 130, 149, 164, 176, 190, 211n57, 212n15, 216n13, 219n1
Blow-Up (Antonioni), 87

Blue Angel, The (von Sternberg), 162, 164–65
Boccaccio, 141, 142
Boccaccio '70, 4, 6. See also *Lavoro, Il*
Bogarde, Dirk, 3, 139, 145
Boito, Camillo, 55, 66, 68, 69, 70
Borelli, Lyda, 56
Brancati, Vitaliano, 213n1
Bresson, Robert, 85, 92, 95–96, 97
Brothers Karamazov, The (Brooks), 92
Brothers Karamazov, The (Dostoevsky), 18, 22, 85, 102, 209n3
Bruckner, Anton, 68, 69, 79
Buddenbrooks (Mann), 66, 138–39

Caduta degli dei, La. See *Damned, The*
Cain, James M., 18–19, 21, 34, 38, 86–87, 88, 139
Calamai, Clara, 19–20, 91, 137
Callas, Maria, 56–57, 111, 112
Camus, Albert, 83–89, 94–95, 96, 100–104
Canova, Antonio, 132
Captive, The (Proust), 8
Caravaggio, 101
Cardinale, Claudia, 21, 107, 113–14, 124, 127, 179
Carné, Marcel, 21, 209n15
Castellani, Renato, 14, 49–50
Cecchi d'Amico, Suso, 55, 58, 107, 140, 174, 219n40
Chanel, Coco, 7–10
Chaplin, Charles, 20, 35, 99
Chenal, Pierre, 19, 38
Chion, Michel, 155
Chopin, Frédéric, 176
Clément, René, 92
Clift, Montgomery, 62
Clothing the Naked (Paglerio), 92
Clothing the Naked (Pirandello), 92
Cocteau, Jean, 65, 68, 98, 99–100, 112, 215n35
Colette, 5, 58
Collet, Jean, 107
Conformist, The (Bertolucci), 140, 141
Conformist, The (Moravia), 140
Conversation Piece, 137, 138, 173–75, 178, 181, 185–91, 193, 198, 202–3
Conversation Pieces (Praz), 175
Crime and Punishment (Dostoevsky), 48, 85
Crime and Punishment (Dostoevsky/Visconti), 17
Cristaldi, Franco, 107
Cronaca di un amore (Antonioni), 15
Cronaca familiare (Zurlini), 84
Cukor, George, 6

Dali, Salvador, 86
Dalle Vacche, Angela, 59, 68, 71, 76
Damned, The, 108, 127, 138–40, 142, 149, 154, 159, 160–68, 185
Daney, Serge, 2–3, 14, 29, 34, 142, 145, 146, 186
D'annunzio, Gabriele, 66, 173, 174, 175–78, 182, 187, 192, 197, 199, 204
Davis, Bette, 60
Day in the Country, A (Renoir), 7
Death in Venice (Mann), 139, 143–45, 152–56
Death in Venice (Visconti), 2–3, 137, 138, 139, 140, 141–56, 158, 160, 164, 165, 170–72, 176, 180, 186, 188, 191, 195

Decameron, The (Pasolini), 138, 141, 142, 154
Delon, Alain, 7, 23, 42, 84, 94, 107, 116, 124, 141, 208n23
De Matteis, Maria, 64
Demons (Dostoevsky), 87, 162–64
Dernier tournant, Le (Chenal), 19, 38
De Santis, Pasqualino, 108
De Sica, Vittorio, 7, 27–28, 31–32, 49, 60, 62, 174
Dietrich, Marlene, 162, 164, 165, 168, 185
Disorder and Early Sorrow (Mann), 175
Doctor Faustus (Mann), 139, 156
Dolce vita, La (Fellini), 18, 63, 83, 107, 123
Donizetti, Gaetano, 57, 80
Dostoevsky, Fyodor, 17, 18, 48, 85, 86, 87, 90, 90–97, 99, 162–64, 209n3
Düttmann, Alexander García, 5, 66, 88, 138, 156
Dyer, Richard, 209–10n15

Eagle with Two Heads, The (Cocteau), 65, 67–68
Edipo Re (Pasolini), 87, 112, 165
Eisenstein, Sergei, 11–14, 18, 21, 23, 26, 29–30, 32–33, 71, 76, 112, 140, 157, 158, 160–61, 166–67, 195, 209n5
Ekberg, Anita, 17, 123
Electra (Euripides), 127
Elisir d'amore, L' (Donizetti), 57, 80
Elsaesser, Thomas, 107, 129, 132
Erasers, The (Robbe-Grillet), 105
Escoffier, Marcel, 65, 98
Euripides, 108, 127
Europa '51 (Rossellini), 156

Fall of Man, The (Titian), 52
Fellini, Federico, 7, 17, 83, 84, 123, 174
Fis puni, Le (Greuze), 121–23, 124, 143, 174, 181
Fists in the Pocket (Bellocchio), 88, 126–27
Flaubert, Gustave, 17
Four Nights of a Dreamer (Bresson), 85, 92, 95–96, 97
Four Steps in the Clouds (Blasetti), 72
Francis, Kay, 6
Franck, César, 108–9, 132, 134, 216n12
Freud, Sigmund, 34, 44, 112, 126
Fuoco, Il (d'Annunzio), 197

Garbo, Greta, 60
Garbuglia, Mario, 176
Garnett, Tay, 21
German Ideology, The (Marx), 10
Germany, Year Zero (Rossellini), 34, 156
Gervaise (Clément), 92
Giannini, Giancarlo, 176, 194
Giori, Mauro, 36, 130, 210n18, 219n34
Girardot, Annie, 41, 137
Girotti, Massimo, 19–20, 36, 47, 67, 69, 84, 137, 142, 194, 209n9
Godard, Jean-Luc, 4, 214n21
Gone with the Wind (Fleming), 63–65, 74–76, 212n15

Gone with the Wind (Mitchell), 80
Gorey, Edward, 163
Götterdämmerung (Wagner), 139
Gramsci, Antonio, 1
Granger, Farley, 63, 84
Gray, James, 85, 91
Greuze, Jean-Baptiste, 121–23, 124, 143, 174, 181
Gruppo di famigilia in un interno. See *Conversation Piece*

Heine, Heinrich, 67, 68
Hepburn, Katharine, 60
Higashi, Sumiko, 209n5

Idiot, The (Dostoevsky), 17, 85
Infernal Machine, The (Cocteau), 112
Innocent, The, 173–78, 181–85, 187, 188, 190, 191–98, 201–2
Innocente, L' (d'Annunzio), 66, 173, 182, 198
In Search of Lost Time (Proust), 8, 106, 128, 174
Intervista (Fellini), 123
Iphigénie in Aulis (Gluck/Visconti), 111
Iron Crown, The (Blasetti), 19–20, 72, 209n9
Ivan the Terrible (Eisenstein), 157, 158, 160–62, 167

Jester's Supper, The (Blasetti), 19–20
Job, The. See *Lavoro, Il*
John, Fourteenth Lord Willoughby de Broke and His Family (Zoffany), 219n1
Joseph and His Brothers (Mann), 22, 42–43, 45–46, 54

Killers, The (Siodmak), 123

Lancaster, Burt, 80, 105, 116, 121, 122, 125, 126, 141, 173, 174, 179, 187, 188
Laura (Preminger), 53
Lavoro, Il, 4, 6–10, 12, 105, 132, 141, 149
Leigh, Vivien, 63
Leisen, Mitchell, 6
Leopard, The, 6, 42, 87, 105–6, 109–11, 112, 113, 114–26, 143, 154, 157, 159, 165, 174, 176, 188, 198, 199, 204
Leopard, The (Tomasi di Lampedusa), 105–6, 107, 110–11, 113, 115, 117, 121, 122, 123–24, 126, 141, 181
Leopardi, 108, 119, 125, 129–30, 135, 217n46
Lesaffre, Roland, 209n15
Levi, Carlo, 22
Liandrat-Guiges, Suzanne, 131, 216n12, 217n43
Liszt, Franz, 68
Luce, Clare Booth, 6
Luchair, Corinne, 19
Ludwig, 108, 127, 137, 138, 139–40, 141, 149, 154, 156–60, 164, 165–70, 171, 173, 176, 219n40
Ludwig II: Glanz und Ende eines Königs (Käutner), 157–58
Lumet, Sidney, 133
"Lyrical Intermezzo" (Heine), 67

Macbeth (Shakespeare), 139, 140, 166–67, 168
Magnani, Anna, 14, 56, 58–61, 62–63, 73, 137
Mahler, Gustav, 8, 68, 139, 146, 170–72
Malavoglia, I (Verga), 7, 33
Mancini, Liliana, 14
Mangano, Silvana, 4, 137–38, 152, 154–56, 158, 178, 186–87, 218n26
Mann, Thomas, 2, 8, 22, 45–46, 66, 138–39, 140, 143–45, 149, 152–56, 175
Man with the Movie Camera, The (Vertov), 10–11, 14, 161
Marais, Jean, 65, 95, 98, 99–100
Marcus, Millicent, 57, 61, 72
"Mario and the Magician" (Mann/Visconti), 140
Marquand, Christian, 68–69
Marx, Karl, 10
Mastroianni, Marcello, 83–84, 86, 87, 91, 94, 103, 123
Maupassant, Guy de, 7, 8, 17, 92
Medea (Pasolini), 112
Medioli, Enrico, 107, 140, 174
Merry Widow, The (Lehár), 156
Metz, Christian, 4
Michelson, Annette, 10
Miller, Arthur, 47, 133
Miller, D. A., 1, 3, 4, 29
Minghelli, Giuliana, 41–44
Mitchell, Margaret, 64
Monicelli, Mario, 7
Monnino, Franco, 173
Moravia, Alberto, 4, 140, 177
Mourning Becomes Electra (O'Neill), 126
Murfin, Jane, 6
Mussolini, Benito, 140, 178

Nannuzi, Armando, 108
Nietzsche, Friedrich, 145, 170, 172, 176, 195
Notte, La (Antonioni), 84, 107
Nowell-Smith, Geoffrey, 20, 29, 66, 97, 109, 140, 210n27, 218n26

Odyssey, The (Homer), 154
Oedipus the King (Sophocles), 112
Orestia (Aeschylus), 107–8, 111
Origo, Iris, 119, 217n46
Orpheus (Cocteau), 112
Orpheus and Eurydice (Gluck), 182, 185
Ossessione, 14–15, 18–22, 34–41, 43, 47, 53, 54, 55, 60, 68, 81, 88, 89, 90, 94, 95, 139, 146, 183, 194, 195, 203
Oudart, Jean-Pierre, 2–3, 14, 29, 34, 142, 145, 146, 186

Paisà (Rossellini), 26
Paradine Case, The (Hitchcock), 63
Parsifal (Wagner), 56
Pasolini, Pier Paolo, 2, 138, 141, 142, 174, 175, 177, 213n1
Phèdre (Racine), 128
Piacere, Il (d'Annunzio), 175, 176–77, 187
Piccolo mondo antico (Soldati), 63, 64
Pirandello, Luigi, 92–93, 214n25
Pontecorvo, Gillo, 87
Portrait of Armand Roulin (Van Gogh), 53–54
Possédés, Les (Camus), 87

Postman Always Rings Twice, The (Cain), 18–19, 21, 88, 139
Postman Always Rings Twice, The (Garnett), 21
Pratolini, Vasco, 84
Praz, Mario, 175, 177, 181, 187
Prelude, Chorale and Fugue (Franck), 108–9, 132, 134
Proust, Marcel, 8–9, 34, 53, 58, 61, 104, 106–7, 176, 200, 201
Psyche Revived by Cupid's Kiss (Canova), 132, 133

Red Desert (Antonioni), 87
Red River (Hawks), 61–62, 146
Red Shoes, The (Powell/Pressburger), 58
Renoir, Jean, 7, 8, 18
Ricci, Nora, 57, 137, 152
Ricordanze, La (Leopardi), 108
Riefenstahl, Leni, 161–62
Rimbaud, Arthur, 66
Ring of the Nibelungen, The (Wagner), 139
Rizzuto, Anthony, 102
Rocco and His Brothers, 1, 3, 4, 6, 17, 21, 22–25, 26, 29, 40–54, 55, 62, 64, 83, 84, 87, 91, 101, 106, 107, 116, 125, 127, 129, 132, 133, 138, 145, 147, 163, 186, 192, 196.
Rohdie, Sam, 17, 23, 45, 122
Romantic Agony, The (Praz), 177
Rome, Open City (Rossellini), 34, 59, 60
Rosi, Francesco, 55, 174
Rossellini, Roberto, 26, 27, 34, 43, 59, 62, 156, 157, 173
Rota, Nino, 105
Rotunno, Giuseppe, 86, 90, 108, 109
Rules of the Game, The (Renoir), 8

Sade, Marquis de, 174, 175, 176, 177, 186–87
Said, Edward, 106
Salò, or the 120 Days of Sodom (Pasolini), 174, 175, 176, 177, 186–87, 197, 200, 201, 203
Sandra. See *Vaghe stelle dell'orsa*
Sansho the Bailiff (Mizoguchi), 155
Saturn over the Water (Priestley), 105
Scenes from Childhood (Schumann), 159
Schell, Maria, 91–92, 94, 141
Schifano, Laurence, 102, 114, 126–27, 128, 187
Schneider, Magda, 10
Schneider, Romy, 4, 7–10, 12, 141, 208n23
Schwartz, Barth David, 141
Scotellaro, Rocco, 22
Sensani, Gino, 64
Senso, 4, 33, 55–57, 59, 62, 63–80, 81, 85, 86, 87, 106, 110, 113, 117, 129, 130, 135–36, 138, 139–40, 148, 157, 159, 177, 183, 185, 203, 212n15
Senso (Boito), 55, 66, 68, 69, 70
Shakespeare, William, 83, 139, 140, 167
Shattuck, Roger, 104
Shoeshine (De Sica), 31, 32
Siamo donne (Visconti et al.), 62–63
Signora senza camelie (Antonioni), 58, 60
Signorini, Telemaco, 68
Sinfonia Concertante K 364 (Mozart), 180–81

Sleeping Hermaphroditus (Bernini), 190
Soldati, Mario, 63, 64
Solomon, Maynard, 181
Sophocles, 108
Sorel, Jean, 107, 126, 127
Special Day, A (Scola), 84
Spurgeon, Caroline, 167
Stalin, Joseph, 161
Steimatsky, Noa, 29, 86
Sternberg, Josef von, 162, 164–65
Stranger, The, 83–90, 94–95, 96, 100–104
Stranger, The (Camus), 83, 86–87, 88–89, 94–95, 96, 100–104
Streetcar Named Desire, A (Williams/Visconti), 83, 84
Streghe, Le, 4, 137
Stutesman, Drake, 60
Suddenly, Last Summer (Mankiewicz), 102, 103
Svilova, Yelizaveta, 11, 14
Symphony No. 5 (Mahler), 146
Symphony No. 7 (Bruckner), 68, 69, 79

Taking of Power by Louis XIV, The (Rossellini), 157
Teorema (Pasolini), 142, 197
Teresa Venerdi (De Sica), 60
Terra trema, La, 7, 25–34, 36, 39, 40, 43–44, 50–51, 55, 56, 60, 61, 80, 81, 86, 88, 106, 154
Testori, Giovanni, 22
Thérèse Raquin (Carné), 7, 209–10n15
Thérèse Raquin (Zola), 21, 22
Third Man, The (Reed), 63
Thus Spake Zarathustra (Nietzsche), 170, 172
Time Regained (Proust), 53, 58
'Tis Pity She's a Whore (Ford/Visconti), 7, 216n37
toeletta del mattino, La (Matino), 68
Tolstoy, Leo, 18
Tomasi di Lampedusa, Giuseppe, 105, 106–7, 110, 113, 115, 117, 121, 122, 123–24, 126, 141, 181
Tonight We Improvise (Pirandello), 214n25
Tosi, Piero, 60, 66, 67, 176
Trilogy of Life (Pasolini), 138, 174
Tristan und Isolde (Wagner), 164
Triumph of the Will (Riefenstahl), 161–62
Troilus and Cressida (Shakespeare/Visconti), 83, 86, 111
Trovatore, Il (Verdi), 57, 65
Tsivian, Yuri, 11, 157, 158
Turner, Lana, 21
Two Lovers (Gray), 85, 91, 92
Tyler, Parker, 32, 127

Ulysses (Camerini), 154, 156
Under the Sun of Rome (Castellani), 14, 49–50

Vaghe stelle dell'orsa, 88, 107–8, 109, 111–14, 126–37, 140, 154, 160
Valli, Alida, 56, 63, 71, 73, 76
Van Gogh, Vincent, 53–54
Verdi, Giuseppe, 57
Verga, Giovanni, 7, 17, 33, 106
Vertov, Dziga, 10–11, 12, 27, 143
Vie, Une (Astruc), 92, 214n21
View from the Bridge, A (Lumet), 127

View from the Bridge, A (Miller), 41, 127
"Vorrei spiegarivi, oh Dio!" (Mozart), 189

Wagner, Cosima, 158
Wagner, Richard, 56, 139–40, 157–59, 164, 168–69, 171
Wayne, John, 62
We the Women. See *Siamo donne*
White Nights, 56, 83, 85–86, 90–100, 141, 183
"White Nights" (Dostoevsky), 85, 86, 90, 91, 94, 96, 99
Wilde, Oscar, 66, 177
Wilder, Billy, 6
Williams, Tennessee, 83, 102
Winterhalter, Franz Xaver, 65, 66
Witch Burned Alive, The, 4, 137–38, 141, 145, 169
Witches, The. See *Streghe, Le*
Women, The (Cukor), 5–6

Zavattini, Cesare, 49, 55, 62, 80
Zola, Émile, 17, 18, 21–22, 85, 92
Zurlini, Valerio, 84

ABOUT THE AUTHOR

Joe McElhaney is professor of film studies at Hunter College, City University of New York. His books include *The Death of Classical Cinema: Hitchcock, Lang, Minnelli*; *Vincente Minnelli: The Art of Entertainment* (Wayne State University Press, 2009); *Albert Maysles*; and *A Companion to Fritz Lang*. He has published numerous essays on European, Asian, and American cinema.

www.ingramcontent.com/pod-product-compliance
Lightning Source LLC
LaVergne TN
LVHW020432080826
844660LV00034B/1401

* 9 7 8 0 8 1 4 3 4 3 0 8 1 *